LIVING
THE LAZARUS
LIFE

STEPHEN W. SMITH

LIVING
THE LAZARUS
LIFE

a guidebook for
spiritual transformation

David C Cook®
transforming lives together

LIVING THE LAZARUS LIFE
Published by David C. Cook
4050 Lee Vance View
Colorado Springs, CO 80918 U.S.A.

David C. Cook Distribution Canada
55 Woodslee Avenue, Paris, Ontario, Canada N3L 3E5

David C. Cook U.K., Kingsway Communications
Eastbourne, East Sussex BN23 6NT, England

David C. Cook and the graphic circle C logo
are registered trademarks of Cook Communications Ministries.

The Web site addresses recommended throughout this book are offered as a resource
to you. These Web sites are not intended in any way to be or imply an endorsement
on the part of David C. Cook, nor do we vouch for their content.

All Scripture quotations, unless otherwise noted, are taken from the *Holy Bible, New International
Version*®. *NIV*®. Copyright © 1973, 1978, 1984 by International Bible Society. Used by permission
of Zondervan. All rights reserved. Scripture quotations marked MSG are taken from *THE MESSAGE*.
Copyright © by Eugene H. Peterson 1993, 1994, 1995, 1996, 2000, 2001, 2002. Used by permission
of NavPress Publishing Group. Scripture quotations marked NASB are taken from the New American
Standard Bible, © Copyright 1960, 1995 by The Lockman Foundation. Used by permission. Scripture
quotations marked KJV are taken from the King James Version of the Bible. (Public Domain.)
All excerpts taken from *The Lazarus Life* published by David C. Cook in
2008 © Stephen W. Smith, ISBN 978-1-4347-9995-1
The excerpt from "The Lightest Touch" by David Whyte on page 14 taken from
Everything Is Waiting for You (Langley, WA: Many Waters Press, 2003).

ISBN 978-1-4347-6701-1

© 2009 Stephen W. Smith

The Team: John Blase, Jaci Schneider, and Karen Athen
Cover Design: Studiogearbox, Chris Gilbert
Interior Design: Amy Kiechlin
Interior Images: "The Raising of Lazarus" by Giotto di Bondone,
© Veer Images, Gallerist Illustration

Printed in the United States of America
First Edition 2009

2 3 4 5 6 7 8 9 10

090809

CONTENTS

ACKNOWLEDGMENTS

The development and polishing of this particular guidebook is the result of men and women who stepped into this project and into my life to help me. They did their work graciously and lovingly with great skill and care. It does not take one long in life to realize who knows the language of the tomb and graveclothes and life itself! Special thanks to Eric Stanford for his insight and developmental suggestions. Thanks also to Steve Forney for developing the "Ordinary Stories" with me. Special thanks to Dan and Deanne Hemboldt, Gwen Harding Smith, Russell and Kate Courtney, and John and Beth Blackburn for doing the pilot study and greatly improving the questions, exercises, and methods of the guide.

Special friends who are musical artists helped recommend the songs found on the Web site www.LazarusLife.com. Thank you for your knowledge, expertise, and belief in this needed guide. You are: Jim DeJarnette, First Presbyterian Church, Colorado Springs; Dan Smith of Olathea Bible Church, Olathea, Kansas; Dave Bullock, Elmbrook Church, Elmbrook, Wisconsin; and friends who know I love music. Jeff Morrison—who wrote the song "Still Waiting," based on Lazarus's plight—is a gifted songwriter. When I heard Jeff's song for the first time, I wept in recognition of the fact that so many of us are "still waiting" on our transformation, but that God is "still waiting" on us to get out of our own tombs of death.

Special and heartfelt thanks to the team at David C. Cook for believing in this project; for knowing the need for a companion "tool of transformation" for the book *The Lazarus Life*. I am deeply thankful to Amy Kiechlin at David C. Cook for her remarkable artistry with the graphic layout of the guide and who envisioned with me a high-sensory experience in the use of the guide. Without the help of John Blase, my editor and companion on the journey of transformation, this book and even I would still be in the tomb wearing the graveclothes we both know so well.

Stephen W. Smith
August 2008
Potter's Inn at Aspen Ridge
Divide, Colorado

FOREWORD

Our master designer has shaped and formed us with the capacity to experience the world in many different ways. We can know a wide spectrum of thoughts and feelings. Our emotional continuum stretches to vast extremes. We have the capacity to soar with exhilaration and, conversely, we can plummet to depths of despair. We love to laugh. We need to weep. We crave intimacy. We seek stillness. We long to know God. We are intricately complex beings.

God honors our uniqueness. We are designed by this master architect to learn in unique ways. There is no single best way to learn—no "one learning style fits all." Just as God has created us with our own personalities and temperaments, He has embedded within each of us a matrix of possibilities through which we can learn and grow. We are free to experience profound change when we can discover our own personal styles of perceiving, interpreting, and responding to God. As we invite His Holy Spirit to touch all of the multifaceted layers of our human understanding, we can experience conversion at the depths of our souls, for which we are created.

Stephen Smith understands the complexities of the human condition as the creative work of God. In this guidebook, he provides a model for spiritual transformation that is based on an integrative approach to learning. It is designed to meet the diverse needs and interests of learners so that meaningful change can occur. This interactive approach involves the "whole person," because learning does not occur in a vacuum, separated from the rest of our personality. Our intellectual functioning does not operate in isolation, apart from our physical, emotional, social, and spiritual domains. The author taps into all of these spheres of human experience to allow the reader to learn and grow at different levels.

This guidebook incorporates many of the ways in which people actually learn. The reader is encouraged to become an active participant in this "meaning-making" journey. The interactive nature of this guide respects individual variation in learning styles. The broad range of methods allows readers to choose activities for personal exploration, based on individual learning preference and pace. For example, a probing question may spur reflection. One person may be inspired to respond by recording his or her thoughts in a journal. Yet another may relate at a more physical level, by engaging the senses. The beauty of this guidebook is that it helps individuals experiment with multiple ways to express their faith by engaging in a variety of exercises. One may discover new areas of growth by viewing the activity of God from different vantage points.

Stephen Smith explores the boundaries of "emotional intelligences" to advance an integrated model for spiritual transformation. He takes learning to a deeper level. He has tapped into a wellspring of knowledge from ancient wisdom based on experience and intuition to contemporary research findings offered by the brightest in the social sciences. In this resource, Smith connects these sources of insight with profound biblical truths.

On a personal note, I have known Steve Smith for twenty years. Since the first day I met Steve, he has been on a relentless journey to explore the ways in which God shapes and forms us into His likeness. The intense pursuit to expand the parameters for learning has consistently defined his calling. The driving impetus in his ministry has been fueled by a burning desire to engage the whole person in an authentic relationship with Christ. Now, his mission to provide concrete ways to connect with the good news has crystallized in this integrative model for spiritual transformation: *Living the Lazarus Life*. I invite you to experience the process of change. Allow God to stretch your heart and mind.

My prayer for you is that you will allow the words of Scripture to chisel within your soul the unique creation that God would have you become. Permit our resurrected Lord to gently disturb the veil that camouflages your soul-sickness—the malady of suffering we all privately mourn. Accept Jesus' invitation to remove your graveclothes and celebrate genuine soul healing.

Susan Durr, PhD, Macon State College

Macon, Georgia

May 2008

HOW TO USE THIS GUIDEBOOK

This guidebook is designed to help you make the journey from head to heart, body to soul, and intuition to reality. This journey will incorporate many of the proven ways that people actually learn. God made us all unique people; we are all "fearfully and wonderfully made" (Ps. 139:14). We were not scooped out of the clay of the earth, then poured into the same mold and mass-produced. Like great art, spiritual formation allows for individuality, uniqueness, and differences. This guidebook takes all of this into account in how we learn and move forward on our spiritual journeys. While the gate is narrow and the way may be also, our styles, preferences, and strengths of learning about spiritual truth are broad indeed.

HOW THIS GUIDEBOOK ACTUALLY WORKS *FOR* YOU AND NOT AGAINST YOU

This is more than a Bible study. It's more than fill in the blanks. It's more than learning facts and acquiring more information. Think of it as a buffet in a marvelous restaurant. As you walk in, you immediately spot the long counters laden with deliciously cooked meats, a wide array of vegetables, and a host of enticing salads—all waiting to be enjoyed and savored. Although the tendency in buffets is to gravitate to the foods we know and recognize, let me encourage you to try to "taste" a little of each section to get a feel for your own style and preference.

DON'T LET THE SIZE OF THE BUFFET SCARE YOU

You don't have to "eat" everything here. In fact, as you move further along this journey, I believe you'll find yourself moving freely about—knowing more of what to expect from each section. Please don't let the size of the workbook scare you. It's a very friendly guide and you'll quickly learn how to navigate and find your way to what you really want!

Here's how the guidebook is organized:

Excerpt from **The Lazarus Life.** Each of the sessions begins with an excerpt from *The Lazarus Life*. The excerpt is followed by several introductory questions to get your mind and heart focused on the theme of the particular session.

Engaging the Scriptures is the portion of the guidebook centered on a biblical passage. While the story and text of Lazarus is always the larger backdrop, each section has its own different scriptural text to engage. This can be done individually or in a group or class setting. You'll notice footnotes throughout the sessions. These are "leader's notes," which give more insight or material for background. If you're using this guidebook by itself, you'll want to look at the leader's notes, as they contain valuable information not found in the text itself.

Examining My Story is an important part and step of each session. Here you'll find questions to ask yourself. Think of each of the questions as being asked by a friend, teacher, personal pastor, or spiritual director; in other words, people who care about the deepest parts of you. Sometimes, our tendency is to float along on the surface of life without having the courage to take a look at something deeper. The French word for *courage* is rooted in the word for *heart*. *Examining My Story* holds questions that flow into the chambers of the human heart and much deeper into the marrow of our souls, those places where great change and our hope for transformation must take root. If change doesn't occur here, it's nothing more than cosmetic.

An Ordinary Story is a short narrative about very ordinary people whom you will perhaps recognize in your church, small group, or work setting. The purpose of these stories is to help us "connect the dots" from the Bible study to our everyday lives. Do you remember playing "connect the dots"? You begin with the dot 1 and move your pencil or crayon to dot 2, then dot 3, and so on until all the connected dots make a recognizable image that you *finally* figure out. One of the greatest challenges to spiritual growth is our failure to connect the dots and thereby miss what God is truly up to in our lives. The *Ordinary Story* section can help with this by being an important "dot" to consider in each of the sessions.

Making Sense of the Truth is where you are encouraged to think outside the box. Various exercises and suggestions are offered to help you visualize, listen, taste, touch, feel, and smell different aspects of what you're considering in the session. You can do these on your own or in a group setting. It's up to you to decide. Our God-given senses are avenues for us to experience God and know Him more. You may imagine more and different exercises than what I have suggested here. Go for it! Give yourself permission to color outside the lines a little or a lot!

Prayers for Transformation are guided prayers. If the disciples as fully grown adults admitted to Jesus that they did not know how to pray, then we too might consider starting over in our prayer life and learning how to pray. The prayers offered here are actually a variety of exercises to help you pray in different ways—perhaps ways you are not accustomed to. It's my hope that you'll find a way, a model, or a pattern that will enhance your confidence to truly walk with God more intimately.

Further Steps on the Journey are my recommendations about books and ideas to help you explore the themes of a given session more deeply. If you are using this guide in a group setting, ask a group member to read ahead, in advance of the actual session, so he or she can give a report on one of the books or ideas.

A WORD ON "PACING"

Our culture has radically shaped our understanding about how people change. We want it immediately, right now. But transformation does not work according to a cultural or even personal timetable. Each person must proceed at his or her own pace and this guidebook takes this into consideration. You may only want to do a part of each session, then go back and complete other exercises. You may want to move slowly and deliberately through the sessions. It's entirely up to you.

The guidebook is crafted into twelve sessions. You may find that you cannot finish one of the sessions in a week. You may need more time. Or you may decide you need to stop and ponder a session just a little longer. Remember: The goal is not simply to finish the guidebook, but to experience authentic transformation.

WHAT DO I NEED FOR THIS JOURNEY?

- a Bible

- a guidebook

- a pen or pencil

- a journal—even a spiral-bound notebook will do

- a friend, small group, or class to travel with you on the journey

In the silence that follows
a great line
you can feel Lazarus
deep inside.
—David Whyte, "The Lightest Touch"

SESSION 1
UNDERSTANDING SPIRITUAL TRANSFORMATION

Lazarus is a story of true transformation. One person dying and coming back to life is a dramatic example of true change. But before we look at the story of Lazarus, let's look at what we mean by spiritual trans-

formation and how it happens. Author and philosopher Dallas Willard has said that the "greatest need you and I have—the greatest need of collective humanity—is [the] renovation of the heart." Willard goes on to say that the heart is "that spiritual place within us from which outlook, choices, and actions come … now it must be transformed."[1] Willard calls this "renovation," while others call it spiritual transformation. The words are not as important as is the experience of true change! Change is at the heart of the Christian message! We know what it is like not to change. It's misery. It's the tomb.

You probably read *The Lazarus Life* and are using this guidebook because the hope for transformation has caught your eye and fed your heart. Spiritual transformation is the key that unlocks a door that, for many of us, has been locked for too long.

Spiritual transformation is the ongoing process of a person experiencing authentic and lasting change by the power of God in his or her life. This study will examine that ongoing process through the life of Lazarus. As we examine his life and transformation, we will have the opportunity to examine our own need for transformation and diagnose what needs to change in our lives.

---

1. Dallas Willard, *The Renovation of the Heart* (Colorado Springs: NavPress, 2002), 14.

Living the Lazarus Life is a practical way to read the story of Lazarus alongside our own story and understand our longings for change, our repeated failures to change way down deep in the DNA of our souls, and how true transformation can be experienced after all. Haven't we all had repeated chances to try to change, yet ended up in a place filled with failure, regret, and disappointment? How many times have you promised to lose the weight you wanted to, stop losing your temper, quit some addiction that gripped you deeper than you ever thought possible, and more?

We are not alone on our journey. We have a guide, mentor, and friend in Lazarus to show us the way. In *The Lazarus Life* we read, "Like Lazarus, you and I know what it is like not to be transformed: unaffected by the power of God; unaltered by the promises of Jesus; and impervious as a granite slab to the penetrating work of the Spirit." The story of Lazarus is embedded with hope that we must discover for ourselves. Let's get started mining the nuggets of truth that will lead us into the experience of spiritual transformation.

1. How would you define transformation?[2]

2. Why are you interested in studying and exploring spiritual transformation?

2. **Transformation**

Trans`for*ma"tion\, n. [L. transformatio: cf. transformation.] The act of transforming, or the state of being transformed; change of form or condition. Specifically: (a) (Biol.) Any change in an organism which alters its general character and mode of life, as in the development of the germ into the embryo, the egg into the animal, the larva into the insect (metamorphosis), etc. (Dictionary.com accessed May 12, 2008).

3. What is an area in your life in which you long to experience change? Think through your social, emotional, spiritual, and physical life and choose one specific area that you want to focus on for the next twelve weeks and monitor any progress. Why did you choose this one area of potential transformation?

4. On a scale of 1–10, with 10 being "extremely hopeful," where are you in regard to feeling hope about your own transformation?

1 ——2 —— 3 ——4 —— 5 ——6 —— 7——8 —— 9—— 10

ENGAGING THE SCRIPTURES

One of the best ways to explore spiritual transformation is by looking at a passage of Scripture where transformation is actually taking place. The timeless image of the potter and clay is one of the most frequently used metaphors or word pictures in the Bible. Let's look at the passage and explore the process of spiritual transformation.

READ JEREMIAH 18:1–6

¹This is the word that came to Jeremiah from the LORD: ²"Go down to the potter's house, and there I will give you my message." ³So I went down to the potter's house, and I saw him working at the wheel. ⁴But the pot he was shaping from the clay was marred in his hands; so the potter formed it into another pot, shaping it as seemed best to him.

⁵Then the word of the LORD came to me: ⁶"O house of Israel, can I not do with you as this potter does?" declares the LORD. "Like clay in the hand of the potter, so are you in my hand, O house of Israel."

1. Why do you suppose God told Jeremiah to go to the potter's house?

2. How might the image of the potter working on the clay have impacted Jeremiah?[3]

3. Using your five senses, what did Jeremiah

    •   see?

    •   touch?

    •   smell?

    •   taste?

    •   hear?

> *Oh, thou that art unwearying, that does neither sleep*
> *Nor slumber, who didst take*
> *All care for Lazarus in the careless tomb, oh keep*
> *Watch for me till I wake.*
>
> —"THE NAKED SEED," POEMS, C. S. LEWIS

---

3. Other biblical references to the image of clay and the potter can be found in Isaiah 45:9; 64:8; 2 Corinthians 4:7; 2 Timothy 2:20, and more.

4. What happened to the marred clay?

5. What is the role of the potter in this passage?

6. What is the role of the clay in this passage?

> I believe one of the most pervasive problems in contemporary western Christianity is that we mistakenly assume that information automatically translates to transformation.
>
> —GREGORY BOYD

7. How has this passage clarified your understanding of spiritual transformation?

EXAMINING MY STORY

1. What are some common ways you see people, including yourself, trying to change?[4]

2. What feels "marred" or in need of transformation in your life?

3. What would it look like for you to sit upon the Potter's wheel?

4. How would describe your efforts to change over the years? What kinds of activities, programs, and help have you been involved with to experience transformation in the past?

---

4. Some examples are self-help, studying more, making promises, renewing commitment, praying.

AN ORDINARY STORY

Bill lost his temper at his son's baseball game and the officials asked him to leave. His wife, Laura, was humiliated. Laura gave Bill an ultimatum: *Until you address your anger, you're not going back to the ball field.* After several weeks of good behavior and it'll-never-happen-again promises, Bill and Laura attended a game, only to have Bill fly into another rage.

1. Is Bill and Laura's situation uncommon?

2. What advice would you give to Laura?

3. Do you believe true and lasting transformation is possible for people like Bill?

MAKING SENSE OF THE TRUTH

1. Look for a magazine in a grocery store or home that is promising some type of change: weight loss, better sex, transformed house or lifestyle. Explore and examine what myths and realities our culture promises about change. What does modern culture teach us about change and transformation?

2. Use modeling clay to mold something that represents what God is doing in your life now.[5]

3. Find some pictures of a butterfly in various stages of development. What do you notice about these stages? How are they similar or not to a person's transformation?

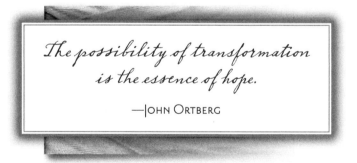

The possibility of transformation
is the essence of hope.

—John Ortberg

---

5. You can purchase modeling clay at a craft store. Play-Doh or Sculpey Clay, which can be baked and preserved as a symbol for you to keep, will also work well.

PRAYERS FOR TRANSFORMATION

King David penned a prayer of transformation in Psalm 139. He concludes his prayer with powerful words that you can consider as your own:

Investigate my life, O God,

   find out everything about me;

Cross-examine and test me,

   get a clear picture of what I'm about;

See for yourself whether I've done anything wrong—

   then guide me on the road to eternal life. (vv. 23–24 MSG)

Try to write your own prayer using David's as a model. Note your thoughts and feelings as you invite God into the process of your spiritual transformation.

Dear God ...

> *The Christian is a person who becomes someone he was not before.*
>
> —DAVID NEEDHAM

FURTHER STEPS ON THE JOURNEY

1. Spend some time looking at the chart (p. 169) comparing authentic transformation with what the author calls pseudo-transformation. You may want to refer to this from time to time.[6]

2. Do a character study of a personality in the Bible. Study this person's life and note the changes in and around him or her. Peter, David, Moses, Ruth, and Naomi are examples.

3. Read Dallas Willard's *The Renovation of the Heart* for a more in-depth study of spiritual transformation.

4. Consider going though the book *Soul Shaping: A Practical Guide to Spiritual Transformation* by Stephen W. Smith. This guide uses the image of the clay and the work of the potter to explain and help the reader experience spiritual transformation. Order online at www.PottersInn.com.

If we always do what we've always done, we'll always get what we've always got and nothing changes. Nothing changes.

—ALCOHOLICS ANONYMOUS SAYING

6. If you are doing this in a group, you may want to make a chart where you can write various definitions and understandings of what transformation means. What is transformation? What are some forms, stages, and seasons of transformation?

Now, with God's help, I shall become myself.

—Søren Kierkegaard

SESSION 2

I AM LAZARUS: FINDING OURSELVES IN THE STORY

Chapter 1 of *The Lazarus Life*

SOUL-SICKNESS

It doesn't take us long in life to realize that what the Bible says is true: No one is sinless. No one escapes being soul-sick. Our sickness seems to repeat itself across the pages and chapters of our lives. It even follows a predictable pattern: We make resolutions and promises to God, and we try to change, but we relapse. We take two steps forward but the one step back nearly always does us in. We muster up the energy to try to break an addiction, to rid ourselves of a self-destructive habit, to not be "so angry, so overweight, so anxious, so doubting, so obsessive, so selfish" or whatever it is (is there ever only one thing?) that brings dis-ease to our souls and makes us desperate.

This is what Dallas Willard calls "sin management"—when we use our own effort to try to control sin rather than dealing with it once and for all. A little bit of cyber-sex isn't as bad as being an addict, is it? A little bit of guilt, a little bit of anger, a little bit of envy is better than a life consumed with it, right? We try to manage our heart, mind, soul, and strength the best we can. All the while, however, the life that Jesus promised seems just beyond our grasp. The joy and passion that God intended for our lives feels like the cookie jar we'll never be tall enough to reach.

Aren't we tired of changing just enough to get by? Change from the outside might look good at church on Sunday, but it leaves us empty and restless the other six days of the week. Pseudo-transformation doesn't touch our deepest soul-sickness. It doesn't move us beyond the issues, problems, and sins that keep us from experiencing the life Jesus promised. Pseudo-transformation leaves us sick because when we don't really change, we have to live with the residue of guilt and shame over our repeated attempts to get life right.

A life outside the tomb is what we want. Real life. Authentic life. The abundant life that Jesus promises. The story of Lazarus offers us an opportunity to explore how transformation really happens—sometimes in the places we least expect it.

(Pages 20–21 of *The Lazarus Life*.)

1. Try putting into a few words or sentences what you believe to be your real soul-sickness.[1] What are your reasons for making this diagnosis?

2. How would you define or describe the healing you seek?

---

1. This question may seem bold at this stage in the guidebook, but the point is to begin to entertain thoughts and concepts over what your own soul-sickness might actually be.

ENGAGING THE SCRIPTURES

Let's read the story of Lazarus as John tells it in John 11. This incredible story of an ordinary man named Lazarus frames our study on spiritual transformation. There may be no other story in all of the Gospels that reveals such dramatic change and transformation. His story becomes a window through which to view our own ongoing story of transformation.

READ JOHN 11:1–37[2]

[1]Now a man named Lazarus was sick. He was from Bethany, the village of Mary and her sister Martha. [2]This Mary, whose brother Lazarus now lay sick, was the same one who poured perfume on the Lord and wiped his feet with her hair. [3]So the sisters sent word to Jesus, "Lord, the one you love is sick."

[4]When he heard this, Jesus said, "This sickness will not end in death. No, it is for God's glory so that God's Son may be glorified through it." [5]Jesus loved Martha and her sister and Lazarus. [6]Yet when he heard that Lazarus was sick, he stayed where he was two more days.

[7]Then he said to his disciples, "Let us go back to Judea."

[8]"But Rabbi," they said, "a short while ago the Jews tried to stone you, and yet you are going back there?"

[9]Jesus answered, "Are there not twelve hours of daylight? A man who walks by day will not stumble, for he sees by this world's light. [10]It is when he walks by night that he stumbles, for he has no light."

---

2. The first Bible study section is intended to be an overview. Later sessions will unpack the meaning and you will be guided to explore other passages outside of the Lazarus story.

[11]After he had said this, he went on to tell them, "Our friend Lazarus has fallen asleep; but I am going there to wake him up."

[12]His disciples replied, "Lord, if he sleeps, he will get better." [13]Jesus had been speaking of his death, but his disciples thought he meant natural sleep.

[14]So then he told them plainly, "Lazarus is dead, [15]and for your sake I am glad I was not there, so that you may believe. But let us go to him."

[16]Then Thomas (called Didymus) said to the rest of the disciples, "Let us also go, that we may die with him."

[17]On his arrival, Jesus found that Lazarus had already been in the tomb for four days. [18]Bethany was less than two miles from Jerusalem, [19]and many Jews had come to Martha and Mary to comfort them in the loss of their brother. [20]When Martha heard that Jesus was coming, she went out to meet him, but Mary stayed at home.

[21]"Lord," Martha said to Jesus, "if you had been here, my brother would not have died. [22]But I know that even now God will give you whatever you ask."

[23]Jesus said to her, "Your brother will rise again."

[24]Martha answered, "I know he will rise again in the resurrection at the last day."

[25]Jesus said to her, "I am the resurrection and the life. He who believes in me will live, even though he dies; [26]and whoever lives and believes in me will never die. Do you believe this?"

[27]"Yes, Lord," she told him, "I believe that you are the Christ, the Son of God, who was to come into the world."

[28]And after she had said this, she went back and called her sister Mary aside. "The Teacher is here," she said, "and is asking for you." [29]When Mary heard this, she got up quickly and went to him. [30]Now Jesus had not yet entered the village, but was still at the place where Martha had met him. [31]When the Jews who had been with Mary in the house, comforting her, noticed how quickly she got up and went out, they followed her, supposing she was going to the tomb to mourn there.

[32]When Mary reached the place where Jesus was and saw him, she fell at his feet and said, "Lord, if you had been here, my brother would not have died."

[33]When Jesus saw her weeping, and the Jews who had come along with her also

weeping, he was deeply moved in spirit and troubled. [34]"Where have you laid him?" he asked.

"Come and see, Lord," they replied.

[35]Jesus wept.

[36]Then the Jews said, "See how he loved him!"

[37]But some of them said, "Could not he who opened the eyes of the blind man have kept this man from dying?"

1. Describe Jesus' relationship with Mary, Martha, and Lazarus.

2. What facts or details seem important to you?[3]

3. What emotions do you sense as the story progresses?[4]

---

3. Consider making a time line that you can refer to in the study. Note the days, people present, when Jesus showed up, the funeral, and the resurrection.

4. As you sit with the story, make note of the emotions you sense: fear of Lazarus's condition, anticipation that Jesus would show up at any moment, disappointment in Jesus, grief at Lazarus's death, etc.

4.   John tells us that Jesus loved Lazarus (John 11:3; 11:5; and 11:35) and called him a friend (11:11). Why do you think Lazarus, Mary, and Martha are the only specific people named as being loved by Jesus?

The continuance of your longing is the continuance of your prayer.

—AUGUSTINE

5.   How do you think Lazarus's life was different after undergoing death and a miraculous resurrection?

6.   Whom do you relate with most in this passage? Why?[5]

---

5. As you enter the story about Lazarus, try to explore whom you relate with most. Is it Lazarus? Mary? Martha? The bystanders? Do you feel like an outsider looking in, or are you already more involved in some way? Lazarus was sick in the opening verses. Can you identify with him in his sickness or later when he actually died?

7. As a modern-day "Lazarus," at what point in the story do you find yourself—Feeling sick? Dying? Lying dead? Hearing Jesus cry, "Come forth"? Walking out of the tomb? Celebrating with Jesus and your sisters? Fully alive? As you find yourself in the story, ask yourself: What is going on in my life that pulls me into this feeling?

8. What's at least one way that Lazarus's resurrection and transformation gives you hope?

> *Homesickness for God is a mark of the life of prayer.*
>
> —JAMES HOUSTON IN *THE TRANSFORMING POWER OF PRAYER*

EXAMINING MY STORY

1. In what ways do you feel more dead than alive; more asleep than awake; more in a posture of surviving rather than thriving? Try to be as specific as you can.

2. What do you feel is preventing you from living the life Jesus wants you to live?

3. What does Jesus want for you that you may not want for yourself?

4. What patterns do you see surfacing when you examine ways in which you have attempted to change, help, or transform yourself?[6]

---

6. Examples might be "I tend to overpromise and underdeliver when it comes to my spiritual life;" "I seem to repeat cycles of trying, then failing, then feeling guilty, and then trying again," etc.

5. As far as you can see, what might an effective treatment plan or action plan for your own spiritual transformation involve?

We can never be lilies in the garden unless we have spent time as bulbs in the dark, totally ignored.

—OSWALD CHAMBERS

AN ORDINARY STORY

After accepting Christ several years ago, Ron experienced tremendous growth in his spiritual life. Church was exciting, the Bible's truths were revealing, and God seemed to be active in answering Ron's prayers. Lately though, something seems to be missing in Ron's life. He has told his friends that he feels lost at work, detached at home, and in a spiritual desert. He's considering dropping out of his small group because he travels and needs to have at least one more night at home. After church last week, Ron thought, *Is this it? Is this the abundant life Jesus promised me? Am I missing something?*

1. Is Ron missing it? What do you think is going on?

2. Think deeper.... What might be the dis-ease in Ron's soul?

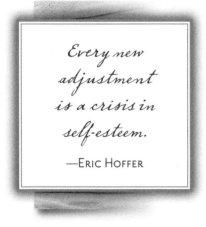

Every new adjustment is a crisis in self-esteem.

—ERIC HOFFER

MAKING SENSE OF THE TRUTH

1. Take a large sheet of paper and have volunteers write their individual soul-sicknesses on it. See if people mention common themes. What soul-sicknesses surprise you?[7]

2. Have the group turn to Jesus' words about sickness and the need for a spiritual physician in Mark 2:17. Have the group repeat Jesus' words three to four times as an affirmation of our need for Jesus. "It is not the healthy who need a doctor, but the sick. I have not come to call the righteous, but sinners." Allow time for group members to give thanks for Jesus' invitation to come and be healed.

3. Listen to "Healer of My Soul" by John Michael Talbot. What does this song stir inside you? Reflect on what the song is saying. (You can find a link at www.LazarusLife.com for this song.)

---

7. If there is a reluctance to this, explore what some of the reasons might be with the group.

PRAYERS FOR TRANSFORMATION

Joseph Hart wrote a hymn in 1759 titled "Come Ye Sinners." Slowly read the words.

> Come, ye sinners, poor and needy,
> Weak and wounded, sick and sore;
> Jesus ready stands to save you,
> Full of pity, love and pow'r.
>
> Refrain:
> *I will arise and go to Jesus,*
> *He will embrace me in His arms;*
> *In the arms of my dear Savior,*
> *Oh, there are ten thousand charms.*
>
> Come, ye thirsty, come, and welcome,
> God's free bounty glorify;
> True belief and true repentance,
> Every grace that brings you nigh.
>
> Come, ye weary, heavy-laden,
> Lost and ruined by the fall;
> If you tarry till you're better,
> You will never come at all.
>
> View Him prostrate in the garden;
> On the ground your Maker lies;
> On the bloody tree behold Him;
> Sinner, will this not suffice?
>
> Lo! th' incarnate God ascended,
> Pleads the merit of His blood:
> Venture on Him, venture wholly,
> Let no other trust intrude.
>
> Let not conscience make you linger,
> Not of fitness fondly dream;
> All the fitness He requireth
> Is to feel your need of Him.

Circle the words of this hymn that seem to speak to you. Write a prayer expressing in your own words your need for change, healing, and transformation.

Dear God:

> Mere change is not growth. Growth is the synthesis of change and continuity, and where there is no continuity there is no growth.
>
> —C. S. Lewis

FURTHER STEPS ON THE JOURNEY

1. Read David Benner's wonderful book *The Gift of Being Yourself*. It may help in some aspect of your own soul-sickness.

2. Ask a spouse/friend/mentor to be a companion in your process of transformation. Your conversation might begin this way: "Here's what I'm looking for in having a companion/ mentor in this process...." Try to be open for feedback as you define this relationship.

3. Ask the person closest to you to give you his or her diagnosis of your soul-sickness.

4. Talk to a trusted/mature Christian about how soul-sickness has been overcome in his or her life. Journal what you discover.

5. Begin to make a list of biblical characters who also experienced spiritual transformation as you proceed through each of the sessions. See how many come to mind while doing this study. You'll be referred to several in the study itself, but your list will hopefully include more characters to know and study at a future time.

SESSION 3

THE LINGERING JESUS: WAITING FOR HIS PRESENCE

Chapter 2 of *The Lazarus Life*

LIVING IN-BETWEEN

As we read the story of Lazarus, we have the advantage of knowing that Jesus *did* show up—eventually. But Mary, Martha, and the dying Lazarus only knew that God was absent. For days of silence, they only knew the tomb.

Just like Mary and Martha, we live in an in-between time in many areas of our lives. In the midst of illness, doubt, and weakness, we try to keep hope in our hearts that when Jesus finally shows up, everything will be all right—but how will we make it through the waiting? "Living by faith is a bewildering venture. We rarely know what's coming next, and not many things turn out the way we anticipate. It is natural to assume that since I am God's chosen and beloved I will get favorable treatment from God who favors me so extravagantly."

This in-between time—this "bewildering venture"—is a necessary experience in the spiritual life. It cannot be skipped or shortened, though many of us try to do exactly that. The invitation is to trust a God who makes us wait. Our fear is that Jesus may not show up for us—not now, perhaps not ever. In this in-between time, seismic earthquakes of doubt can topple our belief systems.

Many of us trade our confidence in God and faith in Jesus for what has been called "functional atheism." Functional atheism says life is up to us and no one else.

We have to do something—anything—to fix our daily crises and spiritual dilemmas. God isn't around; perhaps God doesn't even exist. Author Parker Palmer writes that functional atheism is at work when we say "pious words about God's presence in our lives but believe, on the contrary, that nothing good is going to happen unless we make it happen."

Living in the in-between times can make even the most devout person succumb to these "pious words." Rather than wait for God, we work to bring about our own transformation. Yet the story of Lazarus indicates that in this awkward season, when it seems we are on our own, God is at work. Unseen. Unnoticed. Seemingly uninvolved. Quietly He is "God with us."

The psychiatrist Gerald May founded the Shalom Institute for Spiritual Formation. In the last book he wrote before his death to cancer, he describes how the in-between times, when God seems absent, are precisely when God is at work. May uses nature and the season of winter's apparent dormant power to help us comprehend this important spiritual season. He writes:

> *How long, O Lord, will I call for help, and You will not hear?*
>
> —HABAKKUK 1:2 NASB

Deer and rabbits quiet, fish and frogs and turtles nearly frozen, snakes holed up, summer birds gone away and winter birds now here, trees black and bare, seeds and cocoons and grubs and cicada larvae and everything underground, deep inside, down and in where you cannot see the life happening. Life is rich in the time of keeping still, sap flowing, cells curing, change taking place.... Inside us all, in depths of our winters, things are going on, things we will have no clue of until spring comes, and perhaps, not even then.

(Pages 33–35 of *The Lazarus Life*.)

1. In what way do you find yourself waiting for God right now? Is this something new or a long-term experience?

2. What thoughts or feelings do you have about the "winter of your waiting"?

I believe in the sun when it is not shining.
I believe in love even when feeling it not.
I believe in God even when He is silent.

—INSCRIPTION ON THE WALLS OF A CELLAR IN COLOGNE, GERMANY, WHERE JEWS HID FROM THE GERMANS

ENGAGING THE SCRIPTURES

This is one of the most gripping scenes in the entire account of the life of Jesus. Here we encounter a Jesus who lingers—a Jesus who deliberately chooses not to show up on the timetable offered Him by people He loved. This session will help you explore your own feelings, experiences, and disappointments with a God who works off His own schedule. The lingering Jesus has something to teach us that is valuable and necessary in our understanding of transformation. Let's explore this.

READ JOHN 5:1–15

¹Some time later, Jesus went up to Jerusalem for a feast of the Jews. ²Now there is in Jerusalem near the Sheep Gate a pool, which in Aramaic is called Bethesda which is surrounded by five covered colonnades. ³Here a great number of disabled people used to lie—the blind, the lame, the paralyzed. ⁵One who was there had been an invalid for thirty-eight years. ⁶When Jesus saw him lying there and learned that he had been in this condition for a long time, he asked him, "Do you want to get well?"

⁷"Sir," the invalid replied, "I have no one to help me into the pool when the water is stirred. While I am trying to get in, someone else goes down ahead of me."

⁸Then Jesus said to him, "Get up! Pick up your mat and walk." ⁹At once the man was cured; he picked up his mat and walked.

The day on which this took place was a Sabbath, ¹⁰and so the Jews said to the man who had been healed, "It is the Sabbath; the law forbids you to carry your mat."

[11]But he replied, "The man who made me well said to me, 'Pick up your mat and walk.'"

[12]So they asked him, "Who is this fellow who told you to pick it up and walk?"

[13]The man who was healed had no idea who it was, for Jesus had slipped away into the crowd that was there.

[14]Later Jesus found him at the temple and said to him, "See, you are well again. Stop sinning or something worse may happen to you." [15]The man went away and told the Jews that it was Jesus who had made him well.

Read the passage slowly and reflect on these questions. You may find it helpful to read the passage three to four times, pausing after each reading to listen for a different aspect or emphasis or insight.[1]

1. Imagine this scene. What do you see? Hear? Feel? Smell? Where do you see yourself in this story?[2] With whom do you most identify? What do you imagine this man would have felt after such a long time of waiting?

2. Jesus asked him, "Do you want to get well?" What do you think of Jesus' question?

---

1. Before the printed Bible, people could only listen to the Bible as it was read. It required a more focused way of listening than we are used to today in our busy, noisy world and hearts. This ancient way of reading the Bible is called "Lectio Divina," which means "sacred reading." Rather than quickly reading a passage of Scripture, you intentionally choose to read the Bible slower, more contemplatively. For more information on Lectio Divina, look at *Embracing Soul Care* by Stephen W. Smith, *Too Deep for Words* by Thelma Hall, or Google the term for thousands of Web sites that may have good information.

2. Engaging the senses is an ancient and important way of reading the Scriptures. Ignatius (1491–1556), the founder of the Jesuit movement, is considered by many to be one of the pioneers to help believers use all of their God-given senses to understand of the truth of Scriptures.

3. What similarities do you see between this man's situation and that of Lazarus, Mary, and Martha?

4. What did the waiting accomplish?

5. Recall a time when you had to wait for God to heal or bless. How did it feel when He finally met your need? Or is it still unmet?

> *My God, my God, why have you forsaken me? Far from my deliverance are the words of my groaning. O my God, I cry by day, but you do not answer; And by might, but I have no rest.*
>
> —A PRAYER OF DAVID IN PSALM 22:1–2 (NASB)

EXAMINING MY STORY

1. In *The Lazarus Life*, the author tells the story of L. B. Cowman's experience of waiting on the caterpillar to transform and emerge as a moth (pages 40–41). How does this story speak into your spiritual life?

2. A friend asks, "Where is Jesus lingering in your life?" How do you respond? What are you doing while Jesus lingers?

3. Review "Dealing with Disillusionment" found on pages 43–46 in *The Lazarus Life*. What effect does unexplored disappointment have in your life? Cynicism? Suspicion? Doubt? How does this threaten the biblical beliefs you have adopted?

AN ORDINARY STORY

Jack had applied for six different jobs this week and hadn't heard good news about any of them. As he filled out yet another application, he thought, *What's the point?* With bills mounting and rent due at the end of the month, Jack's anger started to get the best of him. He began lashing out at everyone around him.

1.   What elements of a "lingering" Jesus do you hear in this story?

2.   What might active waiting look like for Jack? (Active waiting is more fully explained in *The Lazarus Life*, page 37.)

Never think that God's delays are God's denials. Hold on; hold fast; hold out. Patience is genius.

—COMTE GEORGES-LOUIS LECLERC DE BUFFON

MAKING SENSE OF THE TRUTH

1. Consider reading aloud Isaiah 40:25–31 in unison. Or use this prayer as an expression of your desire to continue waiting on God.

2. Listen to "Everlasting God." How does this song offer encouragement in the waiting process? There's a line in this song that says, "Strength will come as we wait upon the Lord." How do you relate to strength coming through waiting? (This song is available at www.LazarusLife.com and downloads from iTunes.)

3. Consider lighting a candle and sitting in silence for five to ten minutes. After the silence, ask, "What is it like to wait in silence—but to wait in community? If you're doing this alone, journal your thoughts after a time of silence.

4. Do you recall the scene in the movie *Forrest Gump* when Lt. Dan is tethered to the mast of a shrimp boat in a violent storm? He is lashing out to God. Show this clip in a group setting and say, "Describe a time when you related to Lt. Dan and felt his words and feelings become your own."

5. Make two lists. First, make a list of the things you continue to believe about God even as you are waiting for Him to act (for example, He is good; He is on my side). Second, make a list of the things you think God might be wanting you to do while you wait (for example, be faithful to obey Him; keep seeking Him in prayer).

WHAT I BELIEVE ABOUT GOD	WHAT I CAN DO WHILE I WAIT

PRAYERS FOR TRANSFORMATION

Scripture is filled with examples of desperate people in desperate situations waiting on a God who chose to linger. Yet, they chose to pray. Consider making some of their prayers your own. Here's an example from the life of Jonah generally, and from the belly of the whale specifically:

In trouble, deep trouble, I prayed to GOD.

He answered me.

From the belly of the grave I cried, "Help!"

You heard my cry.

You threw me into ocean's depths,

into a watery grave,

With ocean waves, ocean breakers

crashing over me.

I said, "I've been thrown away,

thrown out, out of your sight.

I'll never again lay eyes

on your Holy Temple."

Ocean gripped me by the throat.

The ancient Abyss grabbed me and held tight.

My head was all tangled in seaweed

at the bottom of the sea where the mountains take root.

I was as far down as a body can go,

and the gates were slamming shut behind me forever—

Yet you pulled me up from that grave alive,

O GOD, my God!

When my life was slipping away,

I remembered GOD,

And my prayer got through to you,

made it all the way to your Holy Temple.

Those who worship hollow gods, god-frauds,

walk away from their only true love.

But I'm worshiping you, GOD,

calling out in thanksgiving!

And I'll do what I promised I'd do!

Salvation belongs to GOD!"

—Jonah 2:1–9 MSG

What words of your own can you add to express your feelings about the lingering Jesus?

FURTHER STEPS ON THE JOURNEY

The Discipline of Disillusionment: This is a worksheet for working through disappointments and practicing the discipline of disillusionment. **Disillusionment means to be "stripped of" a false impression or misconception.** The discipline requires a pursuit of truth as things really are rather than holding on to false impressions and illusions. People can hold false illusions about God, themselves, and each other. When life does not meet our expectations and illusions, disappointment results. Disappointment with God, ourselves, and others can result in bitterness, anger, cynicism, and negative thinking. Use this worksheet to help you work through a particular issue you might be struggling with: disappointment in a friend who let you down; disappointment because you did not get the job you were hoping for; frustration in your spiritual life because of unanswered prayer or thinking that Jesus' lingering caused massive problems for you. An example of Mary and Martha's disillusionment is included here. Additional examples are included in the appendix of the guidebook, along with a "clean" chart for you to use for your own discipline.

Please note: It is understood that some of this content is conjecture, but what follows are definite possibilities as to what may have been going on in Mary and Martha's hearts and minds.

> We must wait for God, long, meekly, in the wind and wet, in the thunder and lightning, in the cold and the dark. Wait, and he will come. He never comes to those who do not wait.
>
> —FREDERICK WILLIAM FABER

INSTRUCTION	EXAMPLE—MARY AND MARTHA	YOUR STORY
1. Identify the issue causing you to struggle. Write out some thoughts on some issue that is causing you to feel disappointed and disenchanted.	We are disappointed that Jesus did not show up and heal Lazarus.	
2. Think more deeply about your disappointment. What is your disappointment really about?	Does He really care? Does He really love me? Why did He not do what I thought He would do? We've got more questions than answers!	
3. Search for the illusion. What is the illusion that feeds your disappointment? It's okay to have more than one, but try to be as specific as you can.	That Jesus would always respond or "show up" when I need Him.	
4. Connect the illusion with feelings and emotions. What surfaces in considering the surrender of this illusion?	Disappointment. Fear. Anger. Confusion. Resentment.	
5. Make an assessment of the root issue. What and where is the root of my disillusionment?	Jesus promised resurrection and it was not experienced. What does it even mean anymore?	
6. What are some possible truths that need to be embraced?	Jesus has a plan beyond my understanding.	
7. Develop an action plan in light of what you have discovered in this discipline. How can I live in light of this truth?	I must wait on the Lord. I need to know more of what it means to practice "active waiting."	
8. Talk plainly to God. Record your thoughts and prayers in your journal.	"Lord, if only You'd been here … Help my unbelief.… Help me learn to wait on You even when I want to give up. Help me to trust You, even when I feel lost inside."	

9. Find a trusted companion to process your heart with in this area.	Rather than building a cynical heart with each other as sisters, we need to consider how we can encourage one another more in the hours and days ahead and practice waiting. Just how can we do this?	
10. Add your own ideas to follow up.	Hear more about others who had to wait for long periods of time, such as Joseph in prison; the children of Israel in the wilderness for forty years; David when he was anointed to be king but had to wait until Saul's death; the Jews' experience of the destruction of Jerusalem and the Temple.	

The Almighty is working on a great scale and will not be hustled by our peevish impetuosity.

—WILLIAM GRAHAM SCROGGIE

SESSION 4

TRAPPED IN THE TOMB: WHEN LIFE COMES TO A DEAD END

Chapter 3 of *The Lazarus Life*

THE NEED FOR TRANSFORMATION

I went through a season in my life when I thought my wife and I were happily married, but I was wrong. We had four young sons and I was called to lead a large church in North Carolina as the senior pastor. It felt like heaven for me. A large staff. A suite of offices. My own assistant. I thought I had arrived.

Because of my own soul-sickness and need for affirmation, I poured my heart and soul into my work. Unaware of what I was really doing, I developed an addiction as nasty as heroin and as dark as meth. My addiction was my work, and the dark side of my own addiction was that I was applauded for working hard. The more praise I got, the more I worked. My church mushroomed, which only affirmed the toxicity of my addiction. Success often has a dark side and my dark side revealed its ugly belly in my marriage and home life. The truth was I really didn't have a home life. I had a work life and a place to change clothes and take a shower.

The tomb began to close in on me one day when my wife went to see her doctor. The doctor took time to ask Gwen questions about her life as the mother of four boys under age ten and the demands of being a pastor's wife. Then at some point during the physical examination, the doctor noticed a rash under her wedding ring. She asked Gwen, "Has this been there a long time?" Gwen sheepishly said, "Yes, a very long time." Then the doctor spoke words that would be a turning point in our marriage. "Gwen, when I see a rash like this, it makes me wonder if there is a rash in the marriage. Is there?"

When Gwen told me this, I barked out that the doctor was a quack. What did a rash on a finger have to do with the intimacy of our marriage? I dismissed this cry for help from my wife and her doctor as nonsense and went on with my life. Then just a few weeks later, the door of the tomb came crashing down.

(Pages 60–61 of *The Lazarus Life*.)

1. According to chapter 3 of *The Lazarus Life*, what is a "tomb time"?

2. Are you currently in a tomb time? If so, describe it. Use as many adjectives as you can to paint a picture of the tomb.

ENGAGING THE SCRIPTURES

How do we learn to speak of the hard times in our lives? Some choose to deny them and embrace more of a "feel good" style of faith. Others seem to be nearly paralyzed by hard times in life. This study will explore how a person on the journey toward spiritual transformation can hold hard times and faith in God hand in hand without giving up one or the other. Paul's own words offer us permission to do this, showing us how to live through a tomb time like Lazarus did yet not abandon hope and faith.

Read the passage and reflect on the questions.

READ 2 CORINTHIANS 1:1–11

¹Paul, an apostle of Christ Jesus by the will of God, and Timothy our brother,

To the church of God in Corinth, together with all the saints throughout Achaia:

²Grace and peace to you from God our Father and the Lord Jesus Christ.

³Praise be to the God and Father of our Lord Jesus Christ, the Father of compassion and the God of all comfort, ⁴who comforts us in all our troubles, so that we can comfort those in any trouble with the comfort we ourselves have received from God. ⁵For just as the sufferings of Christ flow over into our lives, so also through Christ our comfort overflows. ⁶If we are distressed, it is for your comfort and salvation; if we are comforted, it is for your comfort, which produces in you patient endurance of the same sufferings we suffer. ⁷And our hope for you is firm, because we know that just as you share in our sufferings, so also you share in our comfort.

[8]We do not want you to be uninformed, brothers, about the hardships we suffered in the province of Asia. We were under great pressure, far beyond our ability to endure, so that we despaired even of life. [9]Indeed, in our hearts we felt the sentence of death. But this happened that we might not rely on ourselves but on God, who raises the dead. [10]He has delivered us from such a deadly peril, and he will deliver us. On him we have set our hope that he will continue to deliver us, [11]as you help us by your prayers. Then many will give thanks on our behalf for the gracious favor granted us in answer to the prayers of many.

1. Paul speaks of sorrow and comfort in the same sentence (vv. 4–5). How is it possible for comfort to be given to us in the midst of our deepest sorrow? Have you had this experience of receiving comfort in some of the hardest times or places you've been in your life? If so, what happened?

2. Paul describes a dead end or tomb time in his life. He is real, authentic, not trying to cover anything up. In fact he says in verse 8, "We do not want you to be uninformed, brothers, about the hardships we suffered in the province of Asia." What is your reaction to Paul sharing about the reality of his life?

3. Paul seems very free and comfortable in stating how life really is. How comfortable do you feel in doing the same?

4. Put Paul's words of his plight and condition in verses 6–9 into your own words. Make a list of how Paul describes his condition. Make sure you mention his emotional distress as well as the facts that he is sharing.

5. What does a tomb time—a very difficult and painful time—offer us that no other time in life can?

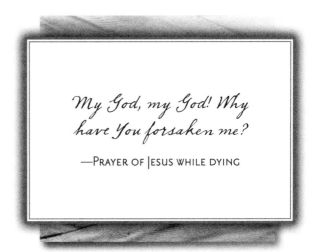

My God, my God! Why have You forsaken me?

—PRAYER OF JESUS WHILE DYING

EXAMINING MY STORY

1. When you are in a tomb, what brings hope and encouragement and fresh insights?

2. What lessons have you learned from a tomb time?

> *His hand is heavy despite my groaning. Oh that I knew where I might find Him, that I might come to His seat! I would present my case before Him and fill my mouth with arguments.... Behold, I go forward but He is not there, and backward, but I cannot perceive Him.*
>
> —JOB 23:2–4, 8–9 NASB

3. On page 52 of *The Lazarus Life*, the author refers to Amy Carmichael's book titled *Things As They Are*. If you were to write a book by the same title, what would the outline look like?

4. **An Exercise in Learning to Speak in Paradox:** During tomb times, many people learn to speak in paradox such as the examples given below. List some of your paradoxes that you are facing right now.

THE REALITY	THE REALITY IN SPIRITUAL PARADOX
My husband left me and divorced me.	I've never felt closer to God than in this dark time.
Work is boring, unrewarding, and makes me feel insignificant.	I am feeling fulfilled in my role as a husband and father.

5. How can speaking in paradox help you in your tomb times?[1]

---

1. Speaking in paradox helps us be true to our own desires and not bury them. It's important to speak in paradox because it helps us know God more and also ourselves. A paradox is a statement that seems contradictory but in reality expresses a truth.

AN ORDINARY STORY

Shawn has been putting in long hours lately at work. When he gets home around 7:30 p.m., he sits and eats dinner, kisses the kids good night, pays some bills, and picks up around the house. He catches a little evening news before going to bed and wakes up to do it all over again. The weekends are filled with soccer games, social activities, and a couple honey-dos. He can't remember the last thing he looked forward to.

1. Do you see any elements of a tomb in Shawn's life?

2. What thoughts or feelings does his story stir in you?

> While he lived on earth, anticipating death, Jesus cried out in pain and wept in sorrow as he offered up priestly prayers to God. Because he honored God, God answered him. Though he was God's Son, he learned trusting-obedience by what he suffered, just as we do.
>
> —HEBREWS 5:7–8 MSG

3. Let's say you're a good friend of Shawn's. How could you encourage him during a time like this?

MAKING SENSE OF THE TRUTH

1. A tomb time can be a season when nothing seems clear. Take a jar with a lid and fill it with water and some dirt. Shake it up and then place it on a table and watch it for a while. Time and stillness help the clarity to return and the muck to settle. What insight can you gain by looking at the jar?

2. Take a hymnal or songbook and read through some of the hymns and songs that speak about God's faithfulness despite hard times.[2] What music gives you comfort in the midst of a very difficult time? What lyrics reassure you of biblical truths relevant to your suffering? How does music comfort your soul? What role does music have in your life in good times and in hard times?

3. On page 59 of *The Lazarus Life*, the author quotes Charles Dickens' famous opening lines in *A Tale of Two Cities*. Experiment with rewriting this line in your own words to describe the tomb time you might be facing now.

4. Listen to the songs recommended for this session at www.LazarusLife.com.

> *It was the worst of times; it was the best of times.... We had everything before us, we had nothing before us....*
>
> —CHARLES DICKENS

---

2. Examples might include: "Great is Thy Faithfulness" and "It Is Well."

PRAYERS FOR TRANSFORMATION

Joseph Bayly, author and former president of David C. Cook, endured the death of each of his three sons. He wrote this prayer:

I cry tears

to you Lord

tears

because I cannot speak.

Words are lost among my fears

pain

sorrows

losses

hurts

but tears

You understand my wordless prayer

You hear.

Lord

wipe away my tears

all tears

not in distant day

but now here.[3]

Write your own prayer here and call it "My Prayer in a Tomb":

3. Joseph Bayly, *The View from a Hearse* (Colorado Springs: Cook Communications Ministries, 1973). Used with permission. May not be further reproduced. All rights reserved.

FURTHER STEPS ALONG THE JOURNEY

1. Consider reading a biography of a well-known Christian such as Amy Carmichael or Hudson Taylor. Underline passages where the author refers to a tomb time in his or her life and how he or she endured it and what was learned. Another book that reveals the tomb times of a great twentieth-century saint, Mother Teresa, is *Come Be My Light: The Private Letters of Mother Teresa*—a true and fascinating account of how one woman faced the prolonged dark night of her soul, how she endured it, and what she learned through such tough times.

2. If you are doing this study in a group, consider having an extended time when group members can each plan on sharing "My most difficult time and what I learned from it." Allow each member to share his or her story in thirty minutes, taking into consideration time for follow-up questions and explanations. This could be a mini-retreat or an extended time on a Saturday or Sunday afternoon ending with a potluck meal.

3. Henri Nouwen has said that "solitude is the furnace of transformation." What would it take for you to plan a time of silence and solitude in the next few days, a time to be still and listen for God's voice? When can you do this in the next seven days?

There are some defeats more triumphant than victories.

—MICHEL EYQUEM DE MONTAIGNE

> When you feel that all is lost,
> sometimes the greatest gain
> is ready to be yours.
>
> —THOMAS KEMPIS

> The kingdom of God is a kingdom of paradox,
> where through the ugly defeat of a cross, a
> holy God is utterly glorified; healing through
> brokenness; finding self through losing self.
>
> —CHARLES COLSON

SESSION 5

THE VOICE OF LOVE: HEARING YOUR SAVIOR CALL YOU BY NAME

Chapter 4 of *The Lazarus Life*

MOVING FROM THE HEAD TO THE HEART

In the Western world most of us build our faith upon a system of beliefs about God. We form these beliefs into creeds and confessions of faith. We say them in our churches. Our pew racks hold them printed on reminder cards. But we need to *experience* God's *love* if we are to be transformed by it.

It has been said, "The longest, most arduous journey in the world is often the journey from head to heart. Until that roundtrip is complete, we remain at war within ourselves." A journey must take place from the head to the heart if we are to be transformed at all. We must truly experience this love that God has for each one of us. Without that experience we will believe we are living, but we'll be void inside of true life. The journey of those eighteen inches between our head and heart is where so many of us get sidelined in our experience of transformation. At some point we have to accept with our heart the mystery of love's power.

When the apostle Paul wrote the believers at Ephesus, he pled with them to know the love of God personally:

I pray that out of his glorious riches he may strengthen you with power through his Spirit in your inner being, so that Christ may dwell in your hearts through faith. And I pray that you, being rooted and established in love, may have power, together with all the saints, to grasp how wide and long and high and deep is the love of Christ, *and to know this love that surpasses knowledge.* (Eph. 3:16–19)

Paul wants us to experience God's love—not just study it or hear about it. We need to taste it for ourselves. We need to feel our own hearts swell inside to know that God loves us as Jesus loved Lazarus. Knowing love personally is different from reading about it. We can have a wealth of knowledge and yet remain unmoved, unalive, and unaltered. Paul knew this all too well because his years of trying to please God as a Pharisee sucked the very life out of him—as human effort always will. Now Paul tells us that love *surpasses* knowledge. Sacred Love cannot be explained. It can only be experienced.

(Pages 73–74 of *The Lazarus Life*.)

1. For what reasons do you need a reassurance of God's loving presence in your life today?

2. How do you see God using these reassurances in your journey of transformation?

ENGAGING THE SCRIPTURES

LEARNING TO LISTEN TO THE VOICE OF LOVE

Knowing that God chose to speak to men and women of old is one thing. We believe this because we believe the accounts in the Bible. Trusting that God still longs to communicate with His children today requires both faith and practice. Learning to listen to the Voice of Love is choosing to believe that the God of the cosmos still longs to speak intimately today.

READ JOHN 10:1–21

¹"I tell you the truth, the man who does not enter the sheep pen by the gate, but climbs in by some other way, is a thief and a robber. ²The man who enters by the gate is the shepherd of his sheep. ³The watchman opens the gate for him, and the sheep listen to his voice. He calls his own sheep by name and leads them out. ⁴When he has brought out all his own, he goes on ahead of them, and his sheep follow him because they know his voice. ⁵But they will never follow a stranger; in fact, they will run away from him because they do not recognize a stranger's voice." ⁶Jesus used this figure of speech, but they did not understand what he was telling them.

⁷Therefore Jesus said again, "I tell you the truth, I am the gate for the sheep. ⁸All who ever came before me were thieves and robbers, but the sheep did not listen to them. ⁹I am the gate; whoever enters through me will be saved. He will come in and go out, and find pasture. ¹⁰The thief comes only to steal and kill and destroy; I have come that they may have life, and have it to the full.

¹¹"I am the good shepherd. The good shepherd lays down his life for the sheep. ¹²The

hired hand is not the shepherd who owns the sheep. So when he sees the wolf coming, he abandons the sheep and runs away. Then the wolf attacks the flock and scatters it. [13]The man runs away because he is a hired hand and cares nothing for the sheep.

[14]"I am the good shepherd; I know my sheep and my sheep know me— [15]just as the Father knows me and I know the Father—and I lay down my life for the sheep. [16]I have other sheep that are not of this sheep pen. I must bring them also. They too will listen to my voice, and there shall be one flock and one shepherd. [17]The reason my Father loves me is that I lay down my life—only to take it up again. [18]No one takes it from me, but I lay it down of my own accord. I have authority to lay it down and authority to take it up again. This command I received from my Father."

[19]At these words the Jews were again divided. [20]Many of them said, "He is demon-possessed and raving mad. Why listen to him?"

[21]But others said, "These are not the sayings of a man possessed by a demon. Can a demon open the eyes of the blind?"

1. Jesus says that the Good Shepherd's voice is identifiable. According to the text, how is this possible?[1]

2. What are other competing and even dangerous voices you encounter today?[2]

1. We're told that Jesus calls and knows the sheep individually and by specific names. They are not herded en mass. God's love is specific and individualized. Just as Lazarus was specifically named to be the recipient of Jesus' love as we have learned in this book, here Jesus tells us of His passion, love, and care for each individual sheep.
2. Jesus uses the word picture of "wolves." This image conjures up ideas of dangerous predators that sheep need protection from in order to live safely.

3. How do people "know" the Voice of Love—the voice of Jesus among other competing voices today?[3]

4. What are the qualities you learn about the Good Shepherd and the Voice of Love of the Shepherd in this text?[4]

5. When you realize that God's love and voice are so specific, so individually focused, and so lavish, how does this make you feel, or what thoughts does it inspire in you?

---

3. Jesus states it as plainly as possible. We can recognize His voice among the other competing voices calling for our attention. His voice is unique, recognizable, and personal. As we journey out of our tombs and closer toward Jesus, His voice makes all the difference in the world. It is interesting that the gospel writer John tells us about the voice of the Good Shepherd prior to telling us about the story of Lazarus where Jesus speaks with the Voice of Love.

4. The extravagant nature of the Good Shepherd's love is seen in the fact that the Good Shepherd knows each sheep, cares for each sheep, and calls each sheep by name. The Good Shepherd's extent of love goes all the way to the fact that Jesus says the Good Shepherd will lay down His life for the sheep (vv. 17–18). Here, Jesus implies that His imminent death was voluntary and He was Himself involved in His own death.

EXAMINING MY STORY

1. When you try to quiet yourself in order to listen to God, what usually happens?[5]

2. How do you experience the Voice of Love today?[6]

3. The psalmist says, "Be still, and know … God" (Ps. 46:10). How does stillness relate to knowing God? To listening to God?

---

5. Often, many people experience a noisy heart when they try to practice silence and solitude. The attempt to be quiet can often lead to disappointment because we hear so many things going on in us: I should be doing this; I could be doing that; I need to answer more e-mails instead of doing this.

6. Not many of us ever hear an audible voice speaking directly to us, but as you think through how you experience God's voice some options may include: through my pastor; through the Scriptures; through music; through a friend's voice saying something that I realize is from beyond my friend's ability to speak a truth to me; through what may seem like a divinely appointed circumstance. Other examples may surface. A simple truth to remember is that God's voice today will never speak something that is contradictory to His Word—already spoken for us.

4. How can you help create space to experience God's love and let yourself be loved?[7]

5. What role do the spiritual disciplines of silence and solitude have in your life today? Why would silence and solitude be called and known as spiritual disciplines?

6. What loving messages has God been speaking to you lately? (Or what loving messages do you *wish* you had been hearing from Him?)

---

7. Spiritual disciplines are exercises that have been practiced for centuries by Christians. Two spiritual disciplines, silence and solitude, are widely recognized as two of the most important for people in the twenty-first century, who live busy and harried lives. The word "discipline" means to "make space." So, the practice of silence and solitude is making space to be quiet—to calm and center our hearts with God. Solitude is making space to be with God alone and to find in His presence the fullness of joy (Ps. 16:11).

AN ORDINARY STORY

Marcy's life is a struggle right now. When she tries to be a good mom, it seems like she's not available to her friends. When she tries to be a good friend, it seems like she struggles with time to be a good wife. Sadly, with all this busyness, she hasn't had time to take care of herself and her weight has gotten out of control.

1. What are the competing voices in Marcy's life?

2. How could Marcy experience the Voice of Love?

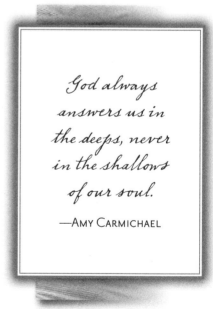

God always
answers us in
the deeps, never
in the shallows
of our soul.

—AMY CARMICHAEL

MAKING SENSE OF THE TRUTH

1. If you are using this guide in a group, consider spending the first fifteen minutes of the group session in total and complete silence. Ask members to be completely still and experience silence together. After fifteen minutes, ask the group to share what this was like for them. Pose questions such as, *What did you feel? What did you think? Was it too long? Not long enough?*

2. Listen to one of the recommended songs for this session (www.LazarusLife.com) and discuss the song's message as a group.

3. Brainstorm possibilities of how silence could be practiced in the ordinary lives of the group members. Is there merit to this? Does it seem like a waste of time?

4. An ancient practice for many Christians was to come together and share a meal in silence. You may want to experiment with this as a group and share a meal without talking. See what stirs in the hearts of the group members when they practice this.

5. Watch the movie *Les Misérables* and discuss the journey of Jean Valjean as a transformed person. What role did the bishop play in Jean's transformation? What role did Jean himself have in his personal transformation?

6. What role does practicing silence have in family life with children and teenagers? What would be the benefits of practicing silence as a family? What are your fears?

PRAYERS FOR TRANSFORMATION

Prayer is not a monologue; it's dialogue. Try writing a prayer that would be God's voice speaking to you. As you think this through, imagine what God might say to you right now and write it down. For example: "Steve, I know you are going through a hard time right now. I want you to know that I am with you every single step. I will be as faithful to you as the rising sun tomorrow morning. In fact, when you see it tomorrow, may the sun remind you of My steadfast love for you. I love you and no circumstance you are going through is going to change My love."

Now you try it. Begin your prayer with God speaking to you,

My child …

What would wordless prayer look like for you?[8]

---

8. Wordless prayer can look like sitting in silence; taking a walk in silence noticing the world around you; lighting a candle and sitting in quiet; listening to instrumental music, etc.

FURTHER STEPS ON THE JOURNEY

1. The following books would be good resources for individual and group use: *Hearing God* by Peter Lord; *Invitation to Silence and Solitude* by Ruth Haley Barton; *The Way of the Heart* by Henri Nouwen.

2. Consider how to incorporate the practice of silence and solitude into your lifestyle and spiritual life. How could you continue to practice the spiritual disciplines of silence in the next week? Month? Quarter?

The core of all prayer is indeed listening.

—HENRI NOUWEN

SESSION 6

THE STENCH OF TRANSFORMATION: THE MESSY REALITIES OF SPIRITUAL CHANGE

Chapter 5 of *The Lazarus Life*

LOOKING FOR THE SOURCE

Many of us have seen Old Faithful in Yellowstone National Park. Every hour or so, this gigantic geyser spews water and steam high into the air as a result of internal pressure building up below the earth's surface. Below the ground, where the eye cannot see, is natural piping that the water has channeled into the soft stone. If you walk by Old Faithful when it's not spewing and sputtering, you wouldn't know that thousands of gallons of steaming hot water are underneath the surface. You would simply see a hole in the ground.

This is a helpful image of the sin and pain in our lives that erupts on a regular basis. Until we look below the surface, we will settle for trying to control the flow of water to make it less messy; remember Willard's phrase—"sin management"? Real transformation requires tracing the hidden piping to the vast reservoirs that have held the water for years. Only then can we do something about the source of the eruptions.

For instance, learning to control anger requires more than counting to ten and trying not to think about whatever makes you angry. This journey requires an in-depth, slow process of exploring reasons for unhealthy anger in the first place. *What am I desiring when I act in rage? What would it look like to acknowledge my feelings without lashing out at someone? What am I really angry about that I'm not addressing?*

79

What am I longing for? Find that reservoir and you'll find the way to be transformed. Greed, food addiction, selfishness, alcoholism, and more all work in a similar way. Something deeper than is visible to the eye is causing us to fall into the same habits again and again.

Jason called me one day from another state to tell me he was in trouble. He asked if he could come visit for a few days. As his story unfolded, I learned that Jason had gotten involved in an emotional affair with one of his staff. His marriage was running on empty, and this new relationship promised a love like he had always envisioned. He considered leaving his wife and kids.

As we talked for hours, it became clear that this woman was offering Jason loving words, promises, and escape. That's exactly what he wanted. But the word got out at home, church, and office. Carnage. Mess. Stink.

(Pages 99–100 of *The Lazarus Life*.)

1. What kinds of carnage, mess, or stink have you or are you experiencing in your life?

2. What do you think God is saying to you through this?

ENGAGING THE SCRIPTURES

ONE PERSON'S SMELLY TRANSFORMATION

This study will help us get to know the smelly side of one of Jesus' best-known followers: Peter. It's tempting to imagine that the characters in the New Testament could not have possibly faced the same issues that we do today. We read the Bible and often forget that the men and women in the pages of Scripture were flesh and blood like us. Peter's journey toward transformation had its highs and lows. His transformation required a step-by-step stumbling just as our own does. In this session, we'll explore a messy situation that Peter had to learn from and one that exposed his own need to be transformed.

READ LUKE 22:31–34, 54–62

31"Simon, Simon, Satan has asked to sift you as wheat. 32But I have prayed for you, Simon, that your faith may not fail. And when you have turned back, strengthen your brothers." 33

But he replied, "Lord, I am ready to go with you to prison and to death."

34Jesus answered, "I tell you, Peter, before the rooster crows today, you will deny three times that you know me."

And

54Then seizing him, they led him away and took him into the house of the high priest. Peter followed at a distance. 55But when they had kindled a fire in the middle of the courtyard and had sat down together, Peter sat down with them. 56A servant girl saw him seated there in the firelight. She looked closely at him and said, "This man was with him."

[57]But he denied it. "Woman, I don't know him," he said. [58]A little later someone else saw him and said, "You also are one of them."

"Man, I am not!" Peter replied.

[59]About an hour later another asserted, "Certainly this fellow was with him, for he is a Galilean."

[60]Peter replied, "Man, I don't know what you're talking about!" Just as he was speaking, the rooster crowed. [61]The Lord turned and looked straight at Peter. Then Peter remembered the word the Lord had spoken to him: "Before the rooster crows today, you will disown me three times." [62]And he went outside and wept bitterly.

> *Accepting the reality of our broken, flawed lives is the beginning of spirituality not because the spiritual life will remove our flaws but because we let go of seeking perfection and, instead, seek God, the one who is present in the tangledness of our lives.*
>
> —MIKE YACONELLI, *MESSY SPIRITUALITY*

1. In what ways do Peter's life and this story illustrate the messy realities of spiritual change?

2. What does Jesus know about Peter that Peter does not know about himself?

3. In Matthew 16:18ff., Jesus calls Peter a "rock," and Peter's confession of faith in Jesus becomes the bedrock for the entire church to be built upon. How does a man go from being called a rock to being called a betrayer? (Luke 22:54–62.)

4. Read Luke 22:61, where we find Jesus turning and looking directly at Peter immediately after Peter denied even knowing Jesus—the One he had pledged absolute loyalty to earlier. What do you imagine Jesus was thinking and feeling when Luke tells us, "The Lord turned and looked straight at Peter"?

> *Messy spirituality is the scandalous assertion that following Christ is anything but tidy and neat, balanced and orderly.*
>
> —MIKE YACONELLI,
> *MESSY SPIRITUALITY*

5. Based on what else you know about Peter from the New Testament, how would you describe his overall progress toward godliness and being a transformed person?[1]

6. How do you relate to Peter's two-steps-forward-one-step-back pattern of obedience?

> *When we sin and mess up our lives, we find that God doesn't go off and leave us—he enters into our trouble and saves us.*
>
> —EUGENE PETERSON, *A LONG OBEDIENCE IN THE SAME DIRECTION*

---

1. Consider Peter's spiritual growth seen in Pentecost and his bold sermon, His vision regarding Cornelius, and Paul's rebuke of Peter for backtracking on the Judaizing issue.

EXAMINING MY STORY

1. What feels messy in and around you?

2. How do you feel about the fact that small groups and churches are made up of messy people—all in process of transformation? What does this tell you about the nature of the people who make up the church?

> *When life becomes all snarled up, offer it to our Lord and let him untie the knots.*
>
> —RICHARDSON WRIGHT

3. How can embracing the messiness of others' journeys help you accept others more and live with more grace?

4. When you face messy situations in your life and in the lives of those you love, what thoughts or emotions stir up inside?[2]

5. How does learning about the messiness of spiritual change make you want to treat others differently?

> It is right that you should begin again every day. There is no better way to finish the spiritual life than to be ever beginning.
>
> —FRANCIS DE SALES

2. Messiness can stir many emotions: fear—because we don't know what the mess will lead to; anxiety—because we worry what God and other people might think if they really knew how totally messy the situation really is; guilt—because we feel responsible and actually may be responsible; scared—because we don't want anyone to find out; shame—because we are embarrassed over what has happened; sad—because we might feel there's no way out or help for us; cynical—because we've given up on hope; etc.

AN ORDINARY STORY

After months of inner turmoil, Abby made a decision to sever a relationship with a good friend. She prayed for guidance, and God seemed to give her the words to say and a peace about moving on. But now, all her friendships have been negatively affected by her decision; some friends talk behind her back or are distancing themselves. This has left Abby very lonely lately, rarely leaving home except for work and church. Even church is difficult because of the looks she gets as she takes her seat in the pew. She now finds herself wondering if she made the right decision.

1. Whether or not she made the right decision, Abby's story has some stench of transformation. What's messy about this story?

2. What kinds of emotions is Abby experiencing?

3. What encouragement would you offer to Abby?

MAKING SENSE OF THE TRUTH

1. Take a "Messy Inventory:"

    •   What mess from your past still exists in the present?

    •   What thoughts or emotions surface as you consider any mess in your life—past or present?

    •   How have others been impacted by your mess?

    •   How has God brought encouragement to you in your messier moments?

    •   What can you do so that a messy situation does not make you feel paralyzed or stagnated?

2. Pass around covered jars containing different smells (some nice, some not) and let people smell them. The goal is to choose a jar whose smell most resembles your spiritual life at the moment.

3. Think about different kinds of artwork or construction projects (painting, sculpting, and so on). What kinds of messes are produced by the artists and workers? How does this relate to your spiritual life?

4. Design an ad for a cleaner that takes care of messy spiritual lives. What promises will the product make? What graphic will the ad include?

PRAYERS FOR TRANSFORMATION

Father,

As I am seeking to love and follow Your Son better, my life has become messy and complicated by
_____ .

For me to confess my messy situation to You, I need to tell You _____
_____ .

I am asking for Your forgiveness and for Your grace to help me live through this mess.

Others don't always understand what I am going through. And so I ask Your help to forgive
_____ for saying/doing _____ .

Even though living with a mess is difficult, I thank You for _____ .

What I want most from You in the midst of my mess is _____ .

I ask this in Jesus' name, not in my own, because on my own I will make even more messes. Amen.

FURTHER STEPS ON THE JOURNEY

1. Consider reading *Messy Spirituality* by Mike Yaconelli. This book is an honest attempt to help us accept the messiness of our lives.

2. For encouragement to persist through the messy changes of life, ask a trusted friend how he or she has seen real progress in your Christian life.

3. Pray and fast for a breakthrough in one particularly smelly aspect of your spiritual life. Fasting is a spiritual discipline that allows us to focus in specific ways on an issue we are facing in our lives. By abstaining from food, technology, or some other necessity in life, we are able to focus, pray, and concentrate on a specific issue that is making life messy. Fasting is a way to see more clearly by giving up something in order to focus on God more.

> No amount of falls will really undo us if we keep picking ourselves up each time. We shall, of course, be very muddy and tattered children by the time we reach home.... It is when we notice the dirt that God is most present in us; it is the very sign of his presence.
>
> —C. S. Lewis

SESSION 7

STEPPING TOWARD LIFE: CHOOSING TO STUMBLE OUT OF DARKNESS

Chapter 6 of *The Lazarus Life*

ONE MAN'S STORY OF THE STEP-BY-STEP JOURNEY

John Newton's life is a story of this stumbling journey toward transformation. Newton was a captain of a ship in the eighteenth century that transported slaves to the New World in exchange for resources discovered in America. The business was lucrative. The life was wretched.

Aboard the slave ship *Greyhound* on May 12, 1748, in a violent storm at sea, John Newton accepted Jesus Christ as his Savior and his Lord. Yet Newton continued in the slave trade for six more years, sailing back and forth from Africa to the New World exchanging chained souls for kegged rum. The transformation that began with accepting Jesus Christ as his Savior was a long, unsteady process.

In 1764, ten years after giving up his profession and sixteen years after his conversion on the storm-tossed sea, Newton became an Anglican priest. In 1787, thirty-nine years after his conversion to Christianity, John Newton wrote a tract titled, "Thoughts Upon the African Slave Trade," which greatly aided William Wilberforce, a member of the British parliament, to campaign against slave trading.

John Newton's story can be disturbing for us if we prefer to imagine a slave-trading captain falling to his knees in the bowels of the ship, praying for God's mercy, asking Jesus into his heart, then getting up and unlocking the chains of captured slaves and sailing home in victory. In fact, many years after his conversion, Newton wrote of that time, "I was greatly deficient in many respects.... I cannot consider myself to have been a believer (in the full sense of the word) till a considerable time afterwards." Newton's "considerable time" becomes permission for each of us to accept the slowness our own step-by-step journeys might take.

Newton wrote a number of hymns that chronicled and celebrated his transformational journey. "Amazing Grace," written in the 1770s, is perhaps his best-known hymn. Later he wrote these words—words that describe the transformation not only of John Newton, but also of Lazarus, myself, and perhaps you as well:

I am not what I ought to be.
I am not what I want to be.
I am not what I hope to be.
But by the grace of God, I am not what I was.

Newton's words speak of a past, present, and future movement in the transformational journey. His life bears witness to an important insight about how ordinary people experience the renovation of their lives. First, we emerge from the tomb, then we take steps—sometimes forward, sometimes wobbly, and sometimes even backward. But we're moving, and ultimately we're moving forward. It is not an instant, total transformation. It's a step-by-step journey of considerable time.

(Pages 115–117 of *The Lazarus Life*.)

ENGAGING THE SCRIPTURES

THE JOURNEY OF TRANSFORMATION: THE STEPS FROM SAUL TO PAUL

The man we now know as Paul had a long life and vocation prior to his conversion. Paul's step-by-step journey toward being a transformed person gives us permission to explore our own journey. Paul—first named Saul—took such a profound journey that even his name changed to fit his new identity.

READ ACTS 9:1–31

¹Meanwhile, Saul was still breathing out murderous threats against the Lord's disciples. He went to the high priest ²and asked him for letters to the synagogues in Damascus, so that if he found any there who belonged to the Way, whether men or women, he might take them as prisoners to Jerusalem. ³As he neared Damascus on his journey, suddenly a light from heaven flashed around him. ⁴He fell to the ground and heard a voice say to him, "Saul, Saul, why do you persecute me?"

⁵"Who are you, Lord?" Saul asked.

"I am Jesus, whom you are persecuting," he replied. ⁶"Now get up and go into the city, and you will be told what you must do."

⁷The men traveling with Saul stood there speechless; they heard the sound but did not see anyone. ⁸Saul got up from the ground, but when he opened his eyes he could see nothing. So they led him by the hand into Damascus. ⁹For three days he was blind, and did not eat or drink anything.

[10]In Damascus there was a disciple named Ananias. The Lord called to him in a vision, "Ananias!"

"Yes, Lord," he answered.

[11]The Lord told him, "Go to the house of Judas on Straight Street and ask for a man from Tarsus named Saul, for he is praying. [12]In a vision he has seen a man named Ananias come and place his hands on him to restore his sight."

[13]"Lord," Ananias answered, "I have heard many reports about this man and all the harm he has done to your saints in Jerusalem. [14]And he has come here with authority from the chief priests to arrest all who call on your name."

[15]But the Lord said to Ananias, "Go! This man is my chosen instrument to carry my name before the Gentiles and their kings and before the people of Israel. [16]I will show him how much he must suffer for my name."

[17]Then Ananias went to the house and entered it. Placing his hands on Saul, he said, "Brother Saul, the Lord—Jesus, who appeared to you on the road as you were coming here—has sent me so that you may see again and be filled with the Holy Spirit." [18]Immediately, something like scales fell from Saul's eyes, and he could see again. He got up and was baptized, [19]and after taking some food, he regained his strength.

Saul spent several days with the disciples in Damascus. [20]At once he began to preach in the synagogues that Jesus is the Son of God. [21]All those who heard him were astonished and asked, "Isn't he the man who raised havoc in Jerusalem among those who call on this name? And hasn't he come here to take them as prisoners to the chief priests?" [22]Yet Saul grew more and more powerful and baffled the Jews living in Damascus by proving that Jesus is the Christ.

[23]After many days had gone by, the Jews conspired to kill him, [24]but Saul learned of their plan. Day and night they kept close watch on the city gates in order to kill him. [25]But his followers took him by night and lowered him in a basket through an opening in the wall.

[26]When he came to Jerusalem, he tried to join the disciples, but they were all afraid of him, not believing that he really was a disciple. [27]But Barnabas took him

and brought him to the apostles. He told them how Saul on his journey had seen the Lord and that the Lord had spoken to him, and how in Damascus he had preached fearlessly in the name of Jesus. [28]So Saul stayed with them and moved about freely in Jerusalem, speaking boldly in the name of the Lord. [29]He talked and debated with the Grecian Jews, but they tried to kill him. [30]When the brothers learned of this, they took him down to Caesarea and sent him off to Tarsus.

[31]Then the church throughout Judea, Galilee and Samaria enjoyed a time of peace. It was strengthened; and encouraged by the Holy Spirit, it grew in numbers, living in the fear of the Lord.

1. As you read Acts 9:1–31, what references to time—days, months, years—do you notice?[1]

2. What impresses you about the process of Paul's conversion experience? How does Paul's journey of transformation compare to what you are studying now?

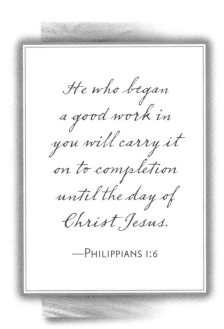

He who began a good work in you will carry it on to completion until the day of Christ Jesus.

—PHILIPPIANS 1:6

1. For more biblical evidence of Paul's conversion, see Philippians 3:4–6 and Galatians 1:11—2:1.

3. In Galatians 1:13–18, Paul describes his own experience and what happened immediately after his conversion. What do you imagine happened to Paul during those three years in Arabia?

4. If you had to label the "Arabia" period or season of time in Paul's life—what would you call it?

5. What role did Paul have in his own transformation? What about the role of others in his life?

6. What encouragement do you derive from learning about Paul's journey?

EXAMINING MY STORY

1. Take some time to consider a "time line of your own spiritual journey"

Write "birth" on the beginning of the line and make the line move up to the right. At the end of that line put "present." Let X's designate the people whom God used to help shape you. Designate "events" that have shaped you with asterisks (*). And exclamation points (!) for "places" that have shaped you. This exercise will foster a reflective awareness, helping you actually get a perspective on how God has been involved in your life—perhaps revealing some steps that may give you an "Aha" moment.[2] Give yourself ample time to do this exercise.

Let us run with perseverance the race marked out for us.

—HEBREWS 12:1

2. What stands out about your time line? Do you see any patterns? Does God's shaping work in your life seem to show up more in one way than another?[3]

---

2. The author has developed this exercise in more detail in Soul Shaping, published by Potter's Inn. For more information, contact Potter's Inn or order a copy at www.PottersInn.com.

3. Consider taking time to hear from one another if you are doing this in a group. If you're doing this alone, ask a friend to do this with you, and over coffee or lunch share your timelines, listening carefully and exploring a bit more with questions to "see" what you might have missed along the way. The benefit of sharing your time line story is that you'll have the opportunity to know each other—perhaps for the first time in context.

3. How does our fast-moving world and ever-changing technology affect your spiritual life
    and perspective on God?

> *Forgetting what is behind and straining toward what is ahead, I press on toward the goal to win the prize for which God has called me heavenward in Christ Jesus.*
>
> —PHILIPPIANS 3:13–14

AN ORDINARY STORY

Mike gets a knot in his stomach every time he thinks of spending Christmas with his folks. It seems like every visit has his parents belittling his career and family, while praising his brother. In years past, Mike silently hated and endured the whole experience. But in keeping with a change of heart, Mike would like to forgive his parents, admit his own failure to them, and make this Christmas different.

1. What small steps could Mike take in moving forward in these relationships?

2. What difficulties will Mike no doubt encounter?

3. What role could Mike's family or friends play in his transformation?

MAKING SENSE OF THE TRUTH

1. Find a clock with movable hour and minute hands and ask participants to set the time according to the time they think it is in their spiritual life. For example: Someone might say, "I think it is 9:00 a.m. in my spiritual life. I'm just beginning and have a long way to go." Or, "I feel like it's 10:00 p.m. I'm tired and need a good sleep to wake up refreshed."

2. In preparation for this week's session, ask participants to bring something from their past that holds meaning for their spiritual journey. Examples could be a photo taken at a camp or other special place you have been where you sensed God's presence, a dish that makes you nostalgic. Share your item with the group. Journal about your feelings and thoughts.

3. Explore and identify the next step in your journey.

PRAYERS FOR TRANSFORMATION

Make a list of stages, seasons, or phases you have completed on your journey to transformation. Write a prayer of thanksgiving specifically for each stage or phase, rather than for specific things you have learned from each phase. Let this be "My Prayer of Thanksgiving for My Journey Thus Far"

A Prayer for the Seasons of My Journey

Lord, in the *winter* of my life, thank You for …

Lord, in the *spring* of my life, thank You for …

Lord, in the *summer* of my life, thank You for …

Lord, in the *fall* of my life, thank You for …

FURTHER STEPS ON THE JOURNEY

1. Consider reading *Deeper Experiences of Famous Christians* by James G. Lawson. In this significant volume, you will read of the events, circumstances, and shaping developments in the lives of dozens of remarkable Christians. If the group should read this together, each person could share a three-to-five-minute overview of one person's life in the book. The group could then discuss common aspects that God uses to shape and transform a life.

2. Do a Google search on "persistence + quotes" and find one just for yourself, a quote about hanging in there when the journey feels too hard.

The great awareness comes slowly, piece by piece. The path of spiritual growth is a path of lifelong learning.

—M. Scott Peck

SESSION 8

NAMING THE GRAVECLOTHES: RECOGNIZING THE THINGS THAT BIND YOU

Chapter 7 of *The Lazarus Life*

THE POWER OF NAMING

After God created the heavens, earth, water, sky, and people, and creatures to populate the earth, He gave a significant instruction to Adam. He told Adam to *name* the animals (Gen. 2:19). By naming the creatures roaming the fresh earth, the first man formed a method of communication and recognition for himself and all humanity. He also showed his domination over the creatures of the world.

We use names today, of course, to identify everything from pets to illnesses. How many times have you heard a toddler ask: "What's that?" From the time we are young, we want to understand our surroundings. *Naming* gives us an ability to understand, associate, and relate to our world around us.

Anyone who has spent time in a foreign country without knowing the language knows that not being able to identify places, people, and objects by name makes one feel incompetent and frustrated. Once we have words to put to our surroundings, we are not as intimidated. The same is true for our thoughts and emotions. If our past relationship with a sibling, for instance, is a vague collection of angry and painful memories, those memories will always have domination over us. If we are able to name those feelings ("I feel like you always have to be better than me" or "I feel hurt that you never take the initiative to come visit"), we are able to address their root and be in better control of them. Naming helps us understand.

Naming helps us overcome. Naming the issue that is really bothering us helps us communicate.

A striking example of this is recorded in Mark 5 when Jesus confronts a nameless, tormented man along the road, in the region of the Gerasenes. This possessed man needed deliverance from an evil spirit; many spirits, in fact. His hands and feet had been chained, but he broke them and lived in the tombs. Night and day he cried and cut himself with stones.

When Jesus encountered the man, He commanded, "Come out of this man, you evil spirit!" The man of the tombs addressed Jesus by one of His names: "What do you want, Jesus, Son of the Most High God? Swear to God that you won't torture me!" To this Jesus countered, "What is *your* name?" The possessed man answered, "Legion," revealing that many demons were tormenting the man (Mark 5:7–8). Jesus then cast out the demons.

Identifying the demons' name and nature reduced their grip on the man. They were no longer mysterious, all-powerful beings; they were demons Jesus could address by name and dominate. As the demons were named, Jesus brought about transformation. Only when the false names were cast out could the man from the tombs embrace his true name: the beloved.

(Pages 136–138 of *The Lazarus Life*.)

1. In chapter 7 of *The Lazarus Life*, the author suggests that we all tend to continue wearing some of our "graveclothes" even after we've begun to be "resurrected." What do you consider to be a few of the graveclothes you seem to carry around—perhaps wearing them on the inside where no one can see?

2. Why do you think those graveclothes are hanging on? What kind of help do you need to take them off for good?

> God in his wisdom only gives the grace of self-knowledge gradually; if he were to show us our true selves suddenly, we should despair and lose all courage. But as we perceive and conquer the more glaring faults, his gracious light shows us the subtler, more hidden imperfections; and this spiritual process lasts all through life.
>
> —Jean Nicolas Grou

ENGAGING THE SCRIPTURES

Scripture encourages us to "take off" certain things in order to move forward in the spiritual life. In the same way, we are told we must "put on" other things to live the life God wants us to live. Paul uses this imagery to help us understand specific things we need to do in the spiritual life that are clearly our responsibility. This session will help you examine your own graveclothes and begin to name them. By learning to name specific things that are holding you back in the spiritual life, you gain clarity of your own heart, which then gives guidance as to how best to remove your graveclothes.

READ COLOSSIANS 3:5–14

[5]Put to death, therefore, whatever belongs to your earthly nature: sexual immorality, impurity, lust, evil desires and greed, which is idolatry. [6]Because of these, the wrath of God is coming. [7]You used to walk in these ways, in the life you once lived. [8]But now you must rid yourselves of all such things as these: anger, rage, malice, slander, and filthy language from your lips. [9]Do not lie to each other, since you have taken off your old self with its practices [10]and have put on the new self, which is being renewed in knowledge in the image of its Creator. [11]Here there is no Greek or Jew, circumcised or uncircumcised, barbarian, Scythian, slave or free, but Christ is all, and is in all.

[12]Therefore, as God's chosen people, holy and dearly loved, clothe yourselves with compassion, kindness, humility, gentleness and patience. [13]Bear with each other and forgive whatever grievances you may have against one another. Forgive as the Lord

forgave you. [14]And over all these virtues put on love, which binds them all together in perfect unity.

1. Why do you think Paul is eager to see people "put to death" these issues in their lives?

2. How do these things restrict life within us and around us?

3. How does a person put these things to "death" according to Paul?

4. How does this passage compare to the graveclothes of Lazarus that the author explores in *The Lazarus Life*?

5. What are the things that Paul encourages us to "put on"?

6. How do we realistically put on these things each day? What would it look like for you to put on forgiveness and then love, which "is your basic all-purpose garment" (Col. 3:14 MSG)?

> The best remedy for those who are afraid, lonely or unhappy is to go outside, somewhere where they can be quiet, alone with the heavens, nature and God. Because only then does one feel that all is as it should be and that God wishes to see people happy, amidst the simple beauty of nature.
>
> —ANNE FRANK

EXAMINING MY STORY

1. As you read through the author's suggestions of possible graveclothes (pages 138–153 of *The Lazarus Life*), which one(s) seem to stand out as possibilities for you? Can you trace the beginnings of this gravecloth in your life and how this happened? This may take some time.

2. What has it been like for you to wear these graveclothes? What is the residue these graveclothes have left on your heart? On the hearts of your family? On the hearts of your friends? Your work?

> *I'm absolutely convinced that nothing—nothing living or dead, angelic or demonic, today or tomorrow, high or low, thinkable or unthinkable—absolutely nothing can get between us and God's love.*
>
> —PAUL IN ROMANS 8:38–39 MSG

3. What would it look like for someone to help you remove your graveclothes? What would this person need to do? What would you need to do to let him or her help you?

4. How do you hope your life will be different after removing these graveclothes?

THE FIVE GRAVECLOTHES: SOME IDEAS FOR REMOVING THEM

1. SELF-REJECTION

Accepting yourself as God made you is one of the most important steps in the journey out of the tomb. In the blanks below, you have the opportunity to be very specific about an area of transformation in your life. For example, you may constantly struggle with your body size; maybe you're large, maybe you're small, maybe you just don't like what you see in the mirror. In number 1, you might say, "I want to accept the size of my body." This is not a resignation, but rather an acceptance of the way your body was created.

1. I want to accept _____ about my body.

2. I want to accept _____about my past.

3. I want to accept _____about my life.

4. I am afraid to do this because …

2. FEAR

1. What is your major source of fear?

2. For me to live without fear in this area of my life, my life would look like …

3. How does God's promise never to leave or forsake us influence or impact your particular fear(s)?[1]

3. GUILT

1. What would it look like for you to wear "forgiveness" rather than the gravecloth of guilt?

2. How powerful is your guilt when you consider the power of Christ's blood and forgiveness? What is the major stumbling block that makes it hard for you to rid yourself of guilt?

3. How can confession become a regular part of your worship and daily experience?

4. BLAME AND SHAME

1. Try to identify any areas of shame in your life. Examples might be economic, racial, spiritual, a wound from the past, sexual.

2. How do shame and blame seem to work together against you in your spiritual life?

3. How can you quiet the voices of shame and blame? Have you been able to do this before or is this an entirely new experience?

5. DISAPPOINTMENT

1. Name a few of your past disappointments.

2. Oswald Chambers reminds us to "let the past sleep but let it sleep in the bosom of Jesus Christ." Explain what you think this means.

3. How do we "leave the irreconcilable past behind and walk into the irresistible future?"[2]

---

1. Matthew 28:20, Isaiah 7:9; 43:1–3, and Psalm 94:19
2. Oswald Chambers uses this expression in *My Utmost for His Highest*

AN ORDINARY STORY

Michelle has been divorced for several years now but is still reluctant to begin dating again. To her surprise, someone at the office asked her out on a date. She said yes, but hasn't slept since. All night she lies awake agonizing over the "what ifs" about dating, relationships, and perhaps even marriage. Even if she should fall asleep, she dreams about making mistakes and scaring him off.

1. How might shame possibly stick its head into Michelle's experience?

2. How would naming these graveclothes improve the situation?

MAKING SENSE OF THE TRUTH

1. If you are using this study in a group setting, take a roll of toilet paper and unwind it into a bag, making it fit loosely inside. When you speak about graveclothes that entangle us and prevent our forward movement to Jesus, lay the toilet paper on the ground in the center of the circle or room. Spread it out to create a visual reminder of the graveclothes. Perhaps try loosely wrapping someone in the symbolic graveclothes and have the group remove particular issues that represent the graveclothes.

2. Give all the group members a piece of paper and ask them to write the name of their number-one gravecloth, the one preventing them from moving toward Jesus and experiencing life. You may want to write the names of some issues that people struggle with today and let people choose the one that seems to fit best. Possible graveclothes to write down could be: lust, anger, pride, envy, jealousy, my thought life, discouragement, or laziness.

3. Have group members write specific issues that relate to their graveclothes. Take all the papers and destroy them—perhaps burning them outside or tearing them up.

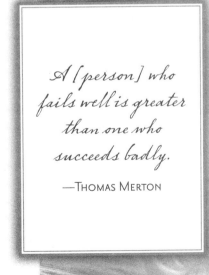

A [person] who fails well is greater than one who succeeds badly.

—THOMAS MERTON

PRAYERS OF TRANSFORMATION

Dear God,[3] You alone are powerful. Nothing can separate me from Your love. As I reflect upon my graveclothes, I'm asking You to take this specific issue of _____ and help me rid myself of it and from it. Far too long this issue has held me back. It has caused me pain and hindered my forward motion of walking toward You. I ask You in Jesus' name to free me from the grip of _____ and to allow me the freedom to walk unhindered toward Jesus Christ. I'm asking You this day to give to me the peace that surpasses my understanding, the faith to believe that You are now at work in my life, and the strength to walk forward and not fall back.

Send to me, O God, friends who will encourage me, truth that will inspire me, and courage to take each step forward in my journey. Thank You that You care not only about the hairs on my head but also the specific issues that hinder my Christian walk. Thank You that You give me strength through Your Holy Spirit to help me when I fall, and give to me the courage to get up again and walk forward.

Thank You for the grace that You give me, which releases me from so much that seeks to hinder me. I need and want that grace.

(Add any thoughts here)

I ask this in Jesus' name. Amen.

---

3. This prayer is loosely based on Romans 8:35–39. Perhaps consider using Paul's words as a prayer for the group to say together. Praying the Scriptures is a beautiful and ancient way of expressing our hearts to God. This passage serves as an affirming and positive message that should offer encouragement and hope.

FURTHER STEPS ON THE JOURNEY

Choose one or two biblical personalities and see if you can determine what graveclothes they struggle with. This exercise presents the opportunity to get to know biblical personalities as real and ordinary people. Gideon is one example. The guide below can serve as a tool for looking at Gideon's life as well as other biblical characters.

GIDEON: JUDGES 6:11–39

1. If you were describing Gideon to someone who'd never heard of him, what would you say?

2. What do you feel Gideon was afraid of?

3. Gideon is called by several names. What are they?

4. Describe God's reaction to Gideon's fear and self-rejection.

5. As Gideon accepts what God has told him, what changes do you see occurring in his life?

6. Don't miss God's promise to Gideon: "The Lord is with you."

7. Hebrews 11:32 includes Gideon in the honor roll of faith heroes. Why do you think he was included in this famous list?

8. What is one thing Gideon learned about God through his experience?

9. How does Gideon's life speak to your life?

You may want to do a character study of Thomas, David, Ruth, Martha, Mary, and others to see what you discover in their lives on this subject.

There is a time to take counsel of your fears, and there is a time to never listen to any fear.

—George S. Patton

SESSION 9

REMOVING THE GRAVECLOTHES: EMBRACING THE HELP OF A LOVING COMMUNITY

Chapter 8 of *The Lazarus Life*

A SOBERING CONFESSION

Here is something that is difficult for me to confess. My experience with community in the transformational process has not been what I thought it would be. Sometimes, in my darkest hours, I have wondered where my friends have gone. I have wondered if anyone really cares about me. At times in my life, I don't feel I am part of an aspen grove at all. I feel like a tender, young pine tree standing alone in a field.

LOOKING FOR FAMILY

When I first became a follower of Jesus, I had high hopes for finding brothers and sisters, even fathers and mothers, who could help me grow as a new believer. The Christian language of family deeply appealed to me. It sounded like a place of belonging. I imagined times when the fatted calf would be roasted for the next few prodigals who arrived home. I looked for small groups, church meetings, and the fellowship of the "one anothers" to offer me what I thought was the norm for the Christian experience of life.

I have found that I am not alone in my quest. Many of us are looking for the same thing. Yet our search for a place to belong and for a people to "do" life with often leaves us disappointed and disillusioned. No matter how hard we try, no matter how many places we look, friendship and community can be a superficial experience that never satisfies the soul. We long for the deep friendships of David and Jonathan and Ruth and Naomi, but with the busyness of life, who has time to foster such friendships? What was meant to be community often turns into "catch up" times over coffee where we share safe stories of vacations and children.

> The best mirror is an old friend.
>
> —GEORGE HERBERT

What God has reminded me is that in every group, every family, and every church, people are wearing their own graveclothes. So am I. But I forget this so often, hoping that *this* group could be *the* place where I can finally deal with something important in my life, and all my needs will be met—finally.

(Pages 157–158 of *The Lazarus Life*.)

1. As you are working toward spiritual transformation, do you feel that you are alone in it? If not, who is on your side?

2. What is hard about having too little help from others as you pursue spiritual change?

ENGAGING THE SCRIPTURES

Mark tells the dramatic story of four people who literally carried someone to Jesus. Their determination, strength, and vigor helped a friend who could not help himself. Let's face it: We need each other on the journey to transformation.

READ MARK 2:1–12

[1]A few days later, when Jesus again entered Capernaum, the people heard that he had come home. [2]So many gathered that there was no room left, not even outside the door, and he preached the word to them. [3]Some men came, bringing to him a paralytic, carried by four of them. [4]Since they could not get him to Jesus because of the crowd, they made an opening in the roof above Jesus and, after digging through it, lowered the mat the paralyzed man was lying on. [5]When Jesus saw their faith, he said to the paralytic, "Son, your sins are forgiven."

[6]Now some teachers of the law were sitting there, thinking to themselves, [7]"Why does this fellow talk like that? He's blaspheming! Who can forgive sins but God alone?"

[8]Immediately Jesus knew in his spirit that this was what they were thinking in their hearts, and he said to them, "Why are you thinking these things? [9]Which is easier: to say to the paralytic, 'Your sins are forgiven,' or to say, 'Get up, take your mat and walk'? [10]But that you may know that the Son of Man has authority on earth to forgive sins ..." He said to the paralytic, [11]"I tell you, get up, take your mat and go home." [12]He got up, took his mat and walked out in full view of them all. This amazed everyone and they praised God, saying, "We have never seen anything like this!"

1. Imagine the emotions of the four men—what were they feeling as they lowered their friend? What about the emotions of their friend? What about the crowd?

2. Which character do you most identify with? Why?

3. Describe the actions of the people who carried their friend to Jesus. What words best describe their action?[1]

4. Mark says that Jesus "saw their faith." What do you think this means?

---

1. These five men, the four who carried the sick man and the sick man himself, all demonstrated faith, determination, resolve, perseverance, and action.

5. Jesus chose to forgive the man's sins. What is this about? What does this tell you about Jesus?

6. What role did the four people who carried the sick man have in his transformation?

7. What was the result of this act of transformation?

8. Who are "four" people who seem to consistently carry you to Jesus?

Walking with a friend in the dark is better than walking alone in the light.

—HELEN KELLER

EXAMINING MY STORY

1. How would you describe your present experience in having a group of people who are committed to your transformation?

2. What part of your life feels paralyzed, incapable of moving toward transformation? What would it take for you to ask for help, for someone to carry you? And what would you ask this person to do?

3. In *The Lazarus Life*, the author lists several characteristics of a "transformational community" (pages 161–169). What are they, and how does your own community compare to what is mentioned there?

4. How aware are you of the graveclothes of others? How could you grow to be more sensitive and helpful in your relationship with their graveclothes?

AN ORDINARY STORY

Compare stories A and B.

A—Eric meets with a group of men from church every other Friday morning for coffee. Their discussion usually remains pretty topical; however, last Friday Eric admitted to difficulties with online gambling. What started innocently had turned addictive. Several of the men admitted to similar vices and agreed to their destructive nature. Eric left the meeting feeling comforted that he wasn't "the only one."

B—Eric meets with a group of men from church every other Friday morning for coffee. Their discussion usually remains pretty topical; however, last Friday Eric admitted to difficulties with online gambling. What started innocently had turned addictive. Several of the men asked Eric to share more of his struggle, his pain, his thoughts, and feelings about gambling. Eric spoke of his hidden life, his loneliness, and his desires. Most of the men remained quiet, listening to Eric's heart for the rest of the meeting.

> *Grief can take care of itself, but to get the full value of joy you must have somebody to divide it with.*
>
> —MARK TWAIN

1. What's different about these two stories?

2. What are some pros and cons of each scenario?

MAKING SENSE OF THE TRUTH

1. Find a blanket strong enough to hold one of the group members willing to be carried. The volunteer should lie down in the middle of the blanket while all the other members grab one of the blanket's edges. Now, as a group, lift the blanket and take a few steps, being careful not to drop the person. Movement requires agreeing on the direction and working together. How does this exercise relate to being "carried to Jesus"?

2. Brainstorm on how the group members can actually commit themselves to becoming a transformational community. What would this involve? What would the group need to commit to do in order to grow in these areas?

3. The "one another" passages are places in Scripture where we are told to help each other do specific things in our spiritual journey. Have the group members read the "one anothers" one at a time, out loud. Just the experience of reading these in a group setting is profound and awakening. Take the time to make sure all of them are read and then ask for responses as to how people feel about them. Which ones does your group do well? Which ones need some attention?

    1. "Be at peace with each other" (Mark 9:50).

    2. "Wash one another's feet" (John 13:14).

    3. "Love one another" (John 13:34).

    4. "Love one another" (John 13:35).

    5. "Love each another" (John 15:12).

    6. "Love each other" (John 15:17).

    7. "Be devoted to one another in brotherly love" (Rom. 12:10).

    8. "Honor one another above yourselves" (Rom. 12:10).

    9. "Live in harmony with one another" (Rom. 12:16).

    10. "Love one another" (Rom. 13:8).

    11. "Stop passing judgment on one another" (Rom. 14:13).

    12. "Accept one another, then, just as Christ accepted you" (Rom. 15:7).

13. "Instruct one another" (Rom. 15:14).

14. "Greet one another with a holy kiss" (Rom. 16:1).

15. "When you come together to eat, wait for each other" (1 Cor. 11:33).

16. "Have equal concern for each other" (1 Cor. 12:25).

17. "Greet one another with a holy kiss" (1 Cor. 16:20).

18. "Serve one another in love" (Gal. 5:13).

19. "If you keep on biting and devouring each other … you will be destroyed by each other" (Gal. 5:15).

20. "Carry each other's burdens" (Gal. 6:2).

21. "Be patient, bearing with one another in love" (Eph. 4:2).

22. "Be kind and compassionate to one another" (Eph. 4:32).

23. "Forgiving each other" (Eph. 4:32).

24. "Speak to one another with psalms, hymns and spiritual songs" (Eph. 5:19).

25. "Submit to one another out of reverence for Christ" (Eph. 5:21).

26. "In humility consider others better than yourselves" (Phil. 2:3).

27. "Do not lie to each other" (Col. 3:9).

28. "Bear with each other" (Col. 3:13).

29. "Forgive whatever grievances you may have against one another" (Col. 3:13).

30. "Teach … one another" (Col. 3:16).

31. "Admonish one another" (Col. 3:16).

32. "Make your love increase and overflow for each other" (1 Thess. 3:12).

33. "Love each other" (1 Thess. 4:9).

34. "Encourage each other" (1 Thess. 4:18).

35. "Encourage one another" (1 Thess. 5:11).

36. "Build each other up" (1 Thess. 5:11).

37. "Encourage one another daily" (Heb. 3:13).

38. "Spur one another on toward love and good deeds" (Heb. 10:24).

39. "Do not slander one another" (James 4:11).

40. "Don't grumble against each other" (James 5:9).

41. "Confess your sins to each other" (James 5:16).

42. "Pray for each other" (James 5:16).

43. "Love one another deeply, from the heart" (1 Peter 1:22).

44. "Live in harmony with one another" (1 Peter 3:8).

45. "Offer hospitality to one another without grumbling" (1 Peter 4:9).

46. "Each one should use whatever gift he has to serve others" (1 Peter 4:10).

47. "Clothe yourselves with humility toward one another" (1 Peter 5:5).

48. "Love one another" (1 John 3:11).

49. "Love one another" (1 John 3:23; 4:7; 4:11; 4:12).

50. "Love one another" (2 John 5).

One loyal friend is worth ten thousand relatives.

—EURIPIDES, GREEK PLAYWRIGHT

PRAYERS OF TRANSFORMATION

Have your group members pair off and share their requests and pray for each other in specific ways. Perhaps the pairs could make an arrangement to keep praying for each other daily for the next week or month.

In your sharing of requests, try to cover these areas:

- Share which of the "one another" passages you most want and value in a friend.

- Confess and share your fears about inviting someone "in" to know your real issues and concerns in life.[2]

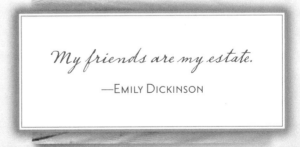

My friends are my estate.

—Emily Dickinson

---

2. As you listen to each other, try to be mindful first to listen without reacting to your friend. A reaction that is strong, judgmental, or disapproving will shut down your friend's willingness to share and confide in you and ask for prayer.

FURTHER STEPS ON THE JOURNEY

1. Consider reading *Sacred Companions* by David Benner. Perhaps assign a group member to read this wonderful book and give a brief report or overview of it.

2. Consider writing a handwritten note to a friend who has helped you remove a gravecloth and encouraged you in your walk toward Jesus. A handwritten note communicates time and determination—true gratefulness in our world.

> *Tell me what company thou keepst, and I'll tell thee what thou art.*
>
> —MIGUEL DE CERVANTES
> (1547–1616) SPANISH NOVELIST

SESSION 10

LIVING IN THE LIGHT: THE POWER OF YOUR TRANSFORMATION

Chapter 9 of _The Lazarus Life_

THE POWER OF STORY

Several times each year I lead a retreat called, "The Transformation of a Man's Heart." It's based on a book I was privileged to work on a few years ago. In this retreat several ordinary men share their true stories of how they have been transformed in a specific area of life. One man will share about how his marriage has experienced transformation after years of infidelity; he will speak about the graveclothes of guilt and shame that he is going to leave at this year's retreat. Another will tell his story of giving up alcohol and restoring his relationships with his grown kids after years of intense gravecloth removal.

Jim, a dear friend of mine, decided at this retreat to begin spending quality time with his wife—something she had been asking him to do for years. Jim loved his wife but always wanted to do one more thing at work before spending time with her. At the retreat he shared with us a decision he made to move toward transformation. Jim doesn't like coffee and never has, but his wife does. In fact she often asked Jim to share a cup of coffee with her and just talk. Jim's decision was to begin this ritual together. Every day they would have a cup of coffee and read a short devotional together. Jim's decision is a simple step forward toward strengthening his marriage. (And now, Jim says, he actually likes coffee!)

At last year's retreat a group of older men, all over the age of sixty, stood and shared their heart-wrenching stories. There was not a dry eye in the auditorium. In the back of the room, a group of men in their twenties stood up and gave their senior brothers a rousing standing ovation. One person's transformation inspires others.

Transformation takes different forms in each of our lives. We have no formula to produce the kind of transformation we want, no twenty-one steps to a transformed life. We only have obedience to Jesus' call. Perhaps God knows that if we had a formula we would worship the formula instead of Him. Instead He calls us to the mysteries of the spiritual life. He asks us to listen to the stories of others and then receive the individual transformation He has for our own lives.

The writer of Hebrews tells us about a host of ordinary, transformed men and women and asks us to remember God's work in *their* lives. We're told to "keep your eyes on Jesus … When you find yourself flagging in your faith, go over that story again, item by item … That will shoot adrenaline into your souls" (Heb. 12:1–3 MSG). I love that line, "shoot adrenalin into your souls." That's how stories of transformation work. They energize us on our way to Jesus.

(Pages 183–185 of *The Lazarus Life*.)

1. The transformation you are undergoing has the potential to impact far more than just your own spiritual life. Due to the changes you are undergoing, what positive effects are you already seeing in the lives of others and in the world at large?

2. What positive effects do you *hope* to see?

ENGAGING THE SCRIPTURES

Most people mistakenly believe that the entire story of Lazarus is contained in John 11. John continues to tell us about the aftermath of Lazarus's resurrection in chapter 12. Here we encounter a fully alive Lazarus. There is a significant "ripple effect" of what happened to Lazarus and those around him after his resurrection. This session will help you explore the "ripple" effect of Lazarus's transformation and your own.

READ JOHN 12:1–19

¹Six days before the Passover, Jesus arrived at Bethany, where Lazarus lived, whom Jesus had raised from the dead. ²Here a dinner was given in Jesus' honor. Martha served, while Lazarus was among those reclining at the table with him. ³Then Mary took about a pint of pure nard, an expensive perfume; she poured it on Jesus' feet and wiped his feet with her hair. And the house was filled with the fragrance of the perfume.

⁴But one of his disciples, Judas Iscariot, who was later to betray him, objected, ⁵"Why wasn't this perfume sold and the money given to the poor? It was worth a year's wages." ⁶He did not say this because he cared about the poor but because he was a thief; as keeper of the money bag, he used to help himself to what was put into it.

⁷"Leave her alone," Jesus replied. "It was intended that she should save this perfume for the day of my burial. ⁸You will always have the poor among you, but you will not always have me."

⁹Meanwhile a large crowd of Jews found out that Jesus was there and came, not only because of him but also to see Lazarus, whom he had raised from the dead. ¹⁰So the chief priests made plans to kill Lazarus as well, ¹¹for on account of him many of the Jews were going over to Jesus and putting their faith in him.

¹²The next day the great crowd that had come for the Feast heard that Jesus was on his way to Jerusalem. ¹³They took palm branches and went out to meet him, shouting, "Hosanna!" "Blessed is he who comes in the name of the Lord!" "Blessed is the King of Israel!" ¹⁴Jesus found a young donkey and sat upon it, as it is written, ¹⁵"Do not be afraid, O Daughter of Zion; see, your king is coming, seated on a donkey's colt."

¹⁶At first his disciples did not understand all this. Only after Jesus was glorified did they realize that these things had been written about him and that they had done these things to him.

¹⁷Now the crowd that was with him when he called Lazarus from the tomb and raised him from the dead continued to spread the word. ¹⁸Many people, because they had heard that he had given this miraculous sign, went out to meet him. ¹⁹So the

[He] is not famous. It may be that he never will be. It may be that when his life at last comes to an end he will leave no more trace of his sojourn on earth than a stone thrown into a river leaves on the surface of the water. But it may be that the way of life that he has chosen for himself and the peculiar strength and sweetness of his character may have an ever-growing influence over his fellow men so that, long after his death perhaps, it may be realized that there lived in this age a very remarkable creature.

—WILLIAM SOMERSET MAUGHAM

Pharisees said to one another, "See, this is getting us nowhere. Look how the whole world has gone after him!"

1. How does it strike you that Jesus is enjoying a dinner party in an intimate setting of the family home of Lazarus?

2. What do you think Mary's act of anointing the feet of Jesus means?[1]

3. Read John 12:9–11 once more. Describe the various reactions to Lazarus's resurrection.

---

1. The act of Mary's anointing Jesus' feet with expensive perfume is intended by John to give his readers an appreciation of the worth of the perfumed oil that Mary used in this act of devotion and love. It's also important here because of Judas's reaction and the timing of what Judas is about to do to Jesus. John's description of the odor filling the house is a description that he wanted to make sure his readers noticed.

4. Read John 12:17–19. John describes the growing ripple effect and aftermath of this important event. The Pharisees said, "Look how the whole world has gone after him!" What do you think they meant by this?

5. Knowing that Lazarus was resurrected only a few days prior to Jesus, what do you imagine Jesus was feeling during this experience?

> *Setting an example is not the main means of influencing another, it is the only means.*
>
> —ALBERT EINSTEIN

EXAMINING MY STORY

1. Describe a person whom you know well who is seeking to live a transformed life. What attributes describe this person's life? What is his or her character like? What is the ripple effect[2] on other people's lives?

2. How is your life different now that you are seeking a transformed life?

3. How many of the characteristics listed in chapter 9 of *The Lazarus Life* do you feel you are experiencing now?

4. A life of *intimacy* with Jesus—what does this look like in your life?

2. By "ripple effect" I mean simply the result of a stone being tossed into a stilled pond making ripples. This image is used to explore impact and influence. A transformed life is not to be lived for one's self. The results of a transformed life are like a ripple that moves outward impacting all of the water in the pond.

5. A life of *gratitude* and *generosity*—what steps are you taking to be more grateful?

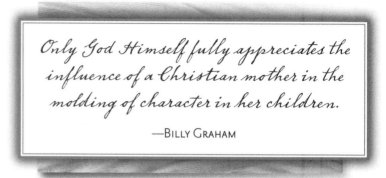

Only God Himself fully appreciates the influence of a Christian mother in the molding of character in her children.

—BILLY GRAHAM

6. A life of *danger*—what is being stirred up in your life as a result of your transformation that feels dangerous?

7. A life of *influence*—whom is God prompting you to influence?

8. Should we *create* a ripple effect as a result of our transformation or does this just happen? Why?

AN ORDINARY STORY

Judy knew her husband, Chris, was terribly frustrated with life. Since being laid off, Chris had aimed most of his anger at God, struggling with anything spiritual: church, prayer, or Bible study. Judy prayed daily for God to show up in a new way in Chris's life, and was hopeful when he went fishing with a couple of friends from church. She certainly was even more hopeful when he came home talking about an encounter with God.

Three months later, Judy continues to see Chris's life changing. He has his moments of frustration, but all in all, he has a new perspective and seems more at peace during the storm of an unstable job market.

Their kids seem to have picked up on the change as well, spending more time with Chris, laughing, smiling, and playing together. Overall, the mood of their home has changed, even to the point that Judy's friends have said she even looks more relaxed and rested. She would have to agree.

1. What ripple effect do you witness in the story?

2. As this ripple continues to flow, what other people might be impacted?

MAKING SENSE OF THE TRUTH

1. Plan a "John-12-style" dinner party for your group. Let each group member bring a dish to share. "John-12-style" means everyone sits on the floor, surrounded by plenty of cushions and pillows to make people comfortable. Put the food in the middle and let the people sit in a circle or lean on one elbow. Enjoy yourselves and notice what happens. Were people comfortable? Did it feel like you needed more space or were people okay with being so close to one another?[3]

2. Have group members share the feelings they have when they see people who are publicly bold in their witness of faith (standing on a street corner passing out tracts, outdoor preaching, holding signs up at sports events, passing out Bibles, etc.). Ask, "When you see people doing this, how does this make you feel?"

3. Consider watching the movie *Shawshank Redemption* and discuss how the influence of one person's life affects others. What do you see in the movie that is good? Redemptive? Discouraging? Encouraging?

> *The people who influence you are the people who believe in you.*
>
> —HENRY DRUMMOND

---

3. Read the section in chapter 9 of *The Lazarus Life* again about the dinner party. This was a custom in the first-century world. In your dinner party, try to re-create the atmosphere, ambiance, and setting to experience a night like Jesus and Lazarus enjoyed.

PRAYERS FOR TRANSFORMATION

Write your own prayer expressing your desire to grow in the following areas:

God, here is my desire to live a more intimate life with Jesus: I want to …

Jesus, here is my desire to live a life of gratitude and generosity: I want to …

Change is the nursery of music, joy, life, and eternity.

—John Donne

God, when I say I want to live a life as dangerous as Lazarus lived, I mean …

Jesus, here is my desire to live a life of influence: I want to …

Now, express a prayer of thanksgiving to God for the influence, impact, and power that one person's life has had upon your own.

God, I want to thank You for _____ because I have seen in him or her …

FURTHER STEPS ON THE JOURNEY

1. Consider reading chapter 1 of *Water from a Deep Well* by Gerald Sittser. The title of this chapter is "Witness: The Spirituality of Early Christian Martyrs." Let someone give a brief report on this and then share your reactions.

2. Go to a pond, lake, or creek and throw rocks in; as you watch the ripples spreading out, contemplate how God is using you, and is going to use you, in the lives of others.

3. Ask a spouse or close friend how he or she has seen you change in the past months. Then ask this person how he or she has seen that change in you affect others.

> *A river touches places of which its source knows nothing, and Jesus says if we have received of his fullness, however small the visible measure of our lives, out of us will flow the rivers that will bless to the uttermost parts of the earth. We have nothing to do with the outflow.*
>
> —Oswald Chambers

SESSION 11

THE LAZARUS LIFE: EXPERIENCING TRANSFORMATION FOR A LIFETIME

Chapter 10 of *The Lazarus Life*

THERE'S MORE

But saying yes to the "more" means saying no to the "less than"; the counterfeit voices that promise resurrection but don't deliver. It's amazing how easily we're convinced that these counterfeit voices are the real thing. Do you find yourself listening to lies and making choices that ignore these truths?

THERE IS MORE TO LIFE THAN MY WORK.

Competing voices will fool us into thinking that power and life—even abundant life—can be found in what we do rather than who we are.

THERE IS MORE TO LIFE THAN ANOTHER PERSON.

A spouse, friend, child, or parent becomes our resurrection and life when we focus our needs, desires, and dreams on him or her.

THERE IS MORE TO LIFE THAN MONEY.

When our sense of significance is attached to money, our true identity is compromised and our integrity hangs in the balance. Jesus gave money a rival god status. We should do the same.

THERE IS MORE TO LIFE THAN SEX.

We live in a culture fixated on sex. This brokenness stems from human hearts that are desperate to be loved. There is a difference between "having sex" as an act and expressing our hearts to our spouses as the Beloved of God.

THERE IS MORE TO LIFE THAN CHURCH.

Even church can become a substitute for true resurrection and life if we are not careful. Our cultural fascination with size, power, and prestige influences our perception of Christian communities. As we have seen, fellowship with others is a crucial part of our spiritual growth. But Jesus never said that church would be our life. Had He meant that, surely He would have mentioned the word *church* more than the couple of times He spoke about it.

Every day offers us the choice to decide what will be our source of life. Poet David Whyte reminds us that "sometimes we must *unmake* a living in order to get back to living the life we wanted for ourselves." What needs to be unmade in our lives? To have the life that Jesus is describing will inevitably require that we "unmake," or change, our ways—which is the literal meaning of the word *repent*. The journey to Jesus requires that we *repent* more than one time in our life. We will need to change our direction and our ways many times on the journey to Jesus. As it was Martha's choice to believe Jesus, it is ours as well. How we choose determines the quality of the life we will live.

(Pages 194–196 of *The Lazarus Life*.)

> The tragedy of life is not that it ends so soon, but that we wait so long to begin it.
>
> —W. M. LEWIS

1. What is keeping you from living the life you want to live?

2. How do the life of Jesus and the story of Lazarus inspire you to really live?

ENGAGING THE SCRIPTURES

This passage of Scripture shows the transformational journey of Paul in his own words. He began his life going one direction. After he met Jesus Christ, his life's course changed. His pleas for us are encouraging words to hear because he speaks of knowing the power of the resurrected Christ and he prays that we would know this power now—not just in heaven.

READ PHILIPPIANS 3:1–14

[1]Finally, my brothers, rejoice in the Lord! It is no trouble for me to write the same things to you again, and it is a safeguard for you.

[2]Watch out for those dogs, those men who do evil, those mutilators of the flesh. [3]For it is we who are the circumcision, we who worship by the Spirit of God, who glory in Christ Jesus, and who put no confidence in the flesh—[4]though I myself have reasons for such confidence.

If anyone else thinks he has reasons to put confidence in the flesh, I have more: [5]circumcised on the eighth day, of the people of Israel, of the tribe of Benjamin, a Hebrew of Hebrews; in regard to the law, a Pharisee; [6]as for zeal, persecuting the church; as for legalistic righteousness, faultless.

[7]But whatever was to my profit I now consider loss for the sake of Christ. [8]What is more, I consider everything a loss compared to the surpassing greatness of knowing Christ Jesus my Lord, for whose sake I have lost all things. I consider them rubbish, that I may gain Christ [9]and be found in him, not having

a righteousness of my own that comes from the law, but that which is through faith in Christ—the righteousness that comes from God and is by faith. [10]I want to know Christ and the power of his resurrection and the fellowship of sharing in his sufferings, becoming like him in his death, [11]and so, somehow, to attain to the resurrection from the dead.

[12]Not that I have already obtained all this, or have already been made perfect, but I press on to take hold of that for which Christ Jesus took hold of me. [13]Brothers, I do not consider myself yet to have taken hold of it. But one thing I do: Forgetting what is behind and straining toward what is ahead, [14]I press on toward the goal to win the prize for which God has called me heavenward in Christ Jesus.

1. Paul says, "All the things I once thought were so important are gone from my life.[1] Compared to the high privilege of knowing Christ Jesus as my Master, firsthand, everything I once thought I had going for me is insignificant—dog dung. I've dumped it all in the trash so that I could embrace Christ and be embraced by him" (Phil. 3:8–9 MSG). How can Paul say this, given his credentials and status? How do you relate to Paul's words?

2. In verse 10, Paul states his heart's desire: "to know the power of [Christ's] resurrection and the power of his suffering." Given what you know about Lazarus's life and experience, what would this look like in your own life?

---

1. Notice the way Paul's words relate to what we have been learning about the transformational journey of ordinary people. Paul came to realize that his life as a transformed person was so much richer and better than the life he was living prior to knowing Jesus Christ.

3. How does Paul's phrase "forgetting what is behind" (v. 13) relate to graveclothes?[2]

4. How is the power of Christ's resurrection linked to the power of His suffering? Do they have to go together? Can we have one without the other?

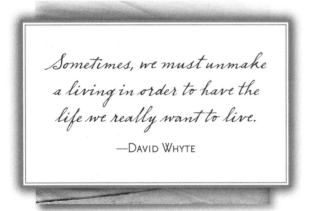

Sometimes, we must unmake a living in order to have the life we really want to live.

—DAVID WHYTE

---

2. Forgetting what lies behind can involve naming our graveclothes of the past and moving on, moving forward without them.

EXAMINING MY STORY

1. In *The Lazarus Life* the author writes, "The greatest spiritual question we can ask ourselves is not, 'Is there life after death?' The real question is much deeper: Is there life before death?" (page 192). What are your thoughts about this question?

2. What makes you feel alive? What does it mean for you to really live?

3. How have your answers to question 2 changed/morphed/transformed over the years? When you were fifteen, what did it mean to live? Twenty-five? Thirty-five? Now?

4. Ziggy says, "In life, the journey is always more important than the destination." What stirs inside you when you apply this to the journey toward being transformed?

5. Read John 10:10 and explore what this means to you in light of *The Lazarus Life* and your understanding and desire for real life right now.

6. What options could you explore in moving toward the transformed life Jesus is calling you to live? Try to be as specific as you can.

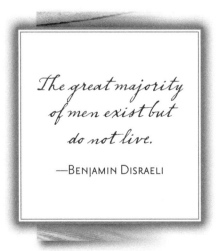

The great majority of men exist but do not live.

—BENJAMIN DISRAELI

AN ORDINARY STORY

Greg has been a worship leader in his church for several years now. Throughout his time there, his greatest spiritual fulfillment came as the congregation members sang to God with their whole hearts. Recently though, Greg has not sensed the same energy during worship. He has prayed about it, asked other leaders, read books, but still the worship time doesn't have the same feel. He wonders if the team needs more practice time, more members, or more of something else.

After months of prayer and discussions with friends, Greg has felt movement away from the options of trying harder or just quitting. Instead, he has felt some change toward connecting with God that's not based on the worship team or the congregation. Greg has felt a new freedom to encounter God outside Sunday morning, releasing him from the need to make worship "work."

1. What made Greg feel alive at the beginning of the story? At the end? What changed?

2. How could Greg have stalled the process of transformation?

3. What is the freedom that Greg feels? How is that connected to the power of the resurrection?

> The same power that brought Christ back from the dead is operative within those who are Christ's. The Resurrection is an ongoing thing.
>
> —LEON MORRIS

MAKING SENSE OF THE TRUTH

1. Consider planting a flower, shrub, or tree as a symbol of your life—the resurrected life. You might want to plant it at your church building or at a group member's home. Notice the care you will give to the new growth. It must be nourished. It must be tended. It must be cared for in order to live—in order to survive—then thrive. Journal your thoughts and experiences about the whole process. Try to pay attention through all the seasons, noting what happens and where your own life is in regard to the new tree or plant.

2. Give all the group members an opportunity to tell the rest of the group what Christ's "come forth" means to them. This is not a time to give feedback. Just listen.

3. Identify a memento of transformation that you can keep as a helpful reminder of the transformation that is taking place in your life. For example, someone who is struggling with her identity in Christ might choose to carry around a white stone (Rev. 2:17). If group members are having difficulty with this, others might "speak into" their lives with what they sense would be a significant memento.

Life is either a daring adventure or nothing.

—HELEN KELLER

PRAYERS FOR TRANSFORMATION

Find Psalm 136 in your Bible. Use this particular psalm as a prayer to pray individually or in a group setting. Notice that there is a refrain used after each statement: "His love endures forever." It is a way to help anchor in your mind and heart the love of God and His steadfast care for us. In your own words, write expressions of praise to God for what He has done in your life. After each statement, use the anchor, "His loves endures forever." Be specific.

An example could be

Thank You for giving me my family!

"His love endures forever."

Thank You for allowing me to meet my wife, who changed my life dramatically!

"His love endures forever."

Thank You for my job and the one I even disliked, because I learned something important about myself.

"His love endures forever."

Etc.

FURTHER STEPS ON THE JOURNEY

1. Do a Scripture study using the footnotes in this chapter on John's use of the word *life* found in *The Lazarus Life.*

2. Once a week—perhaps on your Sabbath or day off—consider lighting a candle as a symbol of life and light to your path.

3. Put on some music and take a journal to record your movement toward Jesus. What things hindered your progress? In what areas did you feel progress and steps of advancing closer?

> *If you want to die happily, learn to live; if you would live happily, learn to die.*
>
> —CELIO CALCAGNINI

Where, O death, is your victory?
Where, O death, is your sting?

—I CORINTHIANS 15:55

SESSION 12

TRANSFORMATION FOR LIFE

> What we're talking about is the Christian life. It's following Jesus. Spirituality
> is no different from what we've been doing for two thousand years just by
> going to church and receiving the sacraments, being baptized, learning
> to pray, and reading Scriptures rightly. It's just ordinary stuff.
>
> This promise of intimacy is both right and wrong. There is an intimacy with God, but
> it's like any other intimacy; it's part of the fabric of your life. In marriage you don't feel
> intimate most of the time. Nor with a friend. Intimacy isn't primarily a mystical
> emotion. It's a way of life, a life of openness, honesty, a certain transparency.[1]
>
> —Eugene Peterson

Spiritual transformation for ordinary people usually happens in very ordinary ways in the midst of, as Peterson put it, "ordinary stuff."

Spiritual transformation happens when God's power converges with our own lives. We participate in the process through opening ourselves to God, making space for God's power to be released in and through us. Spiritual exercises or disciplines such as prayer, Bible study, silence, solitude, and fasting are all helpful in the ongoing journey toward transformation.[2] As we take the step-by-step journey toward

---

1. Eugene Peterson, interviewed by Mark Galli "Spirituality for All the Wrong Reasons," *Christianity Today* 49, no. 3 (2005).
2. An excellent resource to help you survey and study more spiritual disciplines is *The Spiritual Discipline Handbook* by Adele Calhoun and Richard Foster's classic *Celebration of Disciplines*.

Jesus Christ, we are following Paul's lead in Philippians 2:12 to "work out your salvation." This "working out" is not finished until we reach heaven's shore and at last can stand before God fully transformed.[3]

For several weeks now, you have engaged your heart and mind in this guidebook. But now—in the last session, it's important to remember that spiritual transformation is ongoing and unending. Each season of life will reveal more places in your heart in need of transformation.

Lazarus eventually died again. History is silent on his life after his resurrection. Legend tells us that Lazarus went to Cyprus and became a bishop there. There is a Greek Orthodox church in Larnaka, Cyprus, named for Lazarus—the *Agios Lazarus*. In AD 890, a tomb was discovered that bears these engraved words: "Lazarus, the friend of Christ."

While we may never know the facts surrounding his second death experience, what is important for us to remember is the legacy of Lazarus. Unfortunately, Lazarus is usually only invoked at funerals. But as we have seen, the message of Lazarus is not meant for the dead but for the living—for you and me today!

The Dutch artist van Gogh painted his version of the resurrection of Lazarus as his final painting before death. What is striking about van Gogh's account is that he used his own face as the face of Lazarus. It's a fitting image for us to consider. The story of Lazarus is really van Gogh's story, as it is our own—the story of ordinary men and women who meet Jesus Christ and begin a journey of transformation that takes a lifetime to complete.

1. In reflecting back over the course of this study, what changes have you noticed within yourself?

2. What does it mean to you to be transforming in light of your study of *The Lazarus Life*?

---

3. See Paul's description of this in 2 Corinthians 5:1–10.

ENGAGING THE SCRIPTURES

Read Romans 12:1–2 in your Bible translation.

Here is how *The Message* renders this passage:

READ ROMANS 12:1–2 MSG

So here's what I want you to do, God helping you: Take your everyday, ordinary life—your sleeping, eating, going-to-work, and walking-around life—and place it before God as an offering. Embracing what God does for you is the best thing you can do for him. Don't become so well-adjusted to your culture that you fit into it without even thinking. Instead, fix your attention on God. You'll be changed from the inside out. Readily recognize what he wants from you, and quickly respond to it. Unlike the culture around you, always dragging you down to its level of immaturity, God brings the best out of you, develops well-formed maturity in you.

1. What words or phrases stand out to you as you compare the two translations?

> *Keep changing.*
> *When you're*
> *through changing,*
> *you're through.*
>
> —BRUCE FAIRFIELD BARTON

2. What are some ways our culture has shaped your understanding of transformation compared to what you have seen in this study?[4]

3. The *New International Version* says, "Do not conform any longer to the pattern of this world, but be transformed by the renewing of your mind." What does "the renewing of your mind" look like? What is involved in this process of "renewing your mind?"

4. According to Paul, what is God's part in the transformation process?

---

4. Advertisements and media shape our understanding of what is important in life and how we can experience it. Quick fixes, airbrushed looks, the right size, the right job, the right house—all are rooted in our understanding of what "right" really means. Even our understanding and values stand in need of transformation, as Paul clearly says. Having a renewed and transformed mind involves allowing our values, ideas, and concepts about spiritual growth, spiritual transformation, and healing of old wounds to be reshaped and brought in line with a biblical understanding of life and more.

5. What is our role in being transformed? As you have worked through this study, how have you found yourself participating in the process of transformation? What have you noticed?

6. How is a transformed life an act of worship?

EXAMINING MY STORY

1. List five "takeaways" or most important insights you have gained from your study of *The Lazarus Life*.

   1.

   2.

   3.

   4.

   5.

2. How can you celebrate your experience? Commit yourself to one act of celebration in gratitude for the transformation you've experienced during this time.

> *Perseverance must finish
> its work so that you may
> be mature and complete,
> not lacking anything.*
>
> —JAMES 1:4

AN ORDINARY STORY

Write your own story of transformation here in one or two paragraphs. Limit yourself to a story you could tell in two to three minutes—the proverbial "elevator conversation." After you finish your story, ask yourself the following questions:

1. What stage in Lazarus's journey (tomb, the voice, stench, clearly out of the tomb, staggering forward in your graveclothes) does your story reflect?

2. How hopeful are you at this stage?

Hope is an adventure, a going forward—a confident search for a rewarding life.

—KARL AUGUSTUS MENNINGER

MAKING SENSE OF THE TRUTH

1. Give a votive candle to each person in the group. Go around in a circle and have participants light their candles and share "how God is transforming my life." Also include statements of thankfulness for the presence of others in this time. Be specific with each group member, perhaps sharing how Joe has helped you in this area and Betsy in that area....

2. Create a symbol of transformation. This might include a drawing, building something, or molding clay to make a symbolic image that represents "transformation." Make sure each person has a part in the process.

3. If you are leading a group study, plan a worship time to celebrate transformation as worship. Choose songs and Scriptures that are meaningful, and as an offering, ask participants to write their names on small pieces of paper and place them on a special table that might represent an altar. The significance here is "giving yourself to the process of transformation." Use any of the songs and resources found at www.LazarusLife.com that you find beneficial.

> It is a bad thing
> to be satisfied
> spiritually.
>
> —OSWALD CHAMBERS

PRAYERS FOR TRANSFORMATION

Recite the Lord's Prayer (Matt. 6:9–13 KJV) in unison. Before you pray, discuss how the Lord's Prayer relates to the theme of spiritual transformation.

Our Father,[5] which art in heaven,

Hallowed be thy name.[6]

Thy kingdom come.

Thy will be done,[7]

in earth, as it is in heaven.

Give us this day our daily bread.[8]

And forgive us our debts,[9]

as we forgive our debtors.

And lead us not into temptation,[10]

But deliver us from evil.[11]

For thine is the kingdom,

and the power,[12] and the glory,

for ever.[13]

Amen.

---

5. The word *father* was a transformational word that Jesus offered us to call God. *Abba* in Aramaic means "Daddy."

6. Hallowing the name of God requires a transformed understanding of God's holiness. We would not hallow His name if we did not experience Him to be truly holy—different and unique.

7. This phrase asks us a basic question. Do you believe that transformation is one way that God's kingdom will come on earth—in you?

8. What is our daily bread in the journey of transformation? "Man does not live by bread alone." Jesus reminds us of this.

9. What role does forgiveness have in our transformation of our past and present?

10. How does temptation relate to the transformational process? Graveclothes, etc.?

11. How does evil thwart the transformational process?

12. God's power, not our own. Here again we are reminded of what God does and is willing to do in the transformational process.

13. Forever means that our transformational journey will one day be complete in eternity. Up until then, we are still in process.

FURTHER STEPS ON THE JOURNEY

1. As you have witnessed spiritual transformation in the life and legacy of Lazarus, are you noticing the themes of transformation in other literature, sermons, books, conversations, etc.?

2. Consider asking a friend who has graveclothes similar to your own to go through the study with you. This time, you can intentionally become the hand that is lovingly reaching for your friend's gravecloth as well as others that might surface in your own life as a result of a deeper look this time.

3. Consider reading *Your Mind Matters* by John Stott to investigate more of Paul's meaning of "renew our mind."

4. Read a book of fiction and compare the transformational journey offered in fiction and compare it to nonfiction and biblical truth. Try reading Leif Enger's *Peace Like a River* and note the ingredients of the journey of the main characters.

Now the Lord is the Spirit, and where the Spirit of the Lord is, there is freedom. And we, who with unveiled faces all reflect the Lord's glory, are being transformed into his likeness with ever-increasing glory.

—2 Corinthians 3:17–18

APPENDIX

DISTINGUISHING BETWEEN *AUTHENTIC TRANSFORMATION* AND *PSEUDO-TRANSFORMATION*[1]

AUTHENTIC TRANSFORMATION *What our hearts are reaching for—our new frontier*	PSEUDO-TRANSFORMATION *Where we've been before— previously explored territory*
Faces the truth. *(Rom. 7:15–25; John 8:31–32)*	Perpetuates a lie and excuses behavior. *("I don't have a problem."* Or, *"Everyone does this.")*
Realizes the importance of the heart. *(1 Sam. 16:7, Prov. 4:23)*	Lives on the surface and from the surface.
Embraces a process. *(Jer. 18:1–6, Eph. 4:13–15, 2 Cor. 3:18, 1 John 3:2)*	Frantically looks for answers in steps, logic, and laws. Watches the clock.
Requires surrender and humility. Says, "I can't do it alone. God, please help me." *(Matt. 26:39; James 4:10; 1 Peter 5:6)*	Insists on self-help and self-reliance for change.
Inside-out change. *(Matt. 23:25; Mark 7:18–23)*	Outside, external change.
Collaborative and cooperative. *(Phil. 2:12; the fifty-four "one another" statements in the New Testament")*	Competitive and judgmental *(comparing ourselves to others and their progress vs. our own).*
Individually designed process. *(Ps. 139:13–15)*	Cookie-cutter program.
Spirit-driven. *(John 14:26–27; 16:13–15, Rom. 8:9, 23–26)*	Human-driven.
Admits brokenness. *(2 Cor. 4:7–12)*	Portrays polished façade.
Community is valued. *(Eccl. 4:9–12; Matt. 18:19–20)*	Desperado and Lone Ranger mentality.

1. This chart originally appeared in The Transformation of a Man's Heart Series by Stephen W. Smith published by InterVarsity Press, 2006. It gives various expressions on how authentic transformation and pseudo-transformation differ from each other.

DISCIPLINE OF DISILLUSIONMENT

What follows are three examples of different types of disillusionment. A "clean" chart follows and more are available for download at www.LazarusLife.com.

Instruction	Example #1	Example #2	Example #3
1. Identify the issue causing you to struggle. Write out some thoughts on some issue that is causing you to feel disappointed and disenchanted.	I am disappointed in the church/my church.	I am disappointed in my own limited intelligence and abilities and my constant comparison of myself to other men in ministry, including my own father.	There are *never* enough volunteers in our church to do what needs to be done.
2. Think more deeply about your disappointment. What is your disappointment really about?	I feel alone and that no one really knows me. Everyone shakes my hand and seems like they know me and everything is okay.	I feel inferior to others and inadequate to accomplish noble things that others have accomplished. I'm disappointed in not being able to do/be all that I desire to do/be at this point in my life.	I end up doing most of the work and I feel resentful about other people not helping me/ the church.
3. Search for the illusion. What is the illusion that feeds your disappointment? It's okay to have more than one—but try to be as specific as you can.	That church should be family—that we should be really connected as brothers and sisters. The church should be a place where we know others and are truly known.	I have too-high expectations of myself. My illusion is that I am not smart enough and that I'm inferior to others.	I thought that people would care about the church and want to get involved and help out.
4. Connect the illusion with feelings and emotions. What surfaces in considering the surrender of this illusion?	I fear that I will never be known; that I will never be connected. I'm afraid there isn't a place on earth where people really care. I feel lonely. I feel sad about this.	I feel inadequate, jealous of others, like a failure at times. I rarely feel competent spiritually and intellectually enough to be effective in work and ministry. I'm often in search of praise and accolades from others, for validation.	Anger. Resentment. Frustration. Cynical. Depressed. Abandoned.

Instruction	Example #1	Example #2	Example #3
5. Make an assessment of the root issue. What and where is the root of my disillusionment?	I've never felt like I belonged anywhere or to anyone, but I have always wanted to.	I have a problem accepting myself the way God created me. I wish for qualities that others have, ignoring those that God has given me. I've always wanted to be more like the man my father is—and I fall way short of that ideal.	I may have too-high expectations of people and place my own expectations about myself on other people.
6. What are some truths that need to be embraced?	The church is made up of soul-sick people just like me. I was made to live in community. Only Jesus can satisfy my aching heart.	God has created and gifted me uniquely with my own set of qualities—strengths that are unique to me—to fulfill His purposes that are designed exclusively for me. I am not my father or anyone else—I'm my own person according to God's design and desire for me.	I am not responsible for the actions or attitudes of others. I have to "let them go" and entrust them to God. I do not have to assume the role of judge and jury.
7. Develop an action plan in light of what you have discovered in this discipline. How can I live in light of this truth?	Seek out people who have similar desires as I do. Initiate and try to talk on a deeper level than just sports and weather.	Stop emphasizing those areas in which I am weak or not gifted. Stop comparing myself to my father and others. List those gifts and qualities that God has given me and celebrate those, noting how perfectly they fit into my ministry and family dynamics.	I wonder how Jesus dealt with the disappointment He experienced in His closest companions. I want to read the Gospels with this in mind and consider this more. I want to process this with the pastor and express my feelings and also my hope to work through this.

Instruction	Example #1	Example #2	Example #3
8. Talk plainly to God. Record your thoughts and prayers in your journal.	I want to ask God to bring people into my life with whom I can have the life-giving relationships that I want and need.	I want to ask God to accomplish His work and will through me, using those unique personality traits and gifts He has blessed me with. I want to request His help in de-emphasizing my "weak" areas and help me instead to celebrate my "strong" points.	God, help me to let my feelings go, and give me a pure heart to serve You faithfully.
9. Find a trusted companion to process your heart with in this area.	I am going to share all of this with C and ask him to initiate with me in our talks about this area and to check in and discuss my progress.	I am going to share these things with my trusted friend. He will be good to offer advice, accountability, and support on these matters.	I am going to talk this over with our men's group on Thursday morning.
10. Your own ideas to follow up.			Read all four Gospels in the next few months and take notes on how Jesus handled disappointment.

Instruction	My Story
1. Identify the issue causing you to struggle. Write out some thoughts on some issue that is causing you to feel disappointed and disenchanted.	
2. Think more deeply about your disappointment. What is your disappointment really about?	
3. Search for the illusion. What is the illusion that feeds your disappointment? It's okay to have more than one—but try to be as specific as you can.	
4. Connect the illusion with feelings and emotions. What surfaces in considering the surrender of this illusion?	
5. Make an assessment of the root issue. What and where is the root of my disillusionment?	

Instruction	My Story
6. What are some truths that need to be embraced?	
7. Develop an action plan in light of what you have discovered in this discipline. How can I live in light of this truth?	
8. Talk plainly to God. Record your thoughts and prayers in your journal.	
9. Find a trusted companion to process your heart with in this area.	
10. Your own ideas to follow up.	

Potter's Inn is a Christian ministry founded by Stephen W. and Gwen Harding Smith, and is dedicated to the work of spiritual formation. A resource to the local church, organizations, and individuals, Potter's Inn promotes the themes of spiritual transformation to Christians on the journey of spiritual formation by offering

- guided retreats
- soul care
- books, small group guides, works of art, and other resources that explore spiritual transformation.

Steve and Gwen travel throughout the United States and the world offering spiritual direction, soul care, and ministry to people who long for deeper intimacy with God. Steve is the author of *Embracing Soul Care: Making Space for What Matters Most* and *Soul Shaping: A Practical Guide to Spiritual Transformation.*

Potter's Inn at Aspen Ridge is a thirty-five-acre ranch and retreat nestled in the Colorado Rockies near Colorado Springs, Colorado. As a small, intimate retreat, Potter's Inn at Aspen Ridge is available for individual and small group retreats. "Soul Care Intensives"—guided retreats with spiritual direction—are available for leaders in the ministry and the marketplace.

For more information or for a closer look at our artwork and literature, visit our Web site: www.PottersInn.com. Or contact us at:

Potter's Inn
6660 Delmonico Drive, Suite D-180
Colorado Springs, CO 80919
Telephone: 719-264-8837
Email: resources@pottersinn.com

Gasoline

GASOLINE

Edited by
Decio Grassi

Introduction by
Rossana Bossaglia

Texts by
Guido Fisogni

ELECTA/ABBEVILLE
Milan   New York

Photography and Graphics
Decio Grassi
Translation
Jeffrey Jennings
Many thanks to Enrico Castruccio
for his historical research

The first edition of this book was
produced on the initiative of SIRM Nord
Srl., Palazzolo Milanese. All objects
reproduced herein belong to the
collection of Guido Fisogni, on
permanent exhibition at the SIRM
Museum, Via Tirano 18, Palazzolo
Milanese.

ISBN 0-7892-0054-6

First U.S. edition

Contents

To Elena, Rachele, Eugenia

I t is difficult for one who is accustomed to thinking imagistically to find the proper words to introduce a volume of images. But I was so struck by the SIRM (Società italiana ristrutturazione e manutenzione) Museum collection that it seemed important to try to offer, in addition to the photographs, a few suggestions and reflections.

One is immediately surprised by the quantity and the variety of the museum's holdings: gasoline pumps, signs, gas cans, gadgets, street maps, tools, toys— nothing seems to have escaped the eye of Guido Fisogni in his quest to document and narrate the history of this particular industrial product.

The fascination of this incredible collection insinuates itself at a number of the levels, inviting a variety of readings. Technology, design, corporate imagery, nostalgia—these are but a few of the overlapping themes that guide the visitor through the museum. If to some it may seem odd to dedicate a museum to the history of gasoline, the visitor sensitive to the importance of gasoline and road transport in our century will find not oddity but liveliness and substance.

The catalogue moves from personal observations to the photographic documentation of the objects themselves. From the simple and essential lines of the early oil cans to the slender forms of the pumps; from the brilliant contrasting colors of the advertising placards to the unadorned metallic crudity of various tools and mechanisms, these objects testify to the vast formal and esthetic range of 20th-century industrial design. Close inspection of individual objects is rewarded by discoveries of stylistic traces of Art Deco, for example, or by the recognition of the presence of a genuine master of graphic design.

The elegantly solid form of the *Imperiale* pump (Siliam, Italy, 1936) recalls the rhetoric of Modernist rationalism, while an American pump from the same period (Wayne, USA, 1939) playfully miniaturizes the forms of New York skyscrapers. And when a gasoline producer wishes to spread its trademark among consumers and to confer dignity upon its simple industrial products, it turns to visual artists like Marcello Nizzoli, whose design of Fiat's lubricant containers reveals "an able hand and fine taste, optimizing the Futurist vocabulary, with a result worthy of the famous 'rubber man' from Michelin" (Bossaglia).

Advertising also found enameled metal signs and the illuminated globes placed atop the gas pumps to be excellent means of communicating corporate imagery. Aggressive animals (monsters, eagles, tigers, dragons, and Agip's flaming six-legged dog) testify to the potency of gasoline, alternating with more reassuring images (puppets, children, blonde nymphets) or more fantastical ones (Mobil's magnificent Pegasus is the exemplar here). And finally, after the stars, the flags, the crowns and the flames, some companies choose to rely exclusively on the evocative power of their own corporate name, exemplified by the yellow scallop to which Shell entrusts its international message.

The brief overview presented here is but a taste of that which follows, for aside from being a catalogue of the Fisogni collection and an inventory of curiosities for the delectation of the automobile aficionado, the present volume is above all a distinctively new look at the history of industrial design.

Decio Grassi

3

A collection such as this one, along with the book which documents it, pose a series of problems to historians of art, design, and so-called "industrial archaeology" (which would perhaps be better termed "archaeology of the industrial age"). These problems can be boiled down to a single, multifaceted one: at what point does industrial design end and art begin? On the theoretical level, the question is an old one, even if it is still being asked today. On the level of the immediate impact of this "new" group of artefacts (new insofar as it documents our own relatively recent artistic heritage), the question takes on a particularly profound resonance.

We are by now accustomed to studying and cataloguing automobile design, which has long since taken its rightful place in the realm of art as a result of the fact that function has never, or almost never, been conceived as being independent of esthetic value, it being assumed that the potential buyer is or can be seduced to some extent by an attractive form. On the other hand, and in other ways, we are fascinated by tools and machinery that have fallen into disuse, relics of remote cultures and obsolete needs, which we eagerly associate with the notion of an epoch of manual skill obliterated by technology, appreciating their artisanal aspect, believing this to be inherently more creative.

How does a gasoline pump fit into this context? We cannot maintain that esthetic concerns were foremost from the start, since it is clear that the earliest manufacturers sought not so much to attract the motorist as to simply signal the availability of the product. Yet there was a certain degree of esthetic concern even in the early years, both because the dignity of the gasoline distribution facility depended in part on its placement within the landscape, and because of the relatively swift arrival of competition, which brought customer attraction into play, and attraction is of course a direct function of attractiveness.

How did this attraction work? The semiological discussions begun some twenty years ago on the nature and operations of the artistic "sign" brought forth the necessity of ambiguity as a condition of attractiveness—the unambiguous image will signal, but it will not lure. The early manufacturers of commercial products knew this instinctively, as did the first designers of gasoline pumps: a trademark is required which is both immediately recognizable and reassuring, and it must be composed in pleasing colors that can be seen from a distance; and if the product, in this case represented by the gasoline pump, is given certain gracious or seductive peculiarities, the motorist will take deeper satisfaction in the transaction.

However, these last observations refer to the gas pump in use, and thus to the perpetual present. The museum, however, deals inherently with the past, for even the most recent inclusion in a museum collection is instantly rendered a part of history. And in our case, given the rapidity of transformation in the gasoline industry, the museum also deals in large part with objects that are truly obsolete, objects which would otherwise have been lost to carelessness or to the ever- changing urban fabric were it not for the documentary, indeed cultural passion of the museum's founder.

It is here that the discourse becomes complicated and requires a moment's reflection. The field of design is founded upon several ideological principles which, though closely tied to the exigencies of the marketplace, are nonetheless intellectual in spirit. The conviction that the beautiful should not be useless, but must ally itself with function (indeed, beauty is seen as arising directly from function), lay at the core of the most advanced design of the first half of our century, and continues to be valid today. This is not to say that such esthetic purism was always at the fore, but one does see in early serial production, particularly as regards limited editions, the occasional play on the charm of certain traditional forms and ornaments. Gasoline pumps are no exception—the oldest and most modest examples from the beginning of the century demonstrate little overall concern with artistry, yet they indulge every now and then in the charming detail, the unnecessary yet pleasing curve, the ordered rhythm of component parts, the brilliance of contrasting colors. And if we look at the drawings for the Bergomi pumps of the 1920s, or even more tellingly to the pumps themselves, we recognize an overt desire to embellish the object by giving it the form of a fluted classical column—an ambitious and highly apt symbolism which communicates the idea of fuel as the life force, the support upon which the new society rests.

The neatly streamlined forms (that is, without corners) of the pumps of the 1930s, which served important functional ends as well as esthetically suggesting the idea of efficiency and manageability, were to be found the world over, but particularly in Italy, which had by then reached a notably high level of stylistic quality in regard to functional objects, both domestic and technical. The dates given by the museum indicate that only the French were close to matching the quality of Italian design in these years.

Needless to say, Italy would distinguish itself yet further during the 1950s in the field of design. The gasoline pumps began to lose, little by little, the more or less cylindrical structure that had lent them an air of the sacred and the totemic rather than the merely practical, that had rendered them animate, latently anthropomorphic presences, waiting along the roadside, becoming instead more suited to an urban esthetic that had come to view roundness and protuberance as being awkward, favoring flattened, planar forms and spaces.

It is unfortunate that the archival sources do not preserve the names of the individuals responsible for these intelligent designs. It is not uncommon for individual credit to be withheld in the teamwork-oriented sphere of technological research and production, and for this reason the names of the creators of the advertising strategies, particularly of the logos which allow us to immediately distinguish one manufacturer from another, are often obscured by indeterminacy. It is not at all clear, for example, who first dreamed up that jolly man of rubber who has, and will forever, define the corporate identity of Michelin. These ideas and images are so flexible that the gestural, stylistic, and physiognomic changes wrought upon the Michelin man over the years have never threatened his identity in the least; the same holds true for the ever more simplified Shell logo and, more recently, the fabulous Etruscan chimera of Agip and the Pegasus of Mobiloil.

Even such modifications to these emblems, the result of shifts in the temper of the times, constitute part of the historical interest of our *imagerie*. But it is precisely at this point, as suggested earlier, that the contradictions in our attitude toward design enter into the picture. The gasoline pumps collected here are of course appreciated for both their functional and formal qualities. But they are valued above all, as we've noted, for the testimony they offer to a moment in the history of technology that has long been left behind—they are admired all the more because they belong to the past; we enjoy them esthetically because they no longer have any other function. It is the same attitude that moves us to include utilitarian objects from bygone days in the realm of art: the primitivity of their original function renders them admirable, and their present uselessness permits us to locate them in a purely esthetic dimension.

Yet it is perhaps this theoretical contradiction, this impasto of thoughts and emotions, that provides us with the richest and most intense means of confronting a collection such as this one. For gasoline pumps do not presume to pose above and beyond time and contingent circumstance in the manner of the so-called pure arts. Their expressivity is firmly linked to the practical concerns of human activity; the testimony they offer is concrete and physical. And yet at the same time they assume an increasingly symbolic aspect, detaching themselves from practicality so as to find their place in an ideal sphere of esthetic ambiguity, animating themselves with secret life.

They occupy a suggestive, almost sacral archaeological realm, alongside the earliest pinball machines and the first "one-armed bandits," affable in their monstrosity. While the disquieting vision of a future populated by menacing robots may frighten us, these noble old machines instead move us by evoking an innocent past populated by harmless dinosaurs. In a very profound sense, the museum of science and technology moves ever closer to the museum of art.

Rossana Bossaglia

From Kerosene to Gasoline

In the mid-19th century certain chemicals were proven capable of distilling the dense and dark liquid that springs forth from certain parts of the earth. Among the various products that resulted from this process, there was one that was ideally suited for the task of illumination. Kerosene, by contrast to vegetable and animal oils, or to tallow and stearin, offered greater luminosity and gave off no unpleasant odors. Initially the precious liquid was sold loose, in bulk. And though it later came to be packaged, the old sales method survived for decades in the form of travelling vendors who went about in wagons laden with barrels or tanks. Seeking to simplify this system, the American Sylvanus F. Bowser contributed, in 1885, an ingenious idea: to the barrel or the tank was applied a lever-action piston pump with a faucet, not much different from that used to draw water from a well. Bowser's invention happens to be documented, but one can imagine that others as well had devised similar means of simplifying the life of the kerosene vendor—travelling or otherwise. After a short time, in order to reach a broader clientele, the vendors of kerosene and other petroleum products such as lubricants organized complex distribution networks linked by means of transport and storage. These were decentralized to the greatest degree possible, in order to limit the risk of damage caused by fire. In the service of this network were born companies that built the tank wagons, storage tanks, and pumping and measuring facilities, whose main task was for a long time that of perfecting safety and security methods.

The automobile did not just appear in a brief shining instant. The earliest precursor of the internal combustion engine (the igneous-pneumatic device of Luigi De Cristoforis, 1841) utilized a liquid hydrocarbon (naptha) vaporized by a carburetor, while the subsequent inventions of Barsanti and Matteucci (1856), Hugon (1858),

Lenoir (1860), Otto and Langen (1867) preferred a combustible mix already prepared: lamp fuel. These first motors were most often used for static functions, to drive pumps and other fixed machinery, in which case the fuel did not present a tremendous hazard. Mounting it on a moving vehicle, however, was tantamount to carrying a lethal bomb, and this brought with it a certain cause for concern. To eliminate the danger, inventors turned their attention to combustible liquid and addressed the complications of the carburetor, choosing among the available substances a petroleum by-product, familiar to industry as a solvent and to the average household as a stain remover. Karl Benz's motorized tricycle (1886) was not the first gasoline vehicle per sé, but by comparison with earlier attempts it was far more functional. Together with the other "automobile" devices that followed, it helped give rise to the transportation revolution and thereby offered new prospects to the petroleum industry.

Although Thomas Alva Edison was already fabricating light bulbs by 1880, the kerosene market would remain in good health for some decades yet, for the electricity network was slow to expand. But in the long run, kerosene was destined for extinction. The advent of the automobile, however, offered the prospect of a new petroleum product that could gradually substitute it. At first a minor by-product, gasoline would become the principal fruit of oil refining. Over time, the manufacturers modified the process, privileging gasoline above all other by-products; to market it, they simply used the existing kerosene distribution network.

As the number of automobiles grew, one began to find gasoline in the same stores that sold kerosene, and in other places as well: grocery stores, pharmacies, markets, garages, weigh stations, and stables. As sales volume increased, the need to improve the methods of supply and distribution became ever more apparent.

The automobile, in the meantime, had passed 7

through its infancy. Inventors from various parts of Europe had conceived it, the French had given it a successful debut, and the United States of America had opened up the doors of its vast market. That which is considered the first American automobile hit the roads in 1893; by the end of the century there were already thirty car manufacturers and more than eight thousand motor vehicles on the road; within a decade Henry Ford had transformed the automobile into an "everyday" means of transport, while in Europe it remained a luxury of few. Thanks in part to the great distances that the average citizen was required to travel, the motorization of America was precocious in its development. Consequently, the problems associated with gasoline and its distribution became rather urgent and the Americans, by necessity, had to solve them first.

American Origins

The automobile was already a common sight in the streets of St. Louis when, in 1905, Harry Grenner and Clem Laessig founded the Automobile Gasoline Company. The terms of the company charter are indicative: kerosene is not even mentioned there. It focuses instead on the retail sale of gasoline in keeping with the times, using equipment conceived expressly for automobiles. The fuel was dispensed from a raised cylindrical tank oriented vertically, equipped with a glass indicator for measuring the liquid level. The apparatus also included a filter and, naturally, a valve for regulating the flow of the gasoline, which arrived by way of a flexible hose whose end was inserted into the car's gas tank. The company succeeded in establishing around forty distribution stations, with the principal storage facility serving as headquarters.

But by 1905 the revolutionary system of Grenner and Laessig already appeared cumbersome and obsolete in respect to the latest product of S. F. Bowser & Co. Founded by Sylvanus F. Bowser in order to promote his invention of 1885, the company had continued to operate in the petroleum business, developing and perfecting new products. The Bowser Self-Measuring Gasoline Storage Pump was for its time a most manageable and functional apparatus, designed to work independently of the stores and repair shops. In a housing of wood resembling a miniature shed was a metallic tank and a lever-action piston pump, equipped with pressure vents and a hose. To measure the amount dispensed it was enough to bear in mind that each apportionment was always of the same quantity; by inserting

stops one could limit the movement of the piston, thus dispensing predetermined fractions of the maximum capacity of the cylinder. Bowser's offspring is the first of a family of such devices, called self-measuring pumps.

Another step forward was taken in the following year by another pioneer in the field, John J. Tokheim, from whose garage came the Tokheim Dome Oil Pump. To the self-measuring pump he added a mechanical counter that indicated the quantity dispensed, along with a graduated glass vessel into which the liquid flowed before passing through the hose, allowing one to visually verify the exactitude of measure. At first slow to be put to outdoor use, the apparatus was adapted by repair shops and garages, where it enjoyed great success.

The availability of these new pumps, the proliferation of the filling stations, and the general expansion of motorization had a reciprocal multiplying effect: if the growing number of automobiles encouraged the installation of new pumps, the resulting accessibility to gasoline opened the doors for the broader use and diffusion of motor vehicles. In 1908, with the Ford Model T, the automobile ceased to be a privilege, and fuel distribution made giant steps in terms of efficiency and security. The somewhat improvised wooden housing of the first Bowser Self-Measuring Gasoline Storage Pump was replaced by metal ones, more solid and not without a certain elegance. One found the new pumps along the roadside or in specially designated off-road areas where one could refill without hindering the flow of traffic. Other versions without housings were made available to private firms, garages and repair shops, the most simple of which resembled bicycle pumps. The use of underground tanks became common, this being the most secure and also the most logical solution, given that the pumps necessarily had to draw their contents from below.

Around 1919, there appeared the first illuminated globes, which were placed atop a pole and bore generic information such as Gasoline, or Filtered Gasoline. Mobile self-measuring pumps mounted on tank wagons proved to be useful auxiliaries to the fixed pumps, especially for garages and secondary retail outlets.

It seemed that the thirst for gasoline was insatiable, even though more and more was being produced: in 1914 it became the principal product of petroleum refining, percentually overtaking kerosene, thanks to a new process called "cracking." Competition among the producers was becoming stiff, and one began to see the first brand names appearing on the lighted globes. The self-measuring pumps had required that the customer take the word of the vendor on faith as to the quantity of gasoline dispensed. Around 1915, to render the transaction more transparent, a solution foreseen in 1906 by the Tokheim Dome Oil Pump was adopted, whereby a glass vessel was mounted above the hose. The pump continued to do the measuring, but the vessel provided a visual control. As before, there remained the option of predetermining the quantity by limiting the movement of the cylinder.

Eventually, the pump was assigned the single task of drawing the liquid, while the job of measurement passed to the vessel, and thus began the era of "visible pumps." The apparatus was most impressive to behold: a sturdy housing concealed the pumping unit which, no longer linked to measurement, could be driven by an electric motor; above stood the measuring vessel, and on top of it all towered the globe. These vessels were enormous at first: the earliest ones carried five American gallons, by the twenties they grew to ten, and in some cases held as many as fifteen. In Canada, one could find pumps with two vessels of ten imperial gallons each, for the dispensing of two different types of fuel (American gallon = 3.7853 liters; imperial gallon = 4.5460 liters). The classic vessel for what came to be called the visible pump was numerically graduated in increasing order toward the bottom. It functioned by filling itself completely, after which a valve was opened and the fuel began to flow; when the liquid level reached the number corresponding to the amount requested, the shutoff valve—at first positioned above the hose and later (circa 1924) incorporated directly into the nozzle—would close.

The visible pumps were the protagonists of the twenties, a decade in which the progress of motorization and of fuel distribution forged strongly ahead. By 1920, the gasoline pump had become part of the landscape, like street lamps and mailboxes. The number of gas stations on U.S. territory approached fifteen thousand, though at this point one could not yet say that they were esthetically satisfying. They were instead crude and improvised constructions, for which no one took care to coordinate forms and colors, the mentality of their owners still being that of the early days, when the motorist asked nothing more than to have his tank filled.

Against this commercial rudeness grew bodies of opinion which forced everyone, vendors and manufacturers alike, to reconsider the problem, and the great companies began to see that they could improve their corporate image by improving and unifying the look of their outlets. And thus began the flowering of the new service stations, whereby the quest for the beautiful at all costs brought results of every kind, and the design of the pumps themselves, focal point and *raison d'être* of the gas station, became fundamental.

Suddenly the pumps were required to be beautiful in the true sense of the word, sometimes to the extent of being harmonized directly with the architecture of the station. The manufacturers (nearly two hundred in 1925, both large and small) engaged in an all-out battle amongst themselves to find new formal solutions. Not being able to eliminate the glass measuring vessel, its presence was instead exalted.

Supported on a base which contained the pump, decorative accessories in brass, chrome and colored enamel were added to the vessels. In certain cases the pump was replaced by an underground compressor which pushed rather than drew the fuel upward.

But the visible pumps were slow: once the vessel had emptied, one had to wait for it to fill up again. And they were even a bit dangerous: if the vessel broke, the service area would be instantly drenched by a cascade of flammable liquid. When at the end of the twenties there appeared a new means of measuring fuel flow, the era of the visible pump ended almost instantly.

The new electric-powered volumetric pumps delivered the fuel to a measuring chamber, a complex mechanism with many moving parts. The chamber, under the pressure of the liquid, and proportionally to the quantity that entered it, rotated on an axis, along which was mounted a spindle that transmitted the degree of rotation to a clock-face dial. The measuring chamber was much more precise than the previous system, and the dial indicated the amount dispensed to both customer and attendant with great clarity. Those nostalgic for the old visible pumps could still monitor the fuel flow through a transparent gauge on top of the hose if they wished; meanwhile the trigger of the pistol nozzle mounted at the end of the hose was far more efficiently controlling the pump and the rate and quantity of fuel flow by means of electricity.

Much more precise and also much faster, the volumetric pump was the instrument that everyone had always dreamed of. Since then, much has changed as far as the appearance and the precise details of its mechanical function, but the basic principles of the most modern gasoline pump are essentially those of 1928.

The nature of the visible pump obliged it to a certain monumentality: the vessel had to be placed above be- **9** cause the gasoline flowed by force of gravity to the vehicle, and it had to have a large capacity so as to not render the transaction too slow. The designers, in tending to the esthetic aspect of these giants, had emphasized their massive structure, effectively offering them as technological totems.

Some years had to pass before they were liberated from this mindset: the first "clock-face" volumetric pumps are still rather tall and imposing. Then the designers began to exploit the new freedoms offered by the new technology (and perhaps the warehouses had finally been emptied of the older models).

Without the huge vessel, the necessity of great height disappeared (for now it was the pressure of the pump that delivered the gasoline) and the pumps became smaller, more compact, yet at the same time more carefully detailed. This was the great era of styling, in which the reigning Art Deco mode was rendered American by the genius of designers who applied it to every object, from pencil sharpener to skyscraper. Parallel lines, aerodynamic modelling, geometric decorations, immaculate finishes, and vivid colors found their way to the gasoline pump. With most of their mechanisms consigned to the interior, and even the exterior gauges and pistol nozzle incorporated into the formal logic of the object, the gas pumps became (like so many other industrial products) pure expressions of the esthetic sensibility of their time.

Meanwhile another fundamental change was under way. It was 1933 when the Wayne Tank and Pump Company proposed a new mechanism for indicating the quantity dispensed. Instead of being connected to the sphere of the clock-face gauge, the spindle of the measuring chamber set in motion a complex system of clockworks which directed a series of numerated rollers. But the novelty doesn't end here: in addition to indicating the quantity of fuel dispensed, the apparatus also clearly indicated the unit price and the amount due. The early life of the contometric display gauge was difficult: competitors boycotted it in every way, so as to avoid paying the patent royalties, but in the end they had no choice but to accept it. From that moment, the very way in which the motorist expressed himself changed: he no longer asked for ten gallons of gas, but for ten dollars worth.

Italy and Europe

While in the USA the culture of the automobile had long been triumphant, on the old continent it was still an expensive toy reserved for the privileged few.

But something was changing, and these few would multiply rapidly. The success which in America was due to Henry Ford and his economical small cars was in Europe an effect of the First World War. Motor vehicles had performed honorably on the battlefield, demonstrating themselves to be useful and trustworthy, and thus they sparked the interest of the common folk. Gas pumps existed in Europe before and during the war. By 1910 Bowser was selling a simple version of the self-measuring pump in France for installation with an underground tank; some years later, this and other models appeared in other parts of Europe; in 1918 the Italian firm S. A. Bergomi introduced the cumbersome Securitas pump, which was used by some large garages and hotels; equally unwieldy pumps were put to the service of the Parisian Compagnie des Omnibus; the armed forces utilized gas pumps in massive numbers wherever there was a battle. Yet on the streets, nothing: grocery stores and pharmacies were more than up to the job of filling a mere dozen or so gas tanks a day. But as soon as the roads began to fill with automobiles, the *colonnina*—or "little column," as the gas pump came to be called—made its appearance in Europe. With the major technologies having already been developed in America, there was almost nothing left to invent.

In France the automobile was already rather widespread, particularly in the large cities. As soon as the war ended, a certain number of industries intuited the potential of the new market and gave themselves over to the construction of the first European roadside filling stations, in part copying American examples, in part proposing original solutions. One genuine innovation was applied to the visible pumps, insofar as the mono-vessel pump gave way to a completely new type with two vessels, usually five litres each, substituting the large single container. Rather than a graduated numerical index, it used a simple spillway at the summit of the vessels which allowed them to operate in tandem. The attendant began to fill the first, closing it when the level arrived at the spillway, at which point he would then activate a small lever, obtaining a twofold result: the five liters contained in the full vessel took the route of the hose and, recommencing to pump, fresh fuel flowed into the second vessel. Once the latter was refilled, the switch was flipped back, and the process began again. While one tank was being filled, the other emptied itself into the vehicle, and so on in increments of five liters. If the method was conceptually elegant, the dispensing was not very fast. A few years later the process was streamlined by the addition of floating ball cocks which rendered the inversion of the vessels automatic.

The old manual models, considered more durable, nevertheless remained in production, and one continued to find mono-vessel columnar pumps *all'americana* not only in France but in other parts of Europe as well. But it was the double-vessel type that came to characterize for the most part the streets of the old continent.

In Italy, the Milanese Società Anonima Bergomi had been active since 1908 in the field of storage, pumping and measuring of fuels, and held among others some important German patents on fire prevention systems. The end of the war marked the beginning of a period of new and more up-to-date equipment: in 1896, Italy boasted a fleet of forty-five motor vehicles; by 1919, the number had leapt to 23,883 cars, 10,613 trucks and 337 buses. A drawing from that same year, executed by the Ufficio Tecnico Bergomi, shows a little measuring pump, used mostly in garages, with crank and stopping devices clearly inspired by American models. Other pumps of this sort, this time for roadside applications, appear in Bergomi designs from 1922 to 1926, some of which (after 1923) are crowned by one or two glass measuring vessels.

The self-measuring pump, which at the beginning of the twenties was already obsolete in its country of origin, found the possibility of survival in the young European market. It was this type that first appeared on the streets of Italy.

After receiving official metric approval by Royal Decree (no. 2199, September 10, 1923), a number of Gilbert and Barker pumps were immediately installed by Siap (Società Italo-Americana del Petrolio, an offshoot of Standard Oil of New Jersey) which since 1891 had been operating in the Italian market, initially in kerosene and later in gasoline. By the end of 1924 the Siap pumps (Lampo gas) numbered 150, and it was just about this time that the first visible pumps began to appear. Ministerial Decree no. 4574 of May 30, 1924 admitted to the Italian market the "semi-automatic measuring device comprised of two glass vessels equipped with a four-way switch for the filling and purging of each." Built by Bergomi, the Lùmina pump (and the subsequent "Hardoll" models, 1925) entered into service under the insignia of Nafta S.A., founded in 1912 as a subsidiary of the Anglo-Dutch concern, Royal Dutch-Shell.

Siap and Nafta dominated the nascent Italian distribution market, and were soon joined in 1924 by the Società Nazionale Oli Minerali, or Snom, whose gasoline, offered to the public under the auspicious name Victoria, was of Soviet origin.

The name Victoria is encountered in some Bergomi drawings representing roadside pumps of singular character, at least for Italy: the measuring was entrusted to a single twenty-liter vessel with a graded index (every five liters) increasing toward the top. We don't know if these pumps were actually built, but even if they were, there couldn't have been very many of them. The large American-style vessel, which appears in but a few other Bergomi designs and in only three decrees of certification, did not enjoy much fortune in Italy. It had greater success in Great Britain where Bowser marketed an interesting model around 1925.

The Italy of 1929, five years after the first roadside facilities had appeared, counted more than two hundred thousand motor vehicles. At their service were 16,750 gasoline pumps: 6,500 of Siap (Standard gas), 6,000 of Nafta (Shell gas), and 4,000 of Agip (Azienda Generale Italiana Petroli, established in 1926), the firm which had brought Snom and the Victoria trademark into the network.

The remaining 250 were of the Benzina-Petroleum group, founded in 1924, which closed after a short while, ceding its holdings to Nafta and Siap. Of these pumps, those of Siap were generally the self-measuring twenty-liter type: imposing obelisks able to communicate a certain robustness, but without much claim to esthetic merit. The five-liter measuring pumps used by hotels and small retailers (also of the Siap network) had a more pleasing aspect, thanks to a rounded housing surmounted by two spires: from one came the hose, and on the other rested the lighted globe. As for the rest, with rare exceptions (Nafta also used some measuring pumps), the Italian gas pump fleet was of the five-liter double-vessel, or *pentalitri abbinati* type, produced in large part by Bergomi.

Ever since its entrance in the field of roadside gasoline pumps, the Milanese company had established close relations with French producers, and adapted many of their technical and esthetic solutions. One frequently encounters the names of the companies Satam, Arbox and Hardoll in the Bergomi designs of the period. Another Italian company with transalpine relationships—in this case with Boutillon—was Siliam (Società Impianti per Liquidi Infiammabili ed Apparecchi Misuratori), born in Milan around 1928. Sais (Società Anonima Impianti Sicurezza) was founded a few years later, also in Milan, thus completing the roster of major pre-war Italian producers.

The classic Italian pump of 1925 has a "Roman" inspiration mediated through France. The transalpine companies doing business with Bergomi (Hardoll and Satam in particular) were looking for inspiration in the splendors of the Imperial Rome, to the extent that the tank trucks they used for mobile distribution bore a certain family resemblance to Roman chariots. The fixed pumps had a columnar base with pedestal, a tapered columnar body, and a capital upon which rested a large cylinder with double doors, which contained the pumping and measuring mechanisms.

Other French companies went to great esthetic pains, looking at least in part to American examples, designing slender and austere bases with conical or pillar-like shafts, dividing the housing for the mechanisms into various elements, and presenting the double vessels behind screens or protective cages. These more elegant and sumptuous models became the characteristic French gas pumps; the others—the "Roman" type—inundated Italy instead.

Bergomi's principal contribution to the stylistic history of gasoline pumps was the continuous refinement of the profile and the decorative elements of the columnar base, while the upper part, the cylinder with doors, remained monotonously the same. When Siliam and Sais arrived on the market, the esthetic of the pumps didn't change drastically, but there were a few new variations on the profile of the column. One innovative contribution was made by Agip which, a few years after its founding, provided the builders with a drawing of a *colonnina* with a rectangular cabinet as a base.

Bergomi, it must be said, also had creative moments—or at least it tried to stretch itself in different directions to accommodate the demands of its clientele. One surprising example, again in the Roman vein, is that of a pump conceived for Nafta's more prestigious locations along the first superhighways. If the typical pump merely suggests the idea of a column, these incredible exemplars—more than nine feet high and crowned with a lighted globe—truly capture the spirit of an imperial column. Some Bergomi designs combined their rectangular roadside *armadi* with classicizing friezes that were more suitable for living room furniture; others show interesting column-pilasters of square section inspired by the characteristic German pumps which were built at the beginning of the thirties for the Società Anonima Italiana Petrolea (est. 1927) whose network was taken over a bit later by Fiat. One Bergomi design from 1928 documents the attempt to leave the vessels in view and to house the pump and counter in a small cylindrical body, with the classic columnar base still intact and the extremely elaborate lighted globe making a lovely spectacle of itself. More interesting from this point of view—though not up to the level of the French examples—is a pump produced for Fiat in 1931: the column is very slender with a simplified profile, the upper cylinder is rendered more compact, and the whole appears decidedly more refined.

For the most part, the five-liter Italian gasoline pumps were honest industrial products designed to function and to last. And they truly did last, for a long while, though with subsequent modifications and updating.

The first volumetric pumps arrived in Italy in 1932; two years later Bergomi started producing its *Insuperabile* (or Unsurpassable) model; from 1936 come the volumetric pumps by Siliam; and in that same year the first contometric display gauge, imported by the American Wayne, was approved by decree. The official documents of the epoch record a fervent demand for the approval of new devices, but in most places the volumetric revolution was late in arriving. These were difficult years for the Italian economy, during which the consumption of fuel, among other things, was discouraged, imports were reduced to a minimum, and the order of the day was to avoid any form of waste. The clock-face pumps were introduced very slowly, starting with the more important locations where they served considerations of prestige. None of the old models were disposed of: they were simply displaced to secondary locations.

The first volumetric pumps of American provenance (and their Italian counterparts as well) were fashioned *a pilastrino* and made conspicuous show of the clock-face display gauge. Originally circular, its form evolved into a polygon inscribed in a square or rectangle, so the advent of the contometric display gauge didn't bring all that surprising an esthetic change; meanwhile, the spyhole on the exterior flank was incorporated into the logic of the frontal decoration.

The quest for the esthetic perfection of the gasoline pump which was all the rage across the ocean was slow to catch on in Italy. Some of these extremely refined imports made their way onto the streets, but the less sophisticated products of local manufacture prevailed. The exceptions however were not few, first among them being the *Imperiale* model of Siliam: elegant in its sobriety yet forcefully characterized, fruit of that 20th-century style with which the regime so strongly identified.

At the end of 1948, the great oil companies reclaimed the freedom of action lost to them during the war and began to reconstruct their networks in Italy. It was the era of the volumetric pump, and the contometric display gauge became commonplace; the old visible pumps, by now offered only to private businesses and garages, remained in production for a while longer. The fifties saw the first authentic motorization of the masses in the form of economical automobiles but above all of scooters: in the filling stations it became obligatory to have mixing pumps, through which the technology of the visible pump survived for a long while. Following a tendency by now common to all the national markets, the new pumps became ever more compact and rounded; alongside them, in less conspicuous positions, the old five-liter types and self-measuring pumps held on. Then everything suddenly accelerated: the idea of the new at all costs combined with a new awareness of the importance of corporate imagery to form the foundations of the aggressive philosophy of the post-war boom. With the arrival of the sixties no one wanted the old relics in their service station any more, and in the arc of a few years almost all the pre-war equipment was replaced by the new automated pumps.

Globes

Attracting the patronage of the motorized customer began with moderation, but as soon as the mechanisms of competition had been set in motion it became clear that to increase business it was necessary to have good locations and optimal visibility. Attempting to achieve the latter, someone was inspired by the lanterns which in the evening brightened the entrances of other types of establishments, and soon thereafter the gasoline pump came to be illuminated by the globe.

On its surface was indicated the type of merchandise being sold: gasoline, filtered gas, etc., but after a while, such precision became superfluous. Since it was given that the subject at hand was fuel, the globes took to indicating the brand name, or better the company trademark: simple logos, names derived from popular imagery or accordingly invented, linked by strong color combinations to images intended to hook the customer. The practical utility of the trademark globe was undeniable, especially in those stations which offered different brands of fuels: it was enough to glance at the top of the pump to know exactly which would be entering one's tank. For the towering pumps of the epoch,

this pleasing point of attention immediately became an essential element of compositional balance whose presence was assumed and taken as a given in the design phase.

The classic form of the globe is a flattened sphere, with two circular, almost planar faces to host words and images. But the technology of working the glass allowed many variations.

Especially between the second and third decades of the century, one saw globes in the form of ovals and lozenges, with some firms directly materializing their trademarks in the modelled form of a shell, a flame, a crown. The first globes were single pieces of glass, crafted in much the same way as a vase or a lamp. Kiln firing rendered the logos and designs weather resistant. One decidedly more industrial type appeared around 1920, no longer a single piece, but made of five parts. Three metallic parts constituted the structure, while two pieces of glass in the form of lenses served as the illuminated ground on which the trademark was printed. There were also globes made entirely of metal: the serigraphed image on the lenses was visible by day, while by night a system of perforations outlined the image in light. Others, all in glass, had an opaline ring structure which held the two lenses in place. It is difficult to trace a more accurate line of evolution for these fragile objects, for each national market had its own rhythms and its own tastes. Luminous announcements of *Benzina*, *Benzina pura*, *Essence*, *Essence filtrée* appeared in Europe in the early twenties, while across the Atlantic the competition among brands was already fierce.

One-piece globes remained in use longer in some parts of Europe and, aside from Shell Oil's cast scallop shell, simpler types tended to prevail. Meanwhile, in the USA, there began to appear in 1933 (though uncommon until after the war) the first plastic globes.

If the demise of these objects came between the fifties and sixties, the decline had begun, at least in America, almost twenty years earlier. The simple gas pumps placed at the roadside were gradually replaced by more complete facilities, which in the attraction of customers had its own drawing power. The illuminated globe was no longer indispensable now that the image of the filling station depended on the sum of many elements, including the supplementary services they now offered to the public.

Additionally, as the pumps gradually became more compact and less monumental, the presence of the globe became formally superfluous. Placing the trademark on the pump itself was enough, since the most urgent task—that of attracting the customer from afar—had for some time been entrusted to great flags mounted on colossal poles.

Packaging

The barrel was for many decades the standard container for petroleum and its derivatives; only at the beginning of this century was it joined and then replaced with the lighter and sturdier steel drum. They were both (forty-two and fifty-five American gallons respectively) ideal for transport and bulk marketing, less so for small quantity sales. But in the middle of the 19th century the public had precious little experience of packaged goods, and found it perfectly natural to go to a store with a container into which the storekeeper would dispense the kerosene.

With the passage of decades the situation changed, and in the more advanced countries pre-packaged goods began to appear, on the wrapping of which was conspicuously printed the trademark of the producer. Kerosene also came to be packaged, but the first cans, introduced in the last decades of the 19th century, were still too capacious for domestic use, better suited to bulk vendors. Toward the end of the century, the pre-filled can small enough to be carried home was introduced to the market place. A sturdy container with a handle and a threaded cap, one paid a deposit upon purchase which was reimbursed upon the return of the can: the era of the disposable container was still a long way off.

As soon as the automobile became an appreciable phenomenon, gasoline went into the cans as well—the same ones used for kerosene, save for a change of color and label. Prior to the advent of the pumps, they were an efficacious means of refilling one's gas tank. With their notable capacity (in Italy, twenty liters) the cans functioned as reserve tanks to be carried in the car or kept in the garage. In many European countries they didn't disappear immediately with the advent of pumps; in remote areas, they remained an especially long while in service.

The automobile required more than just fuel alone. In particular, it burned large quantities of oil, which was furnished in bulk or in glass containers packaged by the storekeeper. But it was also offered in cans to those who wanted a particular brand of oil, guaranteed by a sealed package. The many other products specific to the automobile, such as additives and grease, came most often in cans or small metal drums.

While the esthetic of the first kerosene and gas cans is rather simple, a great concern for presentation emerged toward the end of the 19th century in the smaller capacity containers. Designed with particular care is the packaging for oil, since the containers had to convince the customer to spend more in comparison to the bulk product, and at the same time to prefer a given brand to that of the competition.

These containers betray a great desire to dazzle, to capture attention with easy and suggestive forms, in keeping with a philosophy of packaging that was both aggressive and ingenious. It's interesting to follow the evolution over time of these logos and images, realized generally with the technique of lithography on tin: although each of the various national contexts had its own traits, they all tended toward communicative efficacy, rejecting descriptive solutions in favor of more synthetic and striking ones, sometimes resulting in genuine masterpieces of graphic design.

In order to render the product more interesting and attractive, some producers experimented with unusual package formats, but these were rather isolated cases: the rectangular and cylindrical can represented the norm. From 1920 on, certain efforts were made to standardize package formats which gave rise to recurrent dimensions and typologies, but forms, capacities, and closure systems remained rather varied even within national markets. Meanwhile, the large-capacity containers destined for the vendors began to be differentiated from the increasingly smaller ones intended for the individual customer.

Progress in manufacturing techniques caused the very function of the containers to undergo a profound transformation: next to the sturdy artisanal can equipped with handle and threaded cap that had to be returned to the vendor, there appeared containers in lighter material, crafted less carefully, which the customer could throw away. The disposable sealed cylinder, which was opened by puncturing one of its ends, appeared in America around the thirties and cleared the way for the first true standardization, though it never completely displaced the earlier types.

Signs

A new culture of brand names pervaded the last decades of the 19th century: the trademark appeared on all forms of packaging; the trademark was the subject of the first color lithograph advertisements; and the trademark was emblazoned on promotional objects which, following the example of the great Parisian department stores, a good number of firms bestowed upon their distributors and customers. Around the 1880s there appeared a new genre of advertisement which, by comparison to its counterpart in paper, was much heavier and sturdier, able to last over time. The support was in cast iron (later to become iron and laminated steel), and the process of fixing the image required the layered application and subsequent kiln firing of semi-liquid vitreous silica.

Invented in central Europe in the early 19th century, perfected and fine-tuned over time, the baked enamel sign entered the world of advertising and remained there for at least fifty years. Ideally suited for outdoor display (even in bad weather) and prized for its sparkling modernity, these signs were used for railroad stations, for trams and steamships, but above all for the exterior walls of retail stores. The message, in this case, was twofold: while it presented in positive terms the idea of a product, it also indicated the place where it could be acquired.

Signs for kerosene began to appear among the others on the walls of grocery stores and emporia; repair shops and gasoline vendors began with placards or signs generally indicating the type of goods on sale, to which were then added those of specific brands. It was, however, a slow process by comparison to the marketing of other products whose consumer base was from the start much more vast. In the United States, where marketing was a serious matter, the first indications of competition among gasoline brands began in the teens. The closest battle was between the producers of lubricating oil, who had already by the first of the century (at least in America) positioned their publicity signs. Not all were in baked enamel: serigraphy on sheet steel and lithography on tin were also used. But for outdoor display, enamel was without rival both in terms of effect and durability. In the American petroleum and automobile markets, the "sign" phenomenon remained contained until the middle of the second decade; Europe would have to wait at least another ten years before seeing the exterior walls of garages, repair shops and filling stations bedecked with signs. When the producers of gasoline, oil, tires and other accessories finally did unleash them, the hapless motorist who stopped by for a tankful of gas was drowned in a flood of brilliant color.

The classic sign was a one-sided, wall-mounted panel. The earliest are convex and often slightly in relief, more exaggeratedly so in the lithographed tin versions.

The forms are for the most part regular—rectangles, squares, and circles—though there is no lack of more elaborate types. In some rare cases (one being that of Mobil's flying horse) the modeling is so accentuated and the relief so deep that the subject represented acquires a sculptural concreteness. Often, especially in America, the sign was detached from the wall and mounted on a stand, pedestal or pole, inserted into the space of the service station, making it yet more effective a means of attraction and prefiguring the giant signs of today. In this case, both faces would be illustrated, or the support would join two separate signs back-to-back.

A separate discussion is merited by another genre of enameled sign, used in Italy not at the sales locus but directly at the roadside: street signs, indications of place, and announcements of services installed at highway exit ramps by the Touring Club, but paid for, totally or in part, by the gas and oil producers who, in exchange, added their trademark to the bottom.

The enameled sign was, in Europe and America, an authentic infatuation, and not without esthetic problems. As the signs gradually crowded the walls, anyone designing a new one was obliged to render it more striking and aggressive than the existing ones.

Seen by itself, a sign may well have been splendid, but a wall jammed with throngs of them in random disposition could become unpleasant both in itself and in relation to its surroundings. Strong opinion arose against the proliferation of signs, but their eventual extinction was determined above all, in the years following the Second World War, by their own specificity.

The signs were expensive to make, and the expense could be justified only so long as the messages they carried remained relevant. But for the by now mature field of advertising, based as it is on the continuous evolution of the message, an indestructible message was the worst that could be imagined. The enameled signs became an old way of valorizing the product and, slowly but surely, they disappeared from the walls of stores. That same specificity that had brought them down from the walls, however, allowed them to survive and evolve in the closed ambient of the service station. As for costs, it was necessary to reduce them: first, baked enamel was replaced by a synthetic version, then the metal support was abandoned in favor of plastic.

Tools and Equipment

From the second decade of the century onward the American filling station underwent an evolution which, in a single decade, would transform it into the service station proper.

To the simple dispensing of fuel was added the checking of oil, water, and tire pressure, the installation of new filters, spark plugs and batteries, the car wash, the lube job, and other services still. At the same time there evolved a concern for the customer, now provided with refreshments, a waiting room, and lavatory services. This didn't begin in Europe until a decade later, but even if the true service station was rare, most of the establishments that sold gasoline were able to provide the more important supplementary services.

This explosion of new commodities for the motorist did not come from the generosity of the vendors: the natural course of things imposed itself on them. As long as the system was limited to the single sidewalk pump in front of store, the sale of gasoline remained only a part of the store's activity, a relative benefit that was more than satisfactory.

But when the vendor found himself selling only fuel, he was forced by necessity to add service upon service in order to increase his income possibilities. It was in this way that the pumps came to be flanked by other equipment, large and small, which also had to make its contribution to the global image of the place and its activity.

These tools and equipment were largely designed strictly for automobile applications; in cases where a tool already existed for other purposes, it was redesigned, in whole or in part, for use in filling stations, service stations, garages and repair shops. Their esthetic evolution generally follows that of other tools: they provide that decidedly industrial fascination which comes from the materialization of a need, of a function, while at the same time trying to achieve a look, in keeping with the forces which transformed household goods, means of transport, and gasoline pumps, to name a few. When the tools or equipment bore the trademark of another product, the intent to ennoble them with interesting forms and colors and other non-functional decorative additions is all the more evident.

The evolution of the fixed tire pump is in some ways parallel to that of the gasoline pump. Those from the twenties have a distinctly vertical orientation which recalls the idea of the column or the *pilastrino*. Later on, their height was modified and they borrowed a bit of the gas pump's modeling and ornament. Finally, in the post-war years, they assumed more austere forms. The mobile air pumps, though sharing the same function, demonstrate a far broader range of both kind and quality. Perhaps less esthetically self-conscious, but not without formal dignity are the pumps for dispensing oil. The rest form a motley group, from the bulkiest contraptions to the smallest gadgets: oilcans, sprayers, oil spouts, funnels, burners, gauges...

Promotional Materials

Promotion is the ultimate weapon, especially for those who deal in precious commodities in highly competitive markets. In the first years of our century this was not the case with gasoline, the sales of which, though still scarce, grew without any need to be pushed.

Lubricants, on the other hand, sold not so much to the housewife or to the rare motorist as to the immense industrial machine, were being marketed by a growing number of companies which, in order to ingratiate themselves with their customers, began offering promotional gifts. And they were rather serious gifts, though they played more on utility than on splendor: pliers, ink blotters, ashtrays, pocket knives, pencils; or perhaps pins and badges bearing the company trademark. The automobile and tire manufacturers also began giving away badges, pins, and pen knives. And eventually, this competition strategy reached the world of gasoline distribution. One of the first promotional initiatives was that taken by Gulf Oil Company which, in 1914, sent more than 10,000 street maps, with promotional material attached, of a part of Pennsylvania to motorists, which was then followed by other maps sent by mail or offered directly at the filling station. Others used similar tactics, focusing always on the practical but pleasing small object. Even the vendors were regaled with plaques of recognition, accessories and trademark-bearing tools to use in their work.

The twenties brought similar promotional schemes to Europe as well: one saw pocket knives in the form of gas pumps, booklets and other little knick-knacks, while the Michelin Bibendum, donated to tire shops in innumerable variations, was rendered more visible every day. But the purest and most spectacular promotional tactic, the hook that would capture the customer's attention by way of his imagination, was still not yet to be seen, not even in America. To unleash it would require the crisis of 1929, which would cause the consumption of fuel to contract dramatically and thus escalate the competition among producers to levels never before seen. So, while the American housewife was beginning to find little gifts in the packaging of many products, he who stopped at the service station for a fill-up could also expect to be delighted by a small gift presented to him by the attendant.

A good luck charm, a key ring, a personalized book of matches, or even a set of salt and pepper shakers in the form of gasoline pumps; or further still a piggybank, an ashtray, a cigarette lighter—all of which, naturally, bore the company trademark, or were indeed modeled in the very form of the trademark. One important aspect of these gifts was that they were made from a revolutionary new material capable of giving life at a reasonable cost: plastic. Promotional gift-giving has been, ever since, a common sales tool in the world of fuels.

Advertising Illustrations

A diffused glow cast by a lamp, around which revolves a homely scene; the atmosphere is meditative, protective. At the end of the 19th century and in the first decades of ours, this was how kerosene and the lamps that used it were advertised. The oil lamp was presented as an efficient instrument at the service of the family, solidly embedded in tradition. A good deal more incisive and disruptive were the messages of its direct antagonist, fast on the rise: the electric light bulb. But when in the teens these same kerosene companies began to promote the sales of gasoline, the message obviously had to be different, at a good distance from the intimacy of the home and the values of tradition.

Since the public identified the automobile with modernity and (especially in Europe) with social distinction, these had to be the focal points of gasoline advertising, and the same went for lubricants. In the Europe of the second decade, still immersed in the softness of Art Nouveau, gasoline advertising focused decisively on the elitist aspect of the automobile and its fuel, and on this button it continued to push at least until the forties. The idea of modernity, already present in the advertising from the teens, was made more evident in the following decades, borrowing expressive motifs from Cubism and Futurism. In the commercial graphics of the epoch, the use of illustrators influenced by the avantgarde connoted two not always coexistent messages: for medicines, for example, it served to underline the modernity of the research from whence the medicines came; for a chocolate or an aperitif, the aim was to identify the product with signs of elitism and refinement. The two needs coexisted perfectly so long as the protagonist was a fuel; in the case of Futurism, the lines of force and the exaggerated perspectives added to the sense of motorized speed.

An exceptional example of advertising philosophy is that of Shell U.K. Ltd. which, from 1932 to 1939, used its brochures as true showcases of graphic design, entrusting their realization to a large number of artists of the most disparate tendencies, some of them of the first order. The quality of the product being a given, the Company sought to consolidate its image by suggesting an idea of seriousness and trustworthiness through the slogan, repeated on all its ad material, *You can be sure of Shell*. The Italian Agip, having decided in 1926 to quickly conquer its share of an already crowded market by capitalizing on the political mood of the time, focused its advertising on the modernity, but above all on the *italianità* of its product—if not of the primary material, at least of the refining and distribution.

But the automobile was not merely a fast-moving modern monster. Little by little it lost its patina of luxury and came to be seen as a practical and useful means of transport.

The idea shone through a certain number of European ads in which car and driver were de-mythologized and rendered more accessible, but this approach found its most coherent and convincing expression in American advertising. And indeed it is logical that we would find a more balanced message in a country where the automobile was already the means of the many, was in fact at the center of a civilization whose great distances were connected by motor vehicles; a message that did not use illustrations to highlight refinement at all costs, but which was posed in more strict relation to the text; which worked in less explicit but more profound ways on the imagination of the consumer. This idea of advertising would become widespread also in Europe, coming at different moments to different countries, and was affirmed definitively after the Second World War. Meanwhile, the unstoppable momentum of photography had come to rival the ad illustration.

Toys

When the first gasoline pumps entered into service, the epoch of the modern toy had been underway for some decades. The perfection of manufacturing technologies and a society-wide increase in the awareness of children's needs favored the establishment in both Europe and America of a good number of companies specializing in dolls, toy trains and sundry other playthings: objects which in most cases offered a reduced version of adult reality for use by children who, confronting that reality through play, could begin to prepare for the complicated life of the grown-up.

One of the most successful toy typologies was that which reproduced means of transport, whose furious pace of evolution sometimes outstripped the limits of imagination. A few years after its introduction, the automobile attracted the attention of toy makers, and by 1898 a German manufacturer was mass-producing miniature cars.

But true success came later, when adult reality included enough automobiles to make toy versions of them desirable to children. The golden age of the toy car began with the twenties. And along with it came, of course, the toy gasoline pump.

Promotional children's toys were for the most part accessories, supplementary pieces intended to accompany toy cars. Technical, esthetic and economic reasons and the spirit of the toy itself did not favor exact fidelity to the actual objects, yet the toy gas pumps of the period do succeed in communicating important information about the characteristics of the real ones, and about the context surrounding them. One can recognize the different national types by the place of manufacture (or by the market for which the toy was destined); in addition to the pumps one finds oil cans, air pumps and, in an American model, a refreshment stand for motorists. Only rarely does the gas pump appear reproduced with exactitude, more in the spirit of a model than a mere toy, but it is easy in any case to see that we are always dealing with promotional objects.

Along with gasoline pumps, toy manufacturers of every period have also offered the vehicles that transport the fuel, of every type and size, from the earliest oil drum-carrying wagons to modern tank trucks. In the absence of the original vehicles themselves, they help to re-evoke the history of petroleum distribution.

Guido Fisogni

Due to lack of precise documentation from the epoch, and to the renovations and restructuring to which many pumps were subjected during their working lives, many of the dates are approximate.

THE SIRM MUSEUM

I f it is true that every manufactured product bears traces of its own historical context, then particularly valuable testimony is provided by mass-produced objects of the past two hundred years, objects which have in unprecedented ways invaded the environment of mankind, giving a shape and an ideology to his civilization. But the industrial product is destined by its very nature to rapid obsolescence, and many risk extinction without even a single surviving exemplar. To recuperate these objects, to preserve them, to reconstruct their genesis and evolution, to restore to them an oft-ignored dignity are the goals of the numerous museums of the "history of things," widespread in the more industrialized countries—museums which, though they deal most often with individual products, jointly serve to preserve and perpetuate, to the benefit of all, the fresh winds of progress that have powered our epoch.

GAS PUMPS

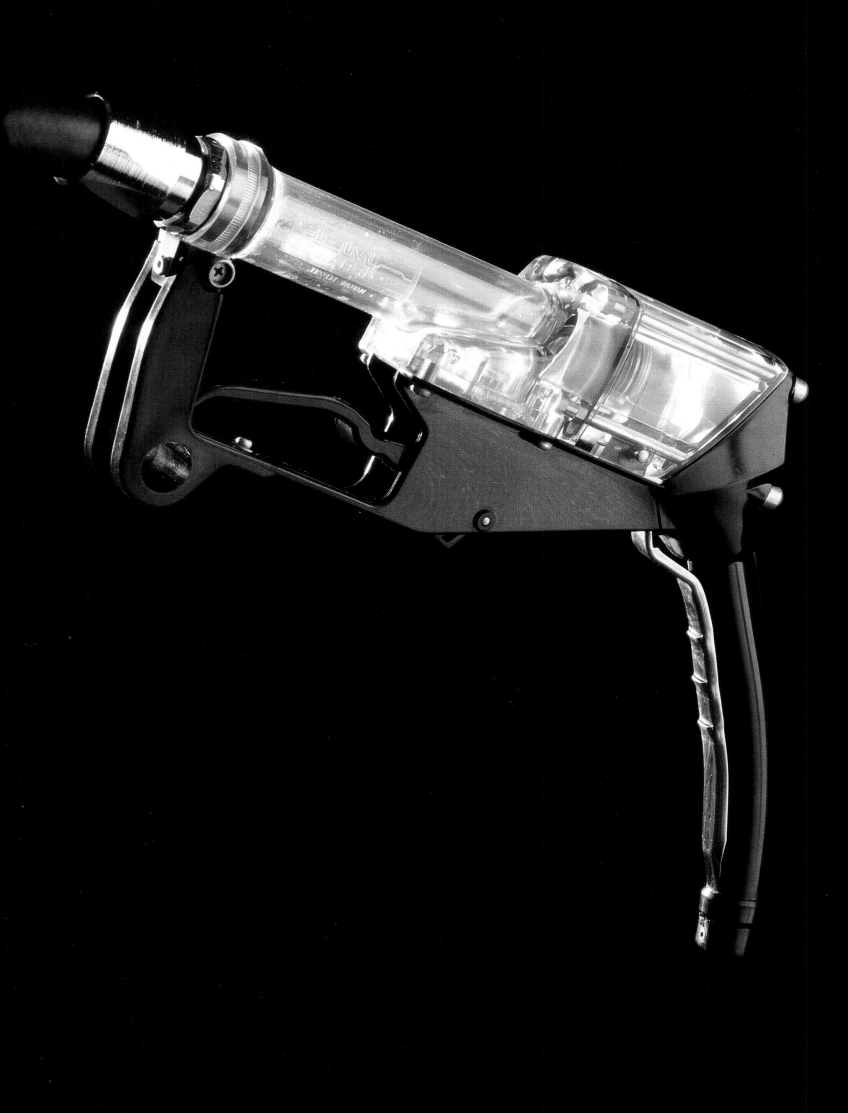

USA 1910

23

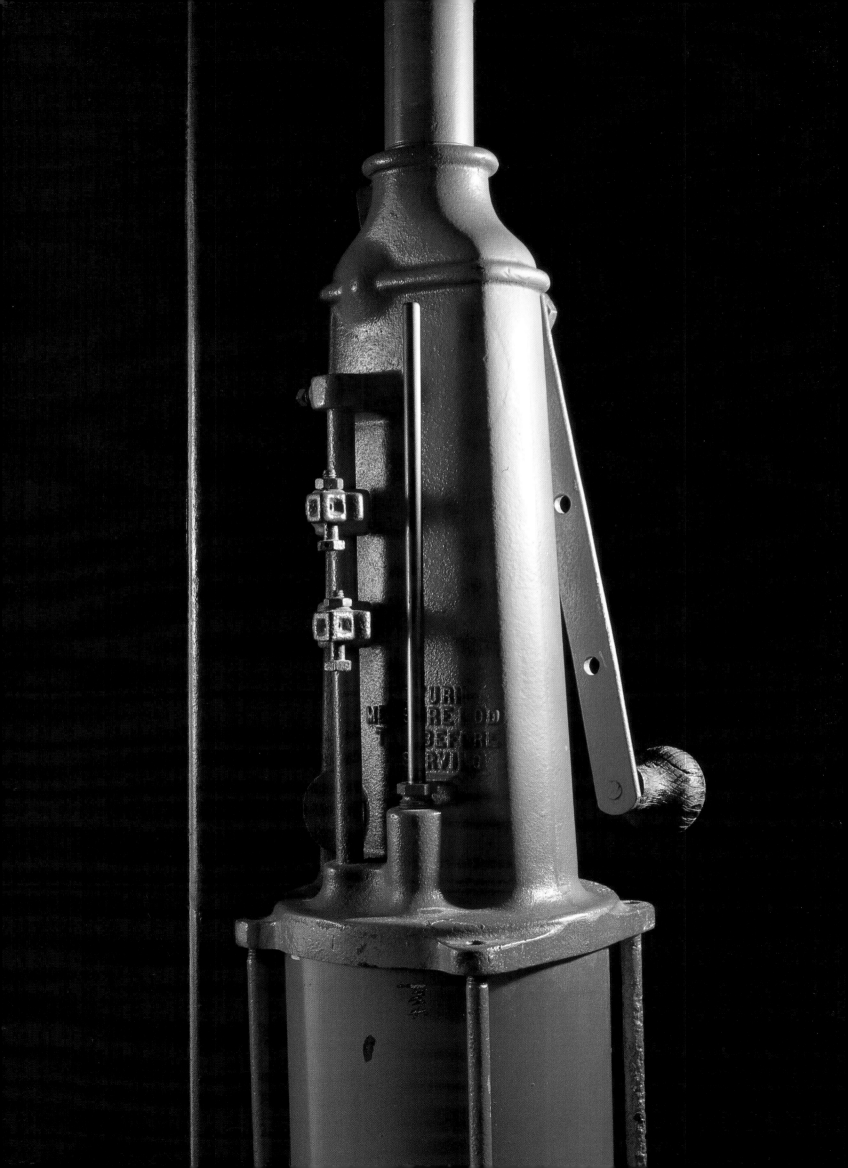

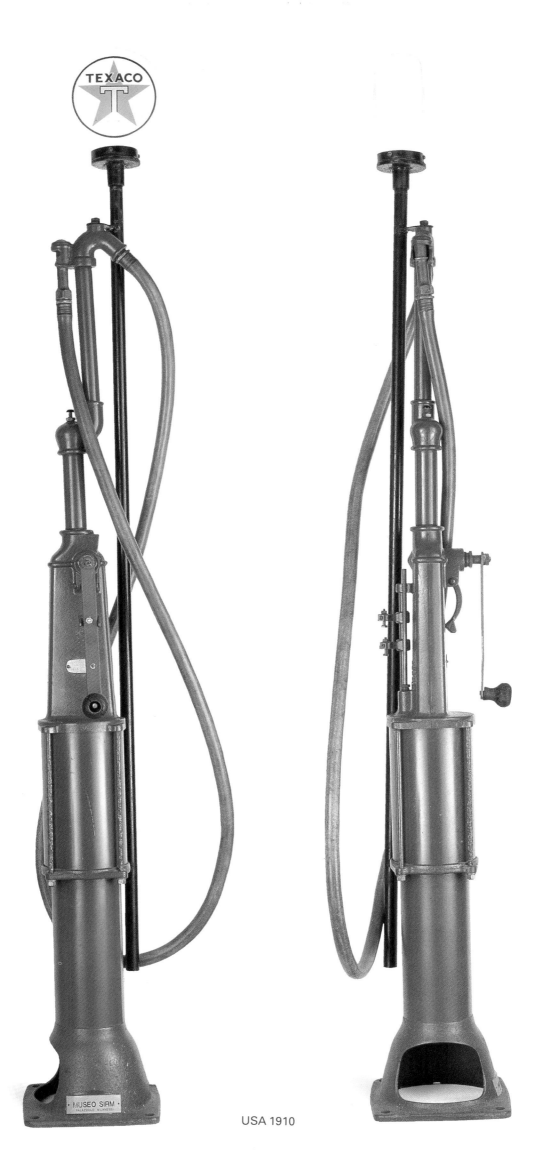

USA 1910

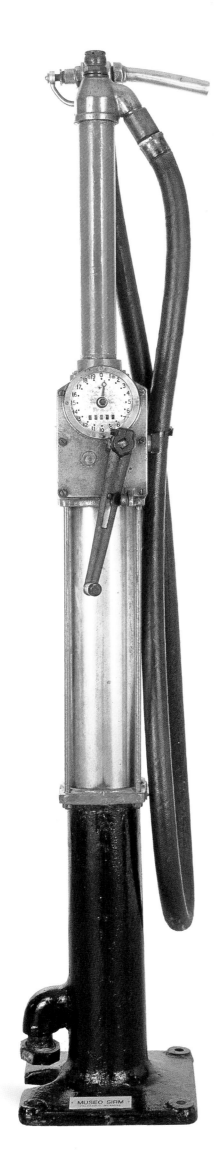
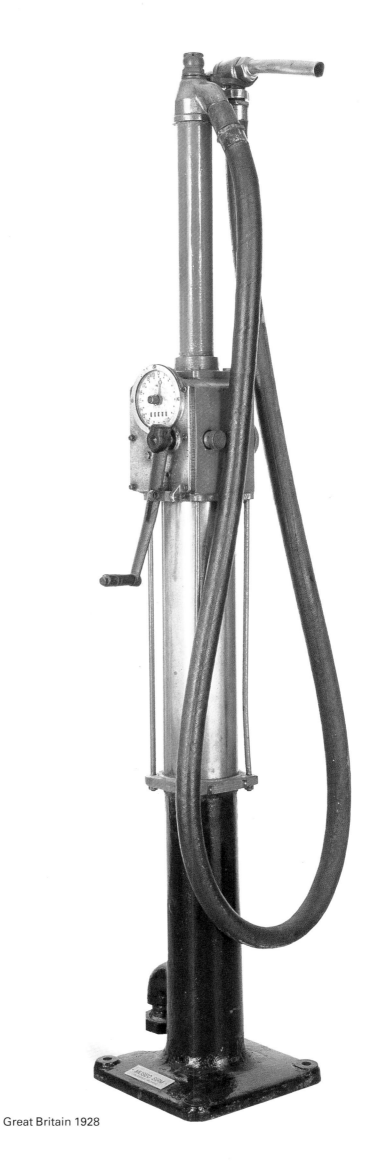

Great Britain 1928

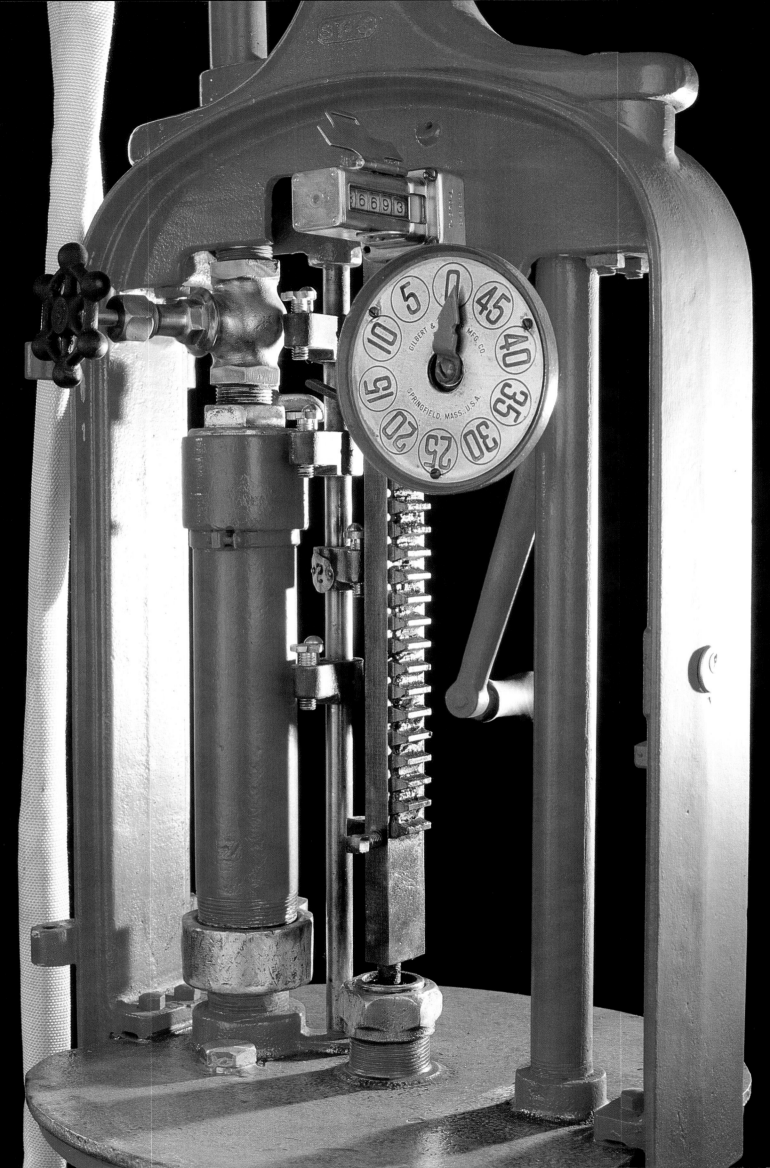

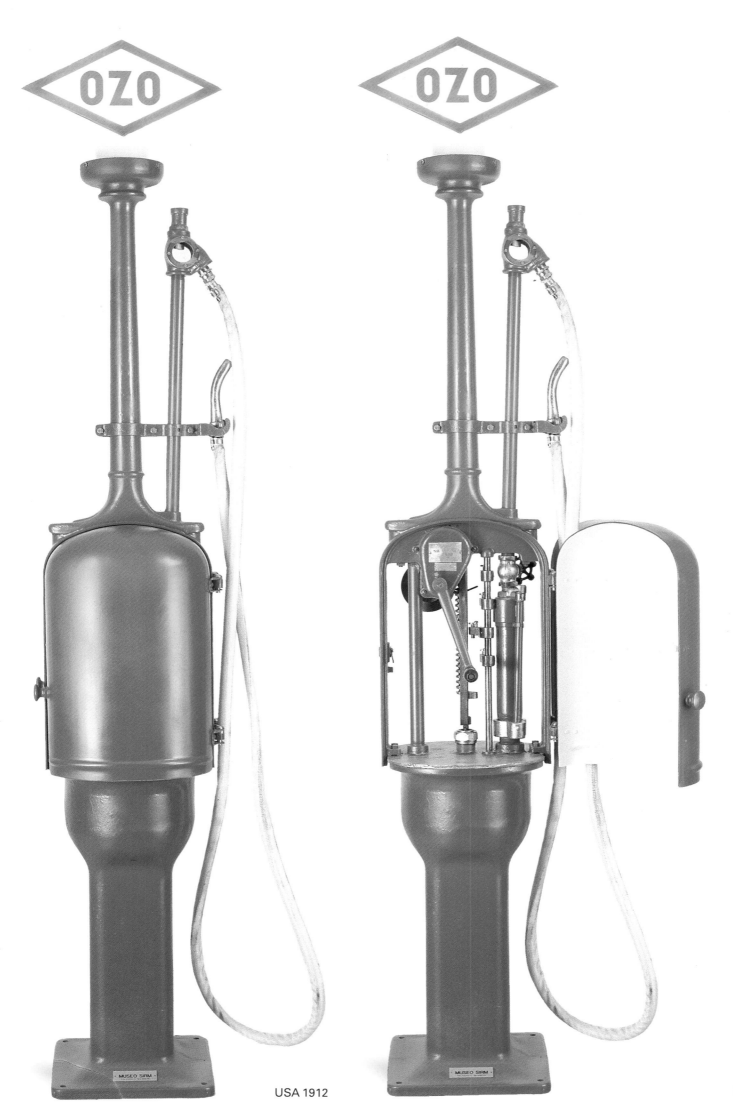

USA 1912

29

USA 1924

7

8

9

10

Bennett
10
MB 74 455

UNDERWRITERS' LABORATORIES
INSPECTED
VISIBLE MEASURE DISCHARGE
FOR HAZARDOUS LIQUIDS
FOR USE OUTSIDE OF BUILDING № 6 5 9 0 2 3

USA 1924

France 1931

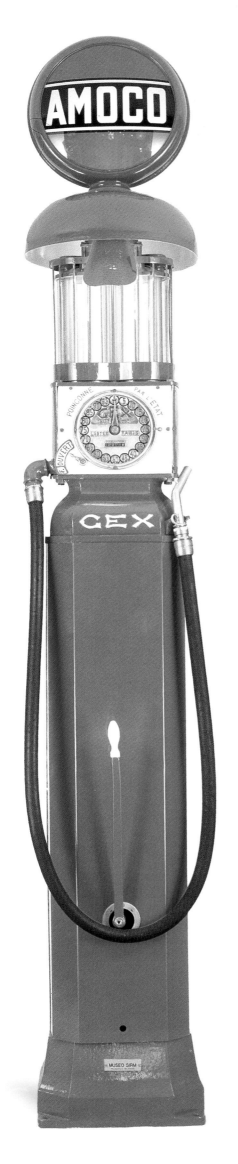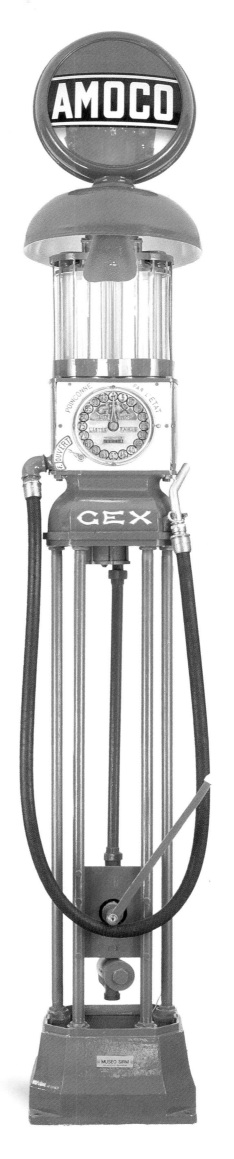

France 1935

France 1934

France 1933

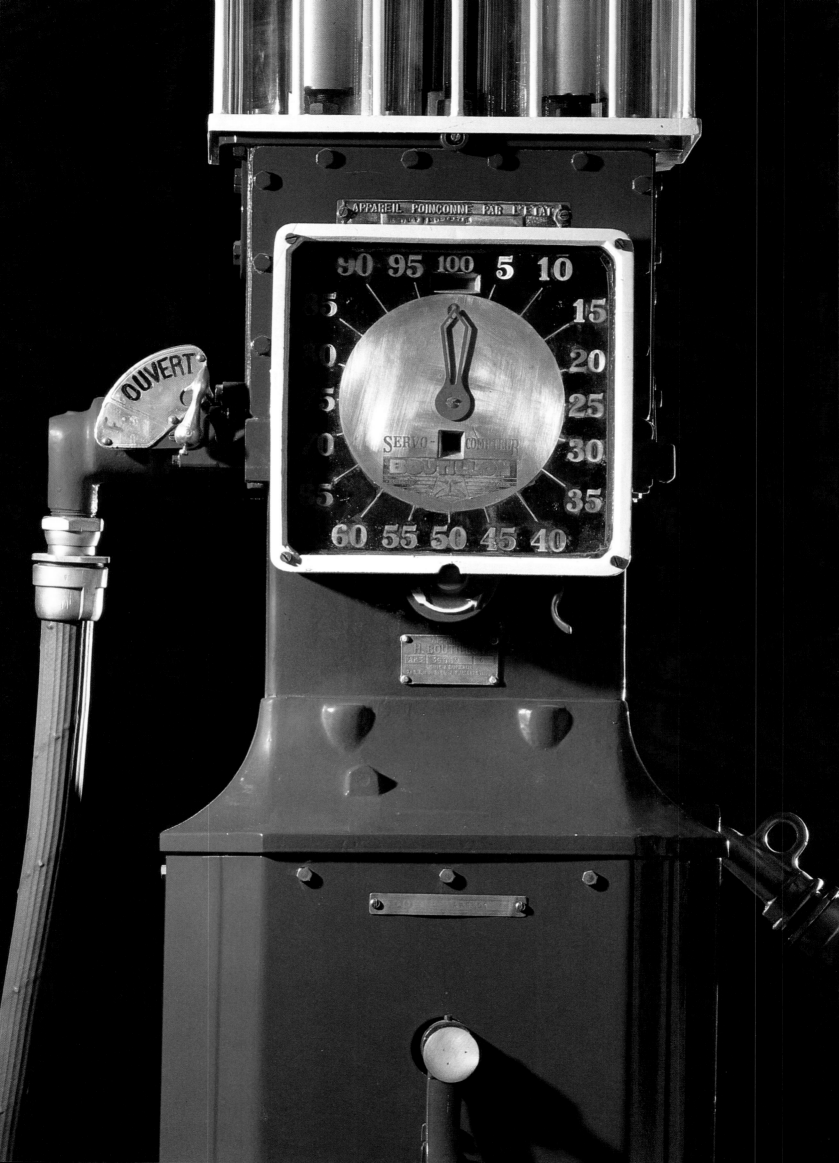

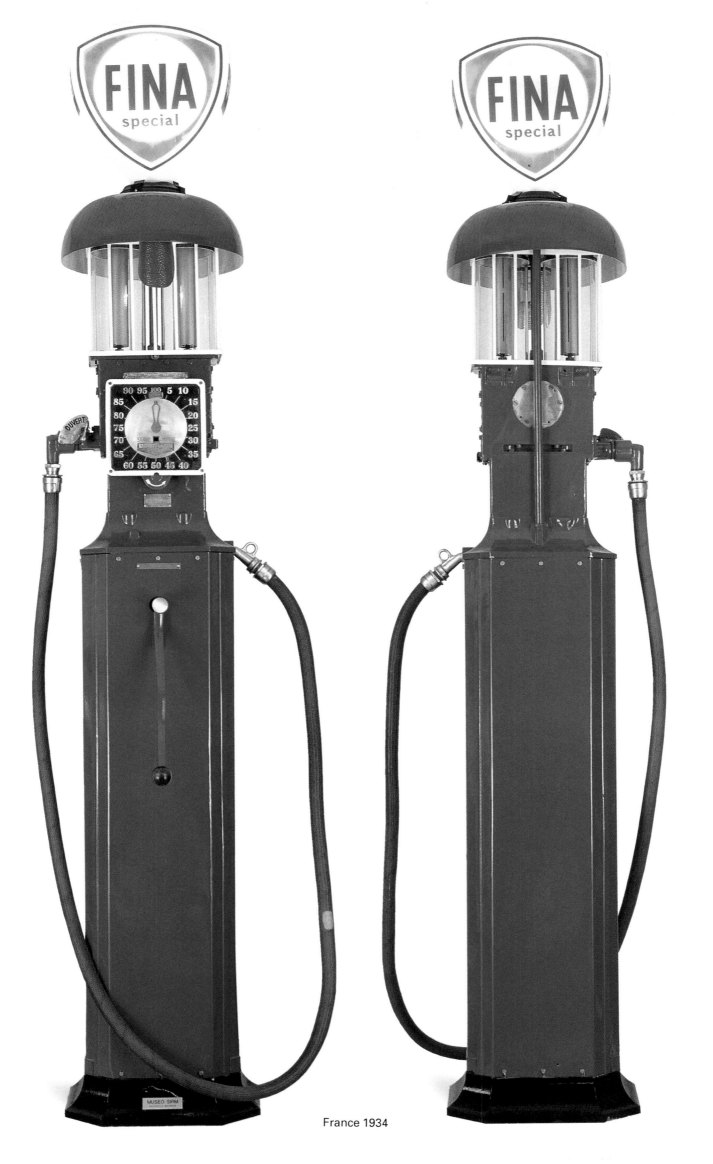

France 1934

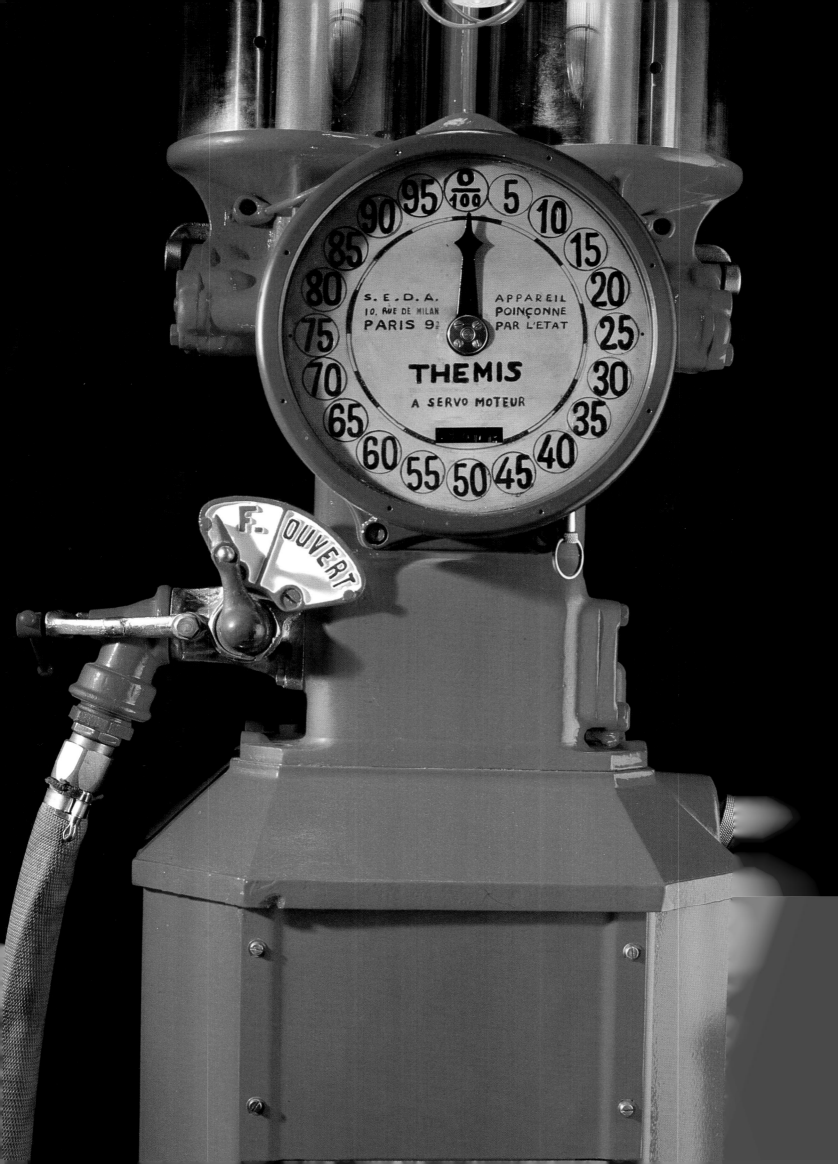

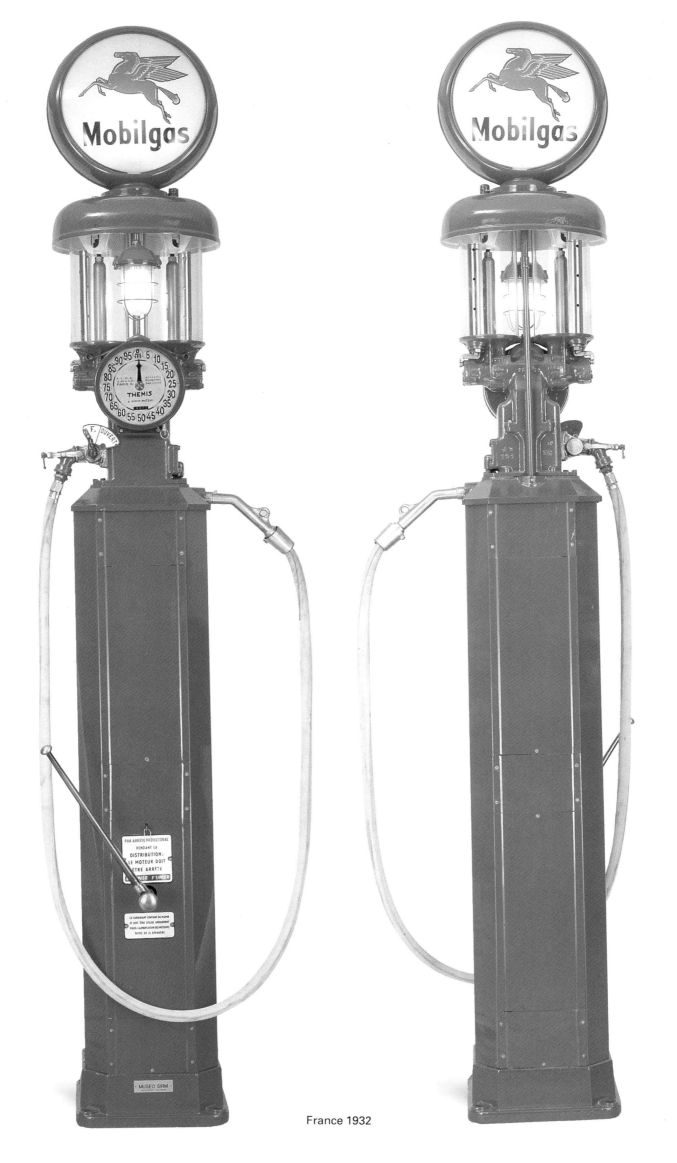

France 1932

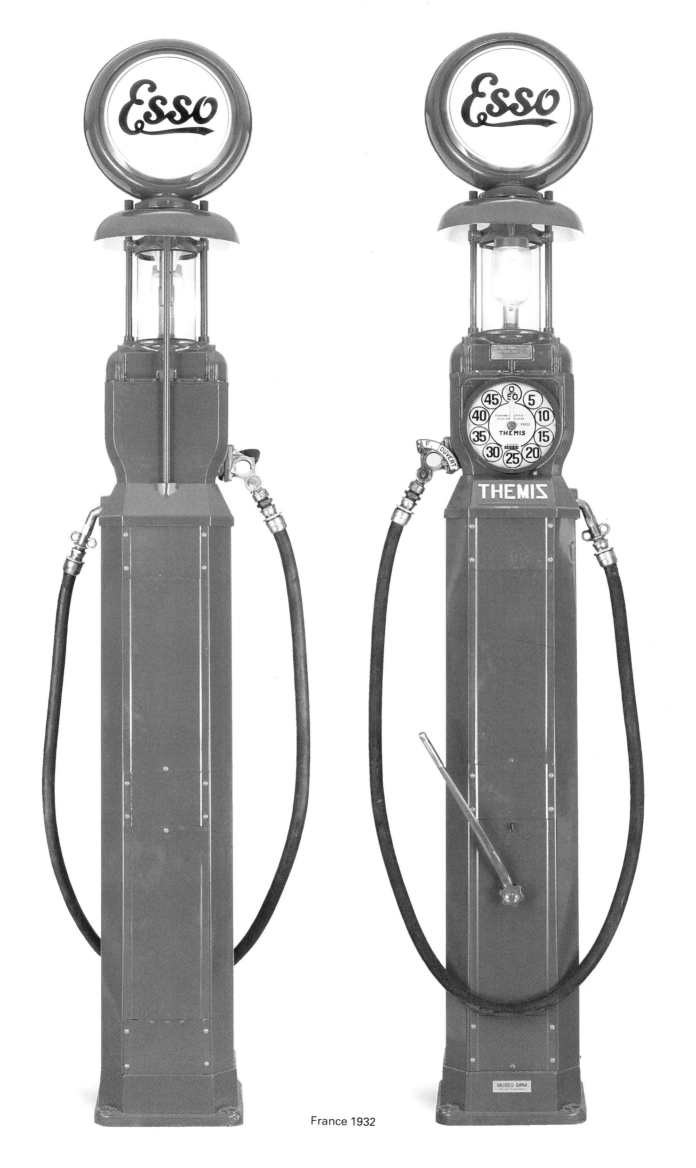

France 1932

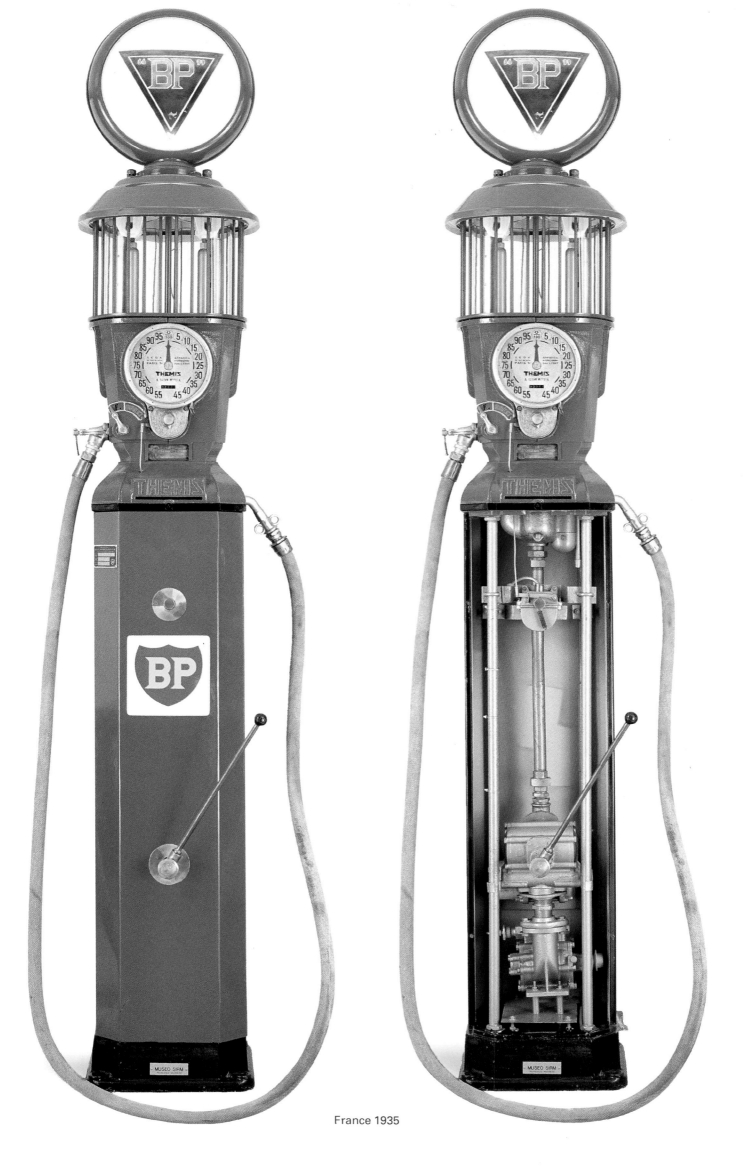

France 1935

France 1924

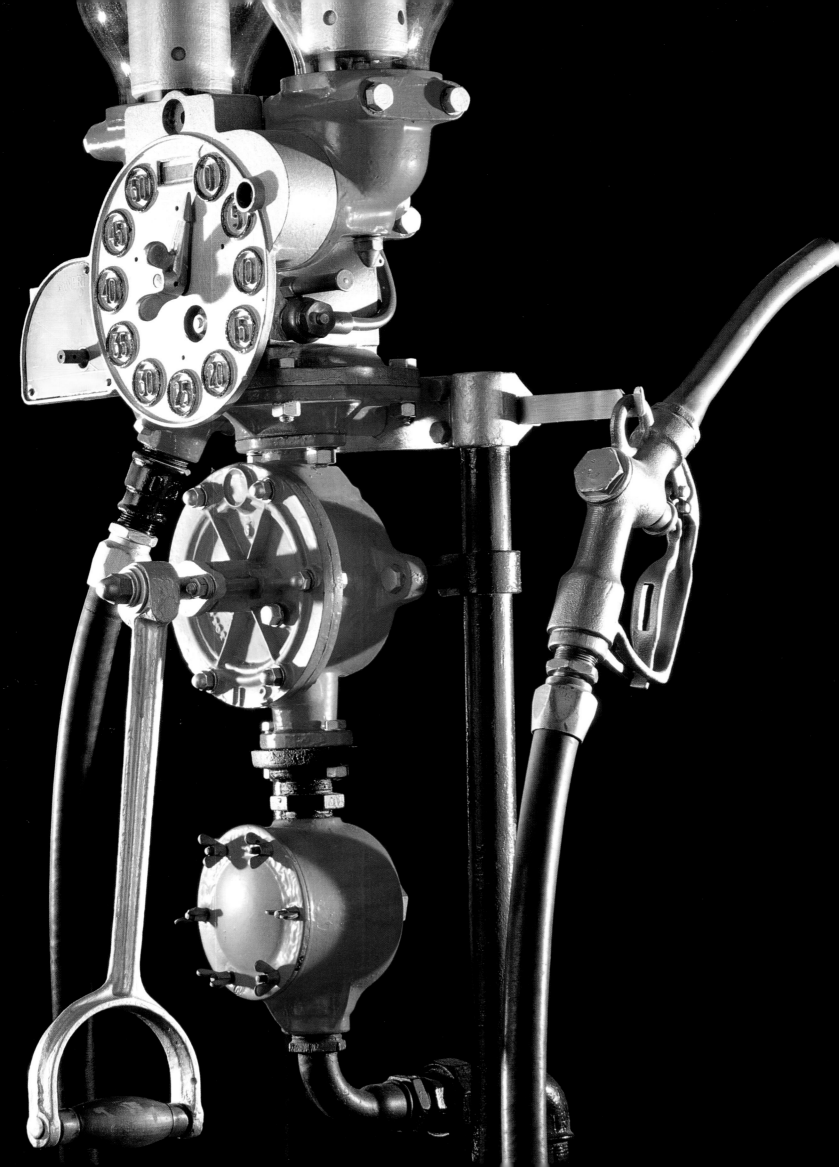

France 1924

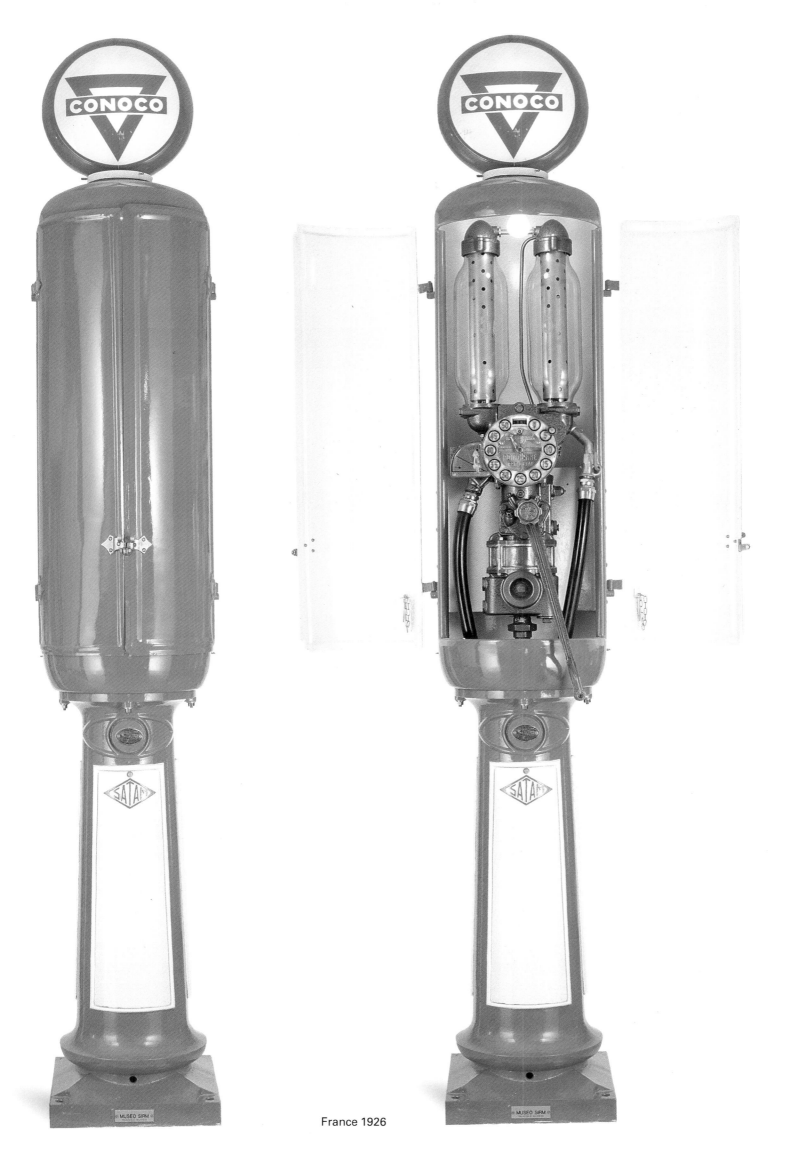

France 1926

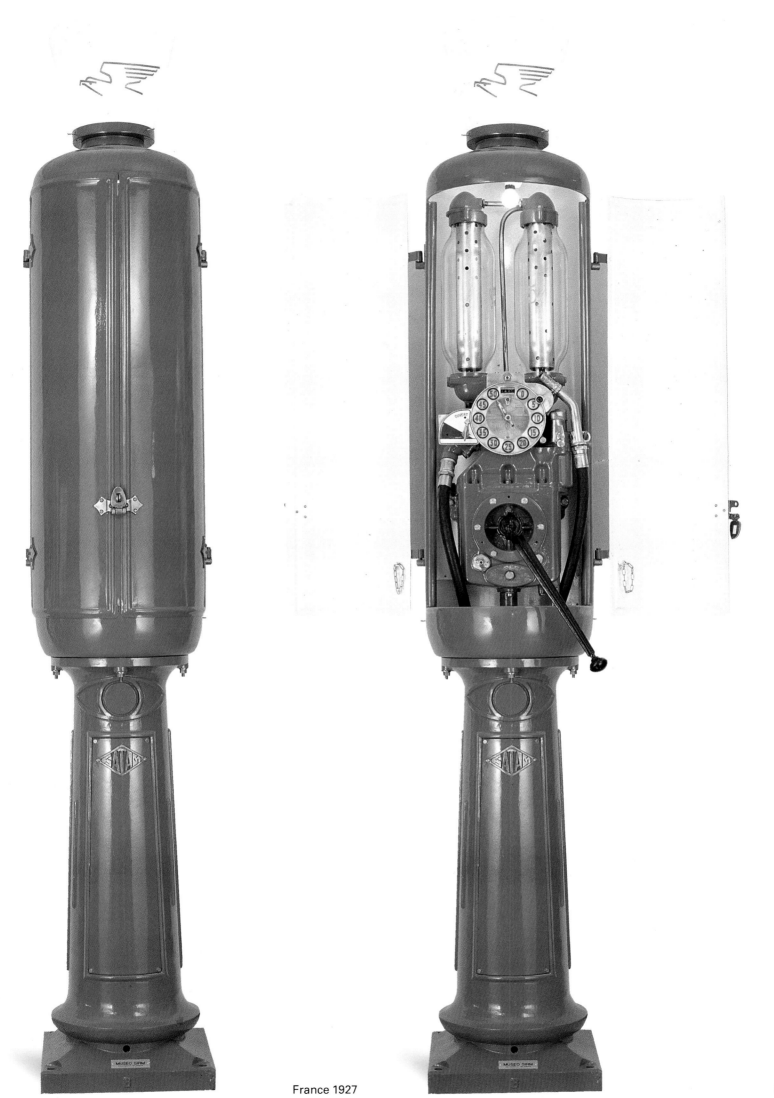

France 1927

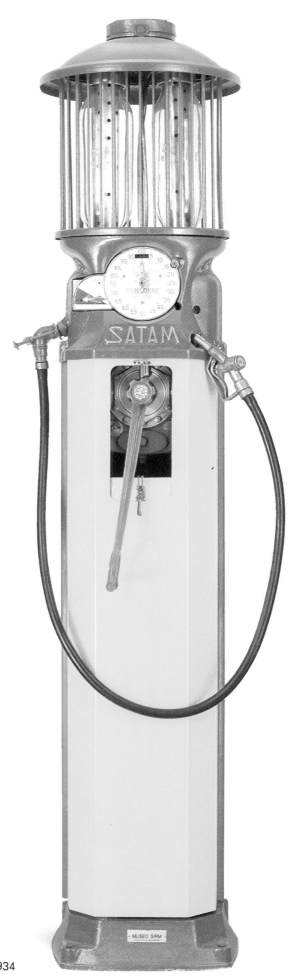

France 1934

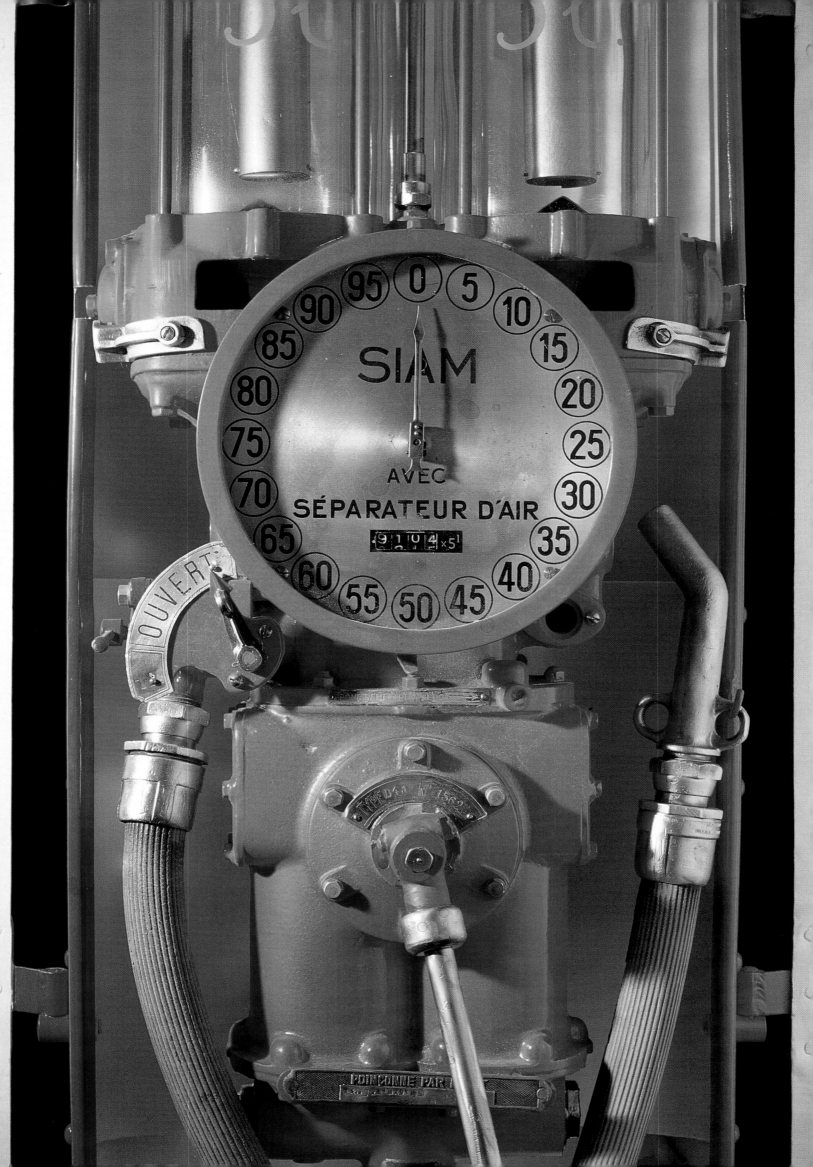

France 1930

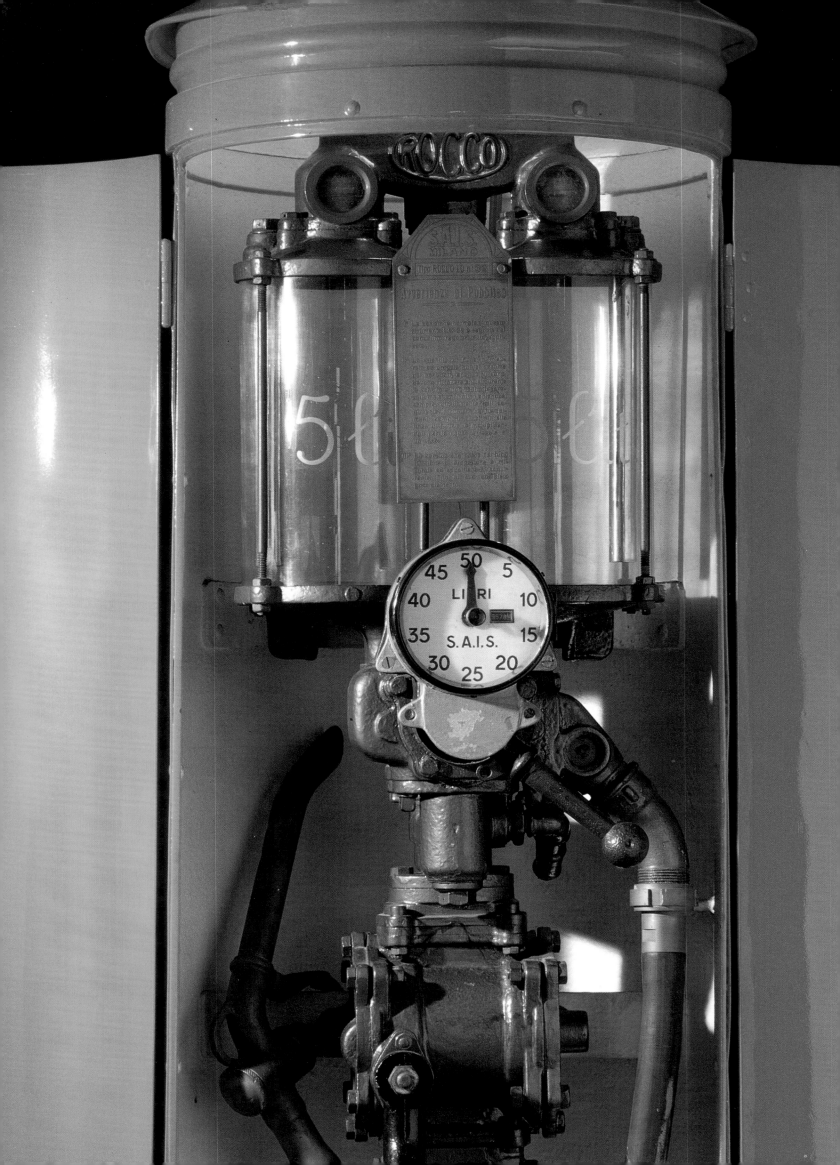

Italy 1933

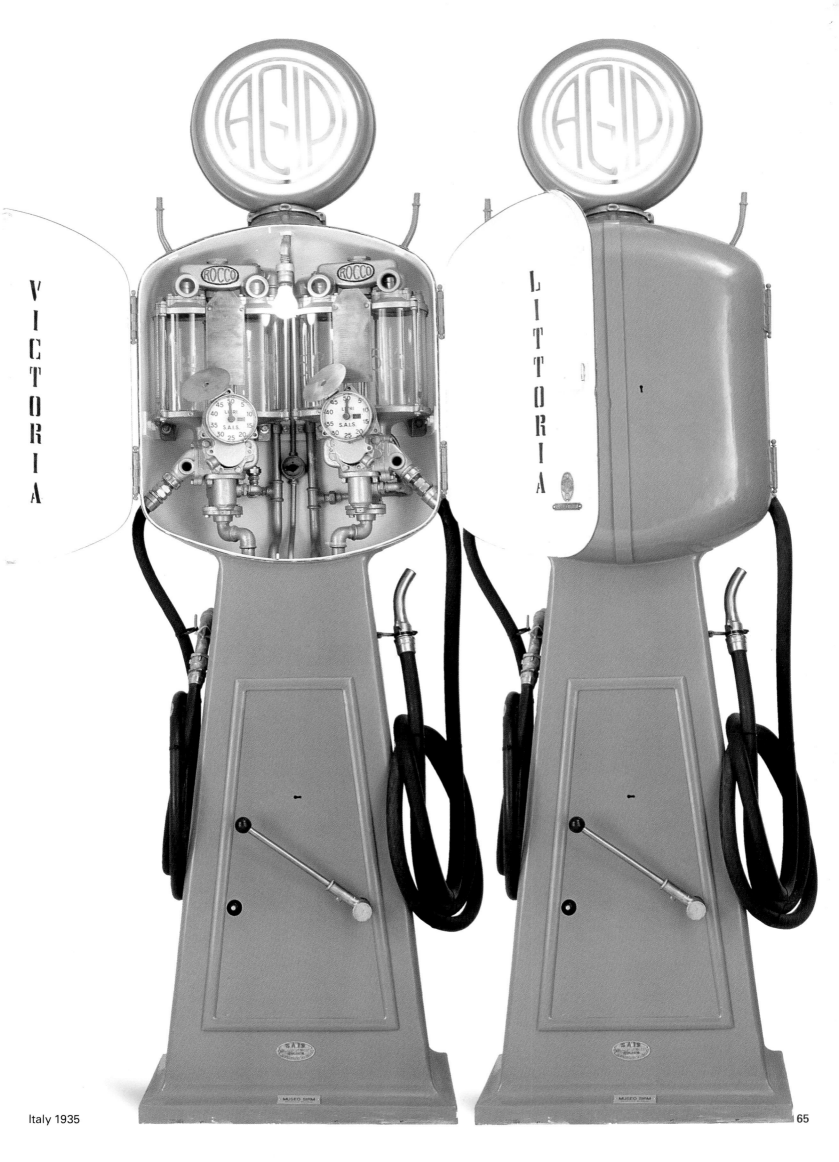

Italy 1935

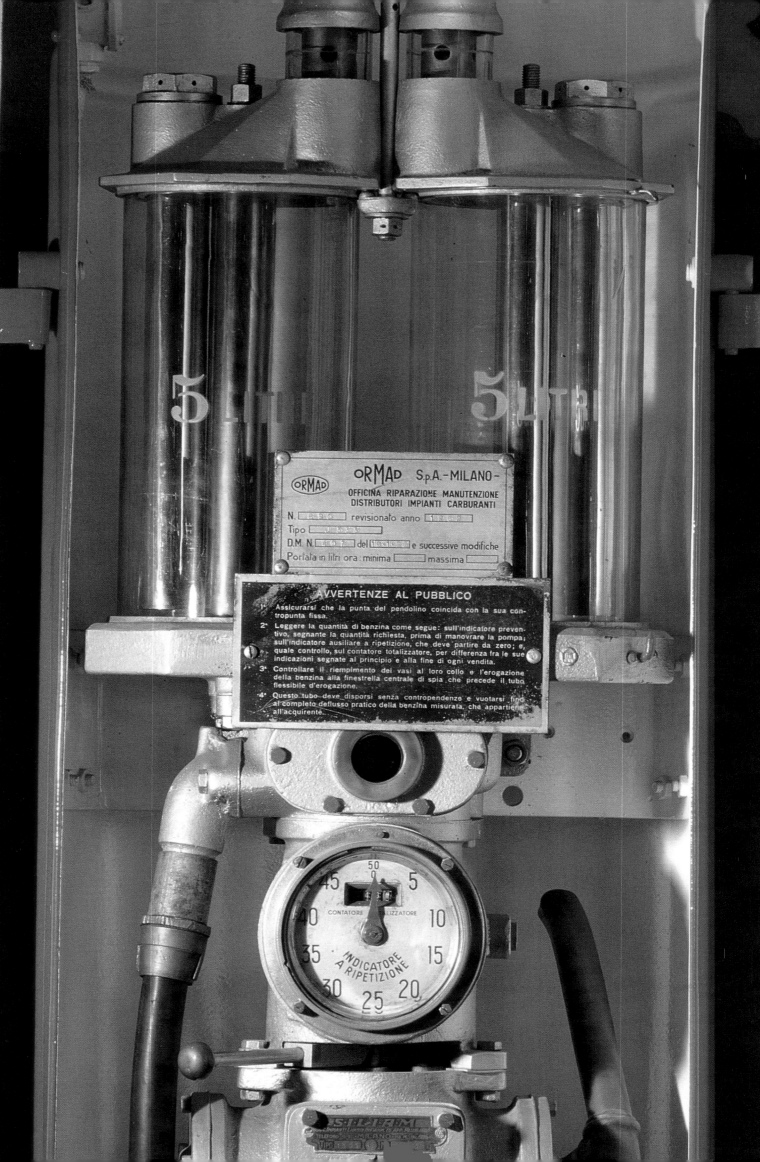

ORMAD S.p.A.-MILANO-
OFFICINA RIPARAZIONE MANUTENZIONE
DISTRIBUTORI IMPIANTI CARBURANTI
N. _____ revisionato anno _____
Tipo _____
D.M. N. _____ del _____ e successive modifiche
Portata in litri ora : minima _____ massima _____

AVVERTENZE AL PUBBLICO

1° Assicurarsi che la punta del pendolino coincida con la sua con-
tropunta fissa.

2° Leggere la quantità di benzina come segue: sull'indicatore preventivo, segnante la quantità richiesta, prima di manovrare la pompa;
sull'indicatore ausiliare a ripetizione, che deve partire da zero; e,
quale controllo, sul contatore totalizzatore, per differenza fra le sue
indicazioni segnate al principio e alla fine di ogni vendita.

3° Controllare il riempimento dei vasi al loro collo e l'erogazione
della benzina alla finestrella centrale di spia che precede il tubo
flessibile d'erogazione.

4° Questo tubo deve disporsi senza contropendenze e vuotarsi fino
al completo deflusso pratico della benzina misurata, che appartiene
all'acquirente.

CONTATORE TOTALIZZATORE

INDICATORE
A RIPETIZIONE

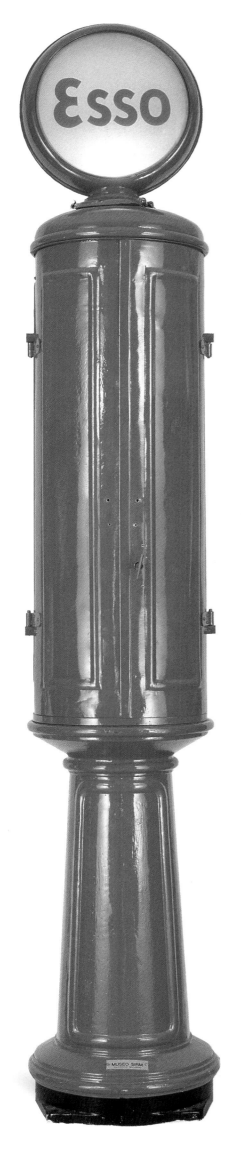

Italy 1930

Italy 1931

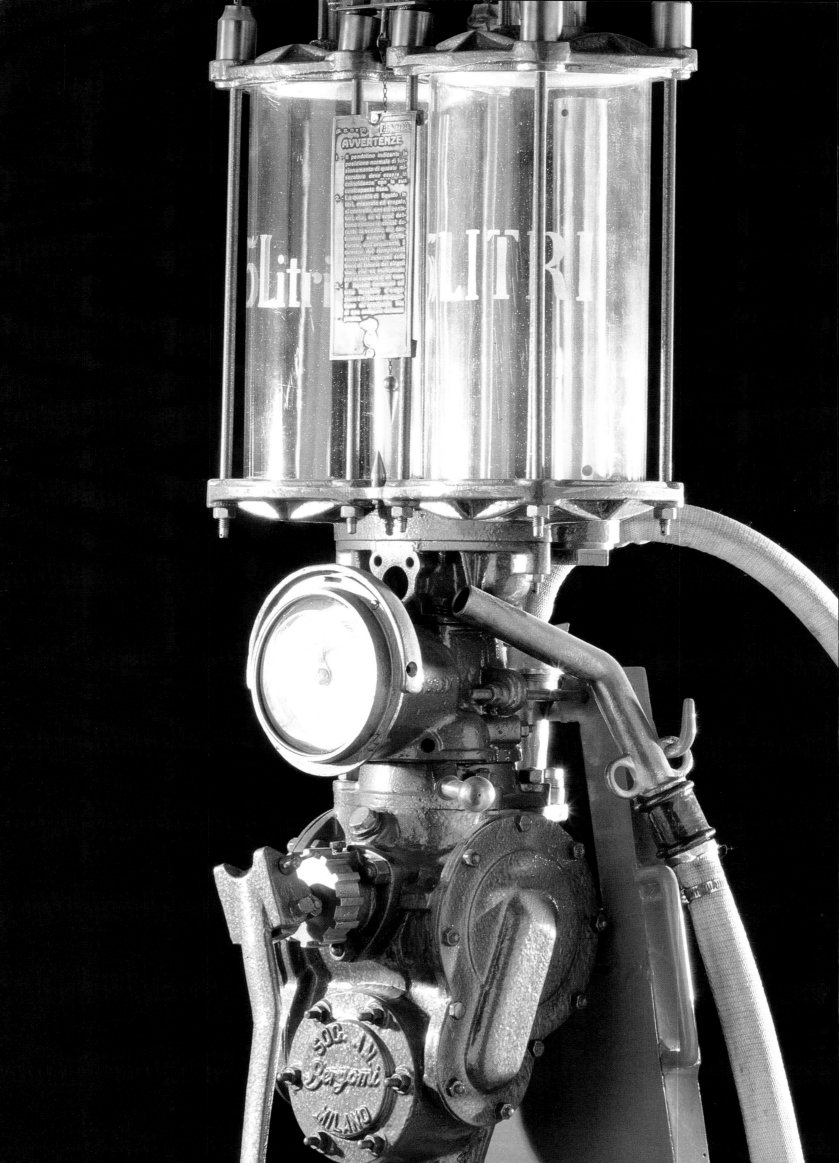

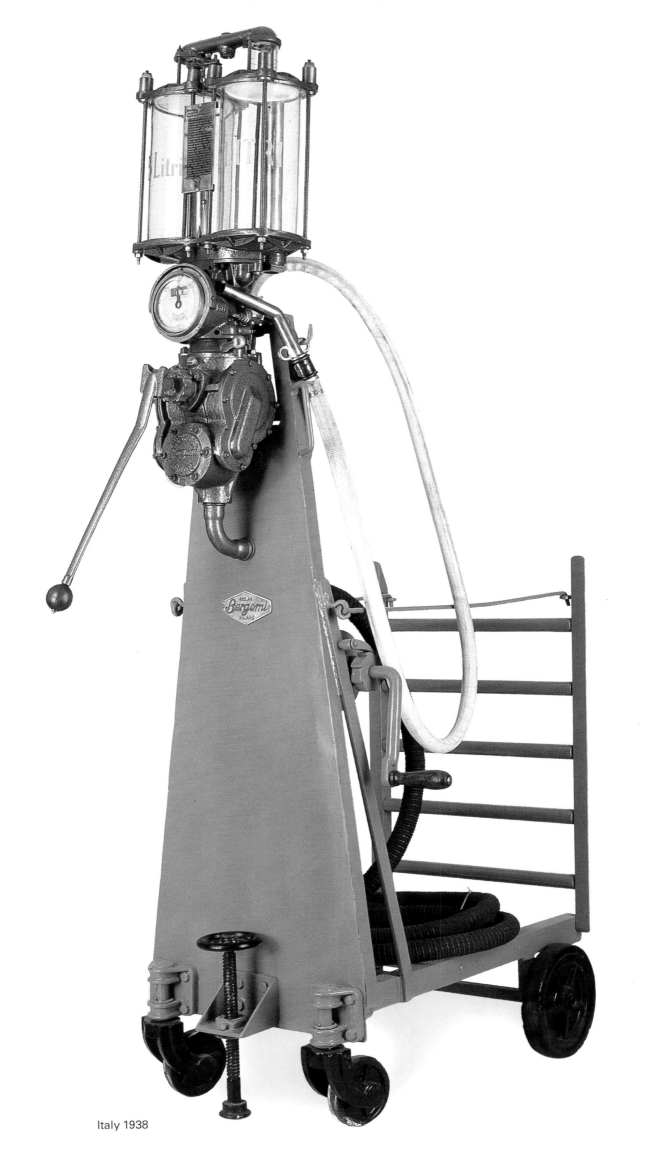

Italy 1938

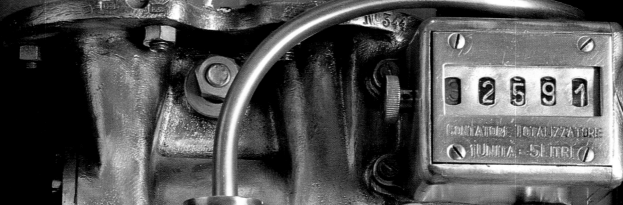

CONTATORE TOTALIZZATORE
(UNITÀ - 5 LITRI)

20 25 30 35 40 45 50
10 5
00 50

INDICA PREVENTIVO
DELLA QUANTITÀ DI
LIQUIDO DA MISURARE
LITRI   LITRI

27   1

DISTRIBUTORE AUTOMATICO DI
BENZINA
LICENZA HARCOLL
BREVETTI - 215820 - 215836 - 215850

SOC. AN. BERGOMI
MILANO

Italy 1935

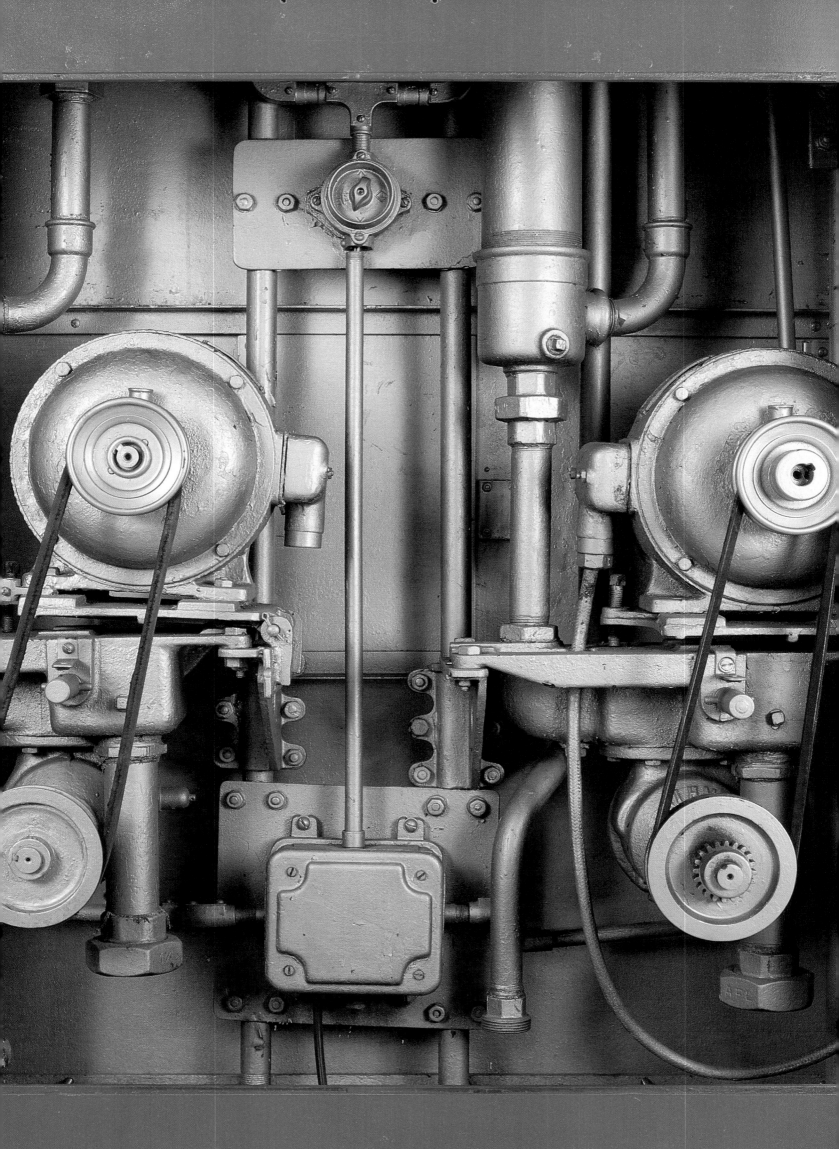

Italy 1935

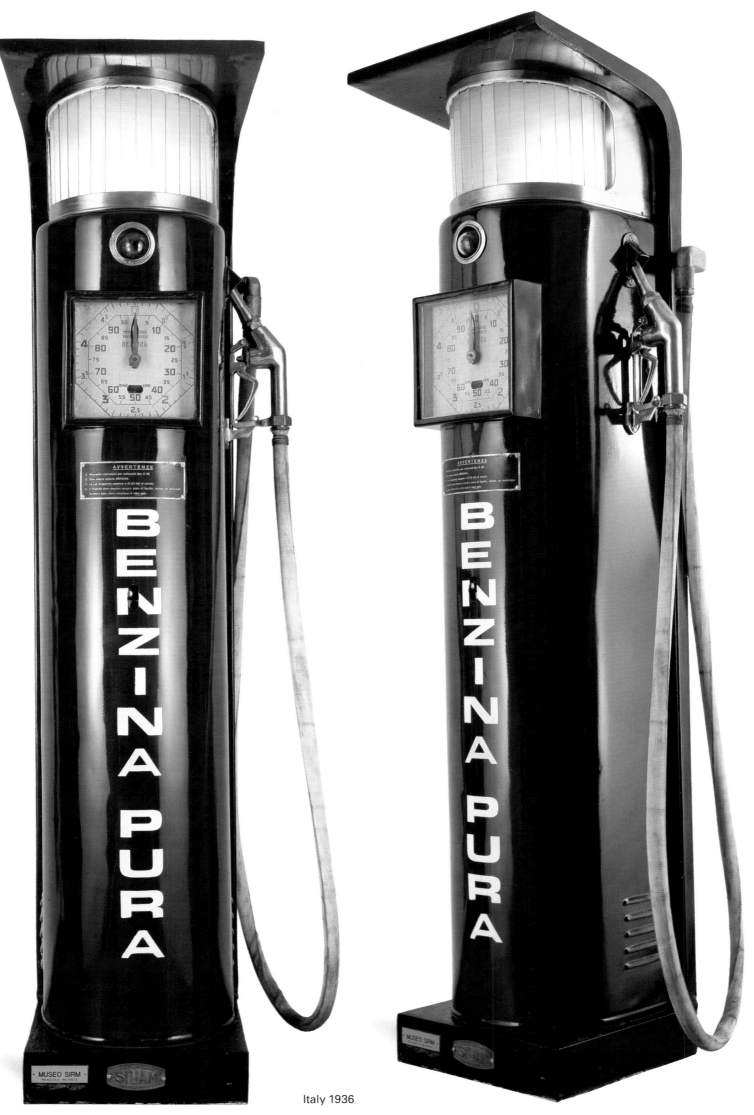

Italy 1936

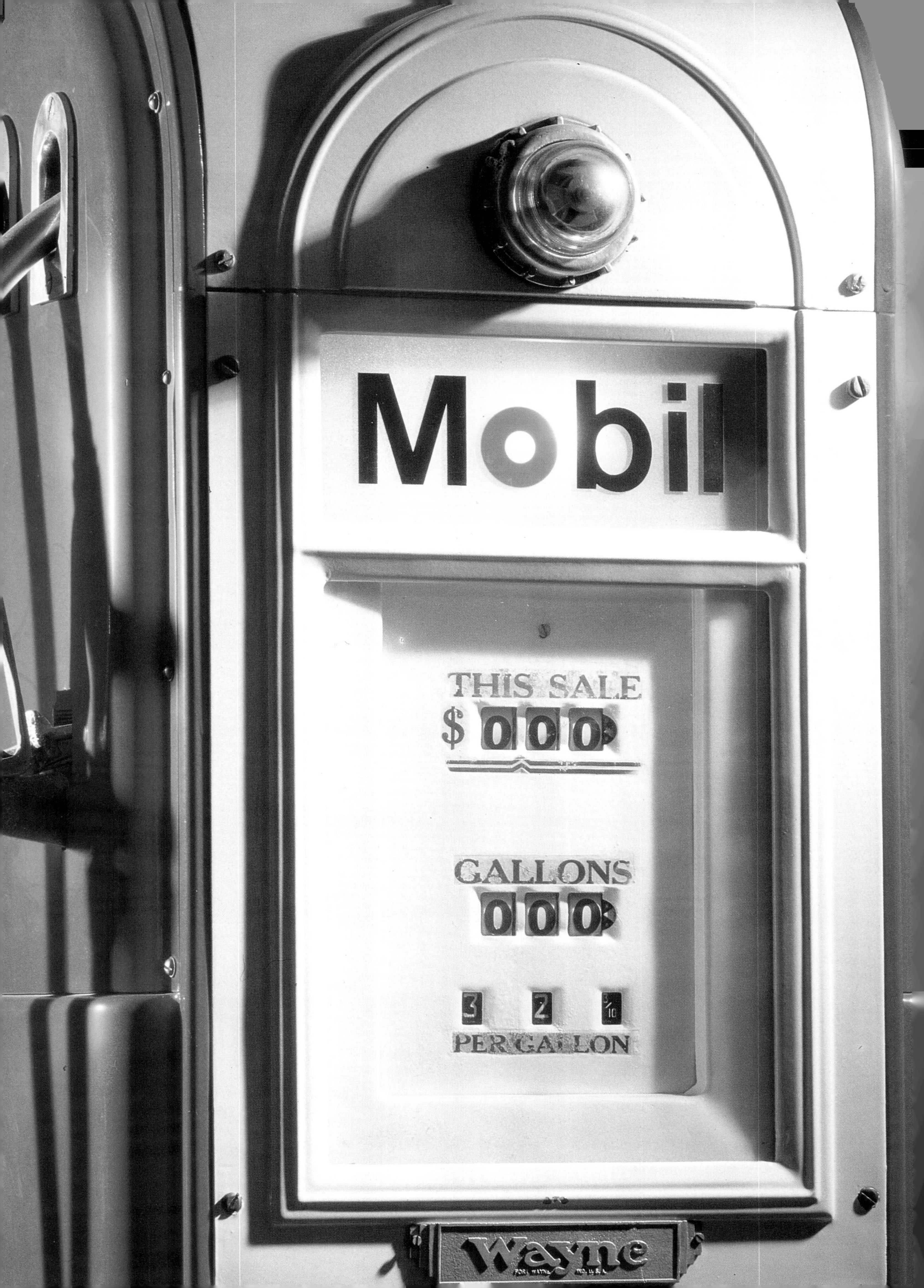
Mobil
THIS SALE
$ 0 0 0
GALLONS
0 0 0
PER GALLON
Wayne

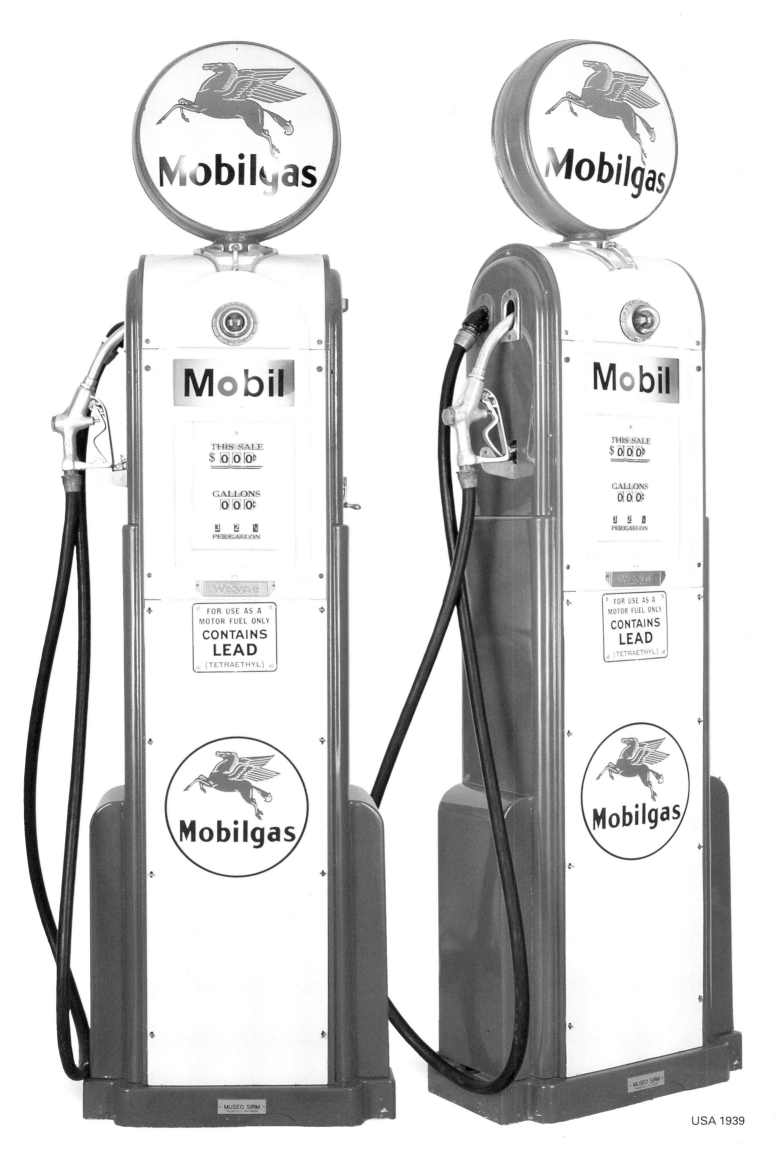

USA 1919

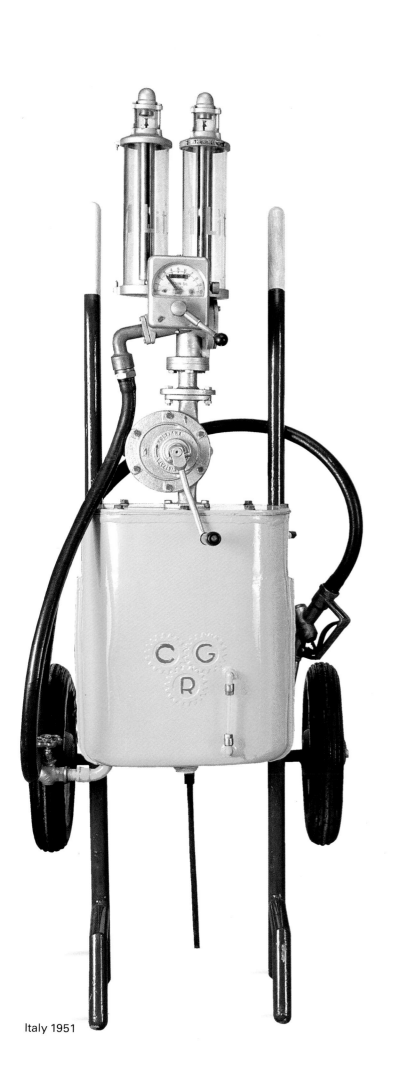

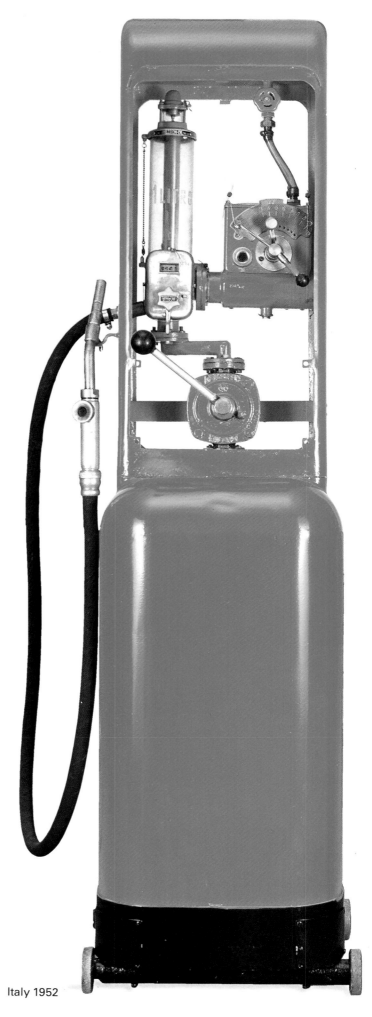

Italy 1951

Italy 1952

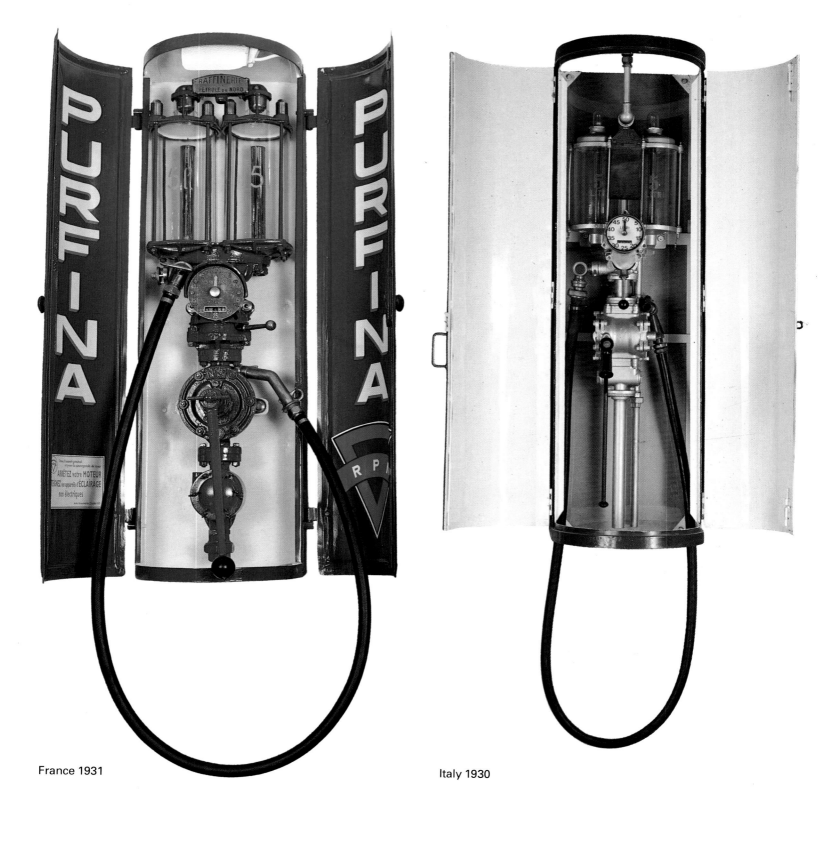

France 1931

Italy 1930

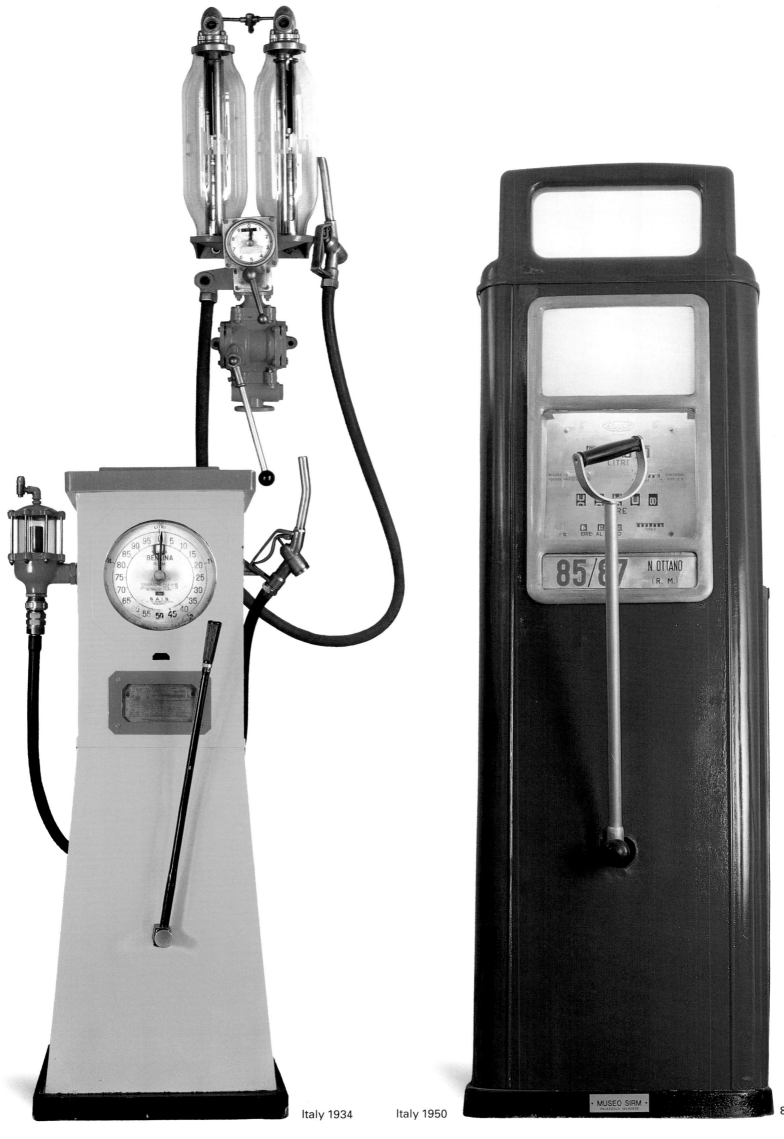

Italy 1934   Italy 1950

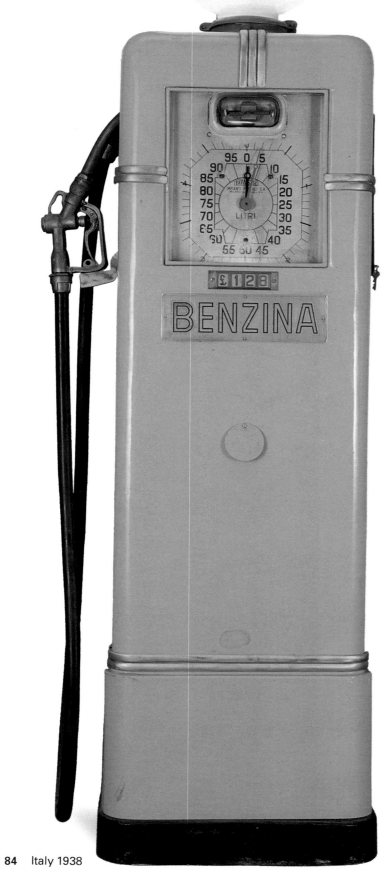

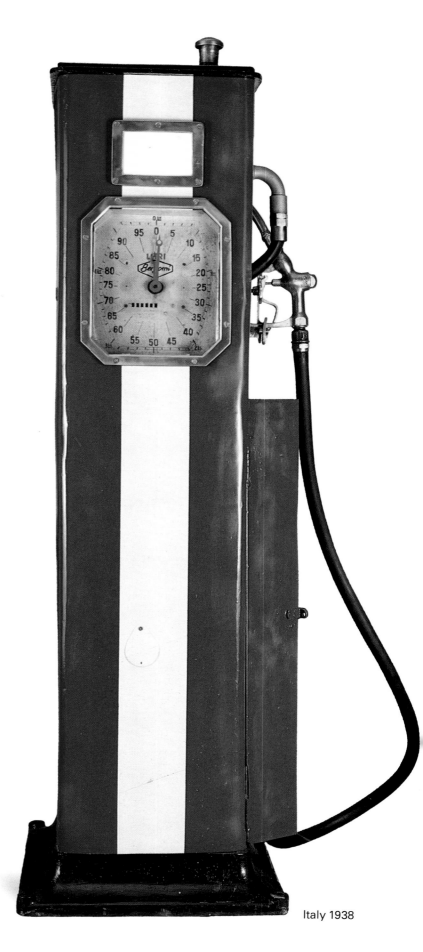

Italy 1938

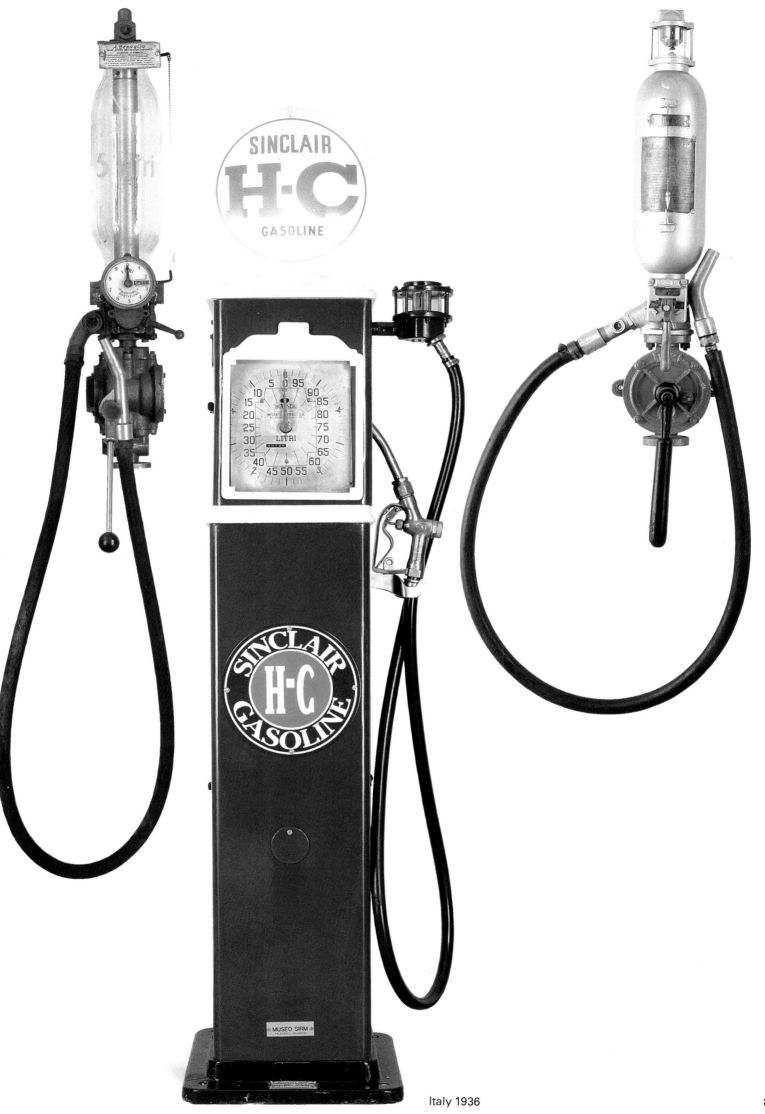

Italy 1936

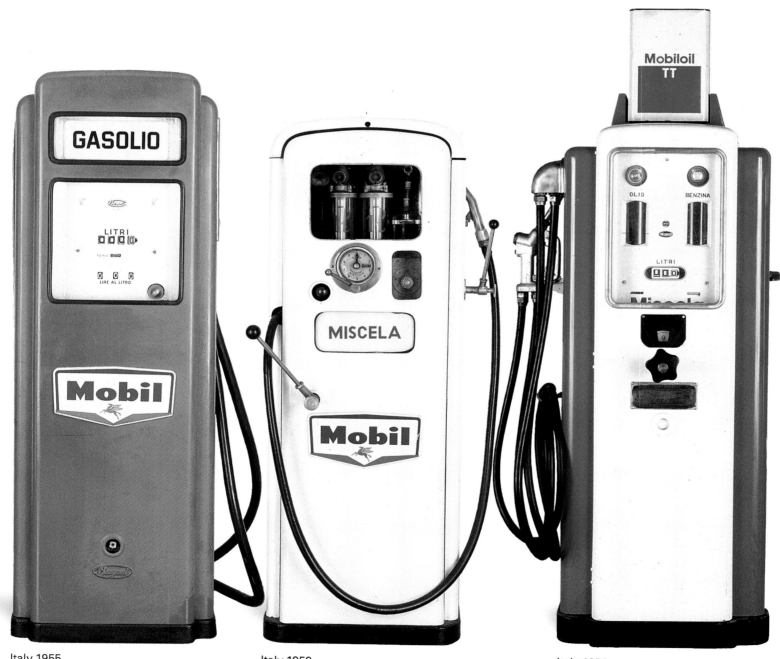

Italy 1959 Italy 1950

Italy 1949

Italy 1950

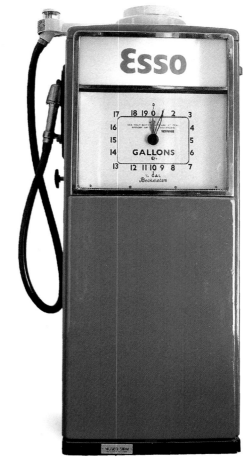

Great Britain 1960

88   Italy 1956

Italy 1962

France 1965

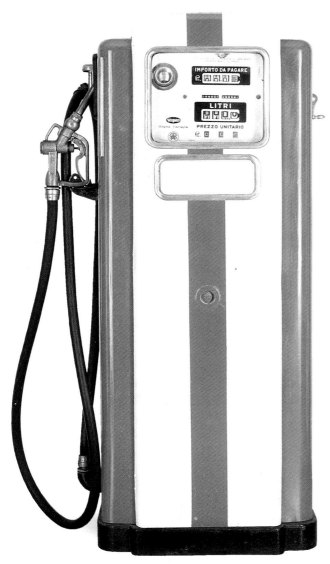

Italy 1950

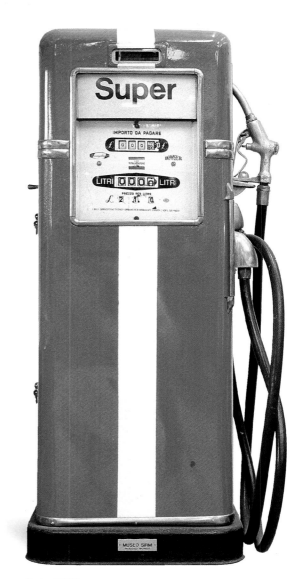

Italy 1950

Italy 1975

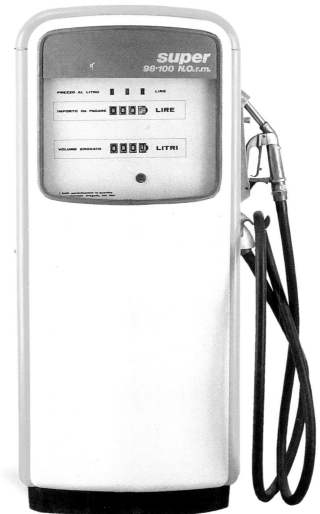

Italy 1960

89

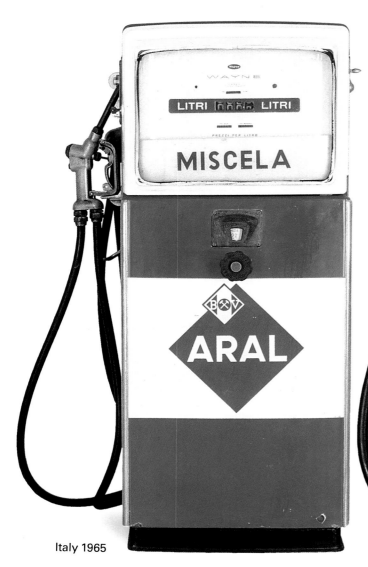

Italy 1965

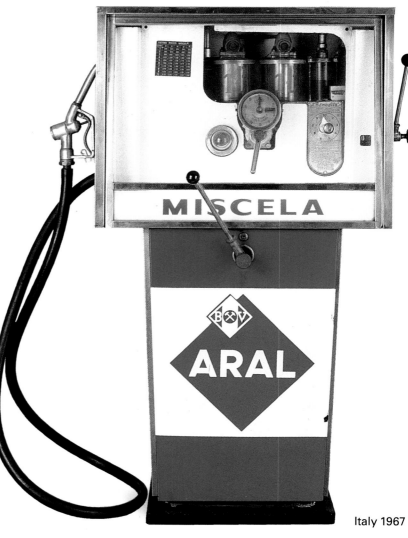

Italy 1967

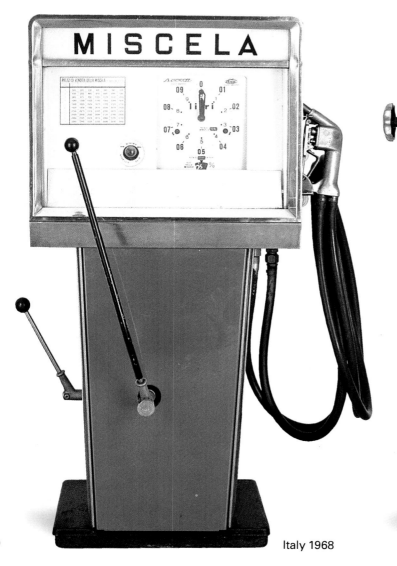

Italy 1968

Germany 1969

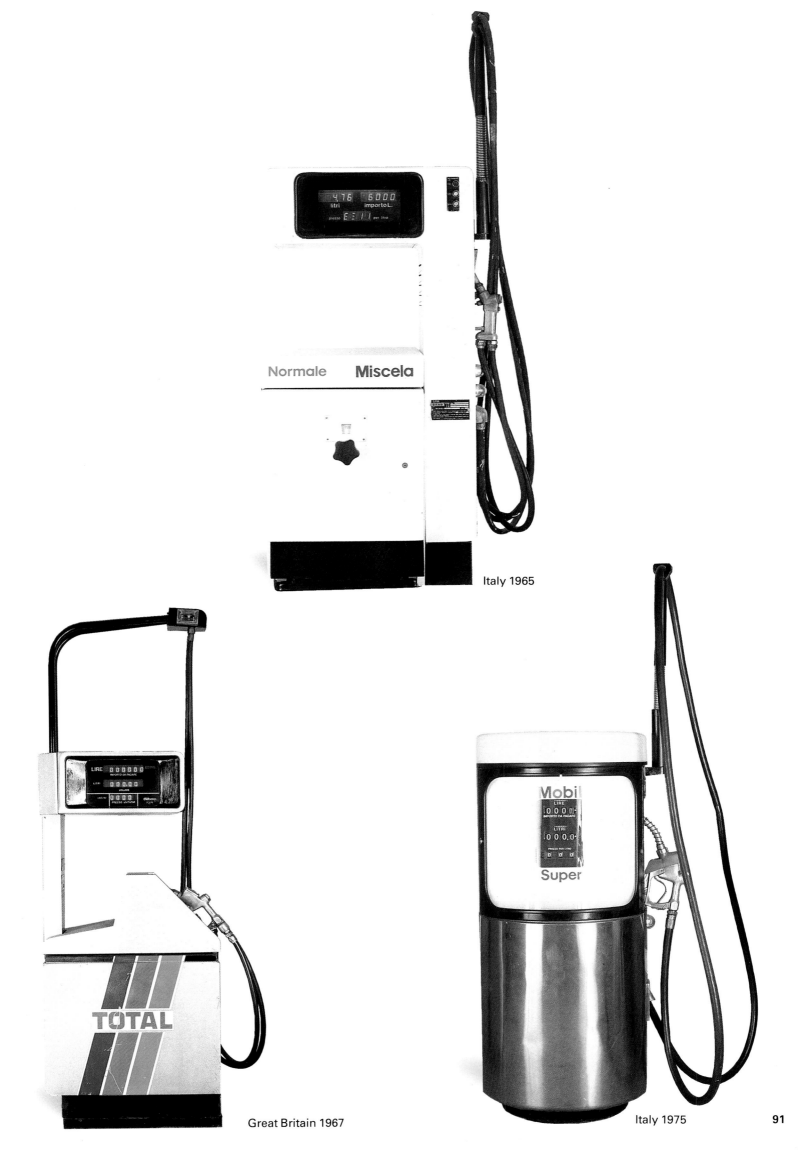

Normale **Miscela**

Italy 1965

TOTAL

Great Britain 1967

Mobil

Super

Italy 1975

91

GLOBES

Italy 1940

USA 1940

USA 1930

Italy 1925

Belgium 1935

USA 1930

USA 1940

Great Britain 1935

Great Britain 1940

Great Britain 1940

Great Britain 1940

taly 1940

Italy 1950

taly 1948

France 1955

JSA 1920

USA 1935

USA 1930

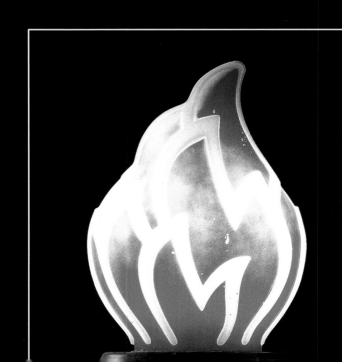

CONTAINERS

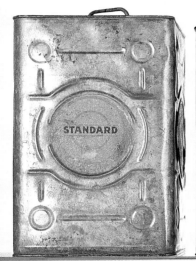

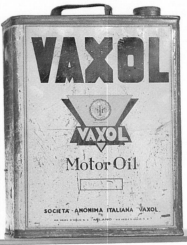

GRADE

XL

GRADE

5   5

GAMAGES

MOTOR

OIL

GALS   GALS

GUARANTEED
SPECIFICATION

COPYRIGHT

GAMAGE

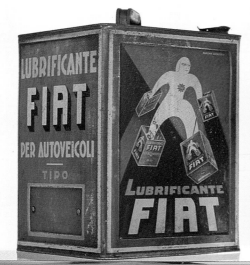

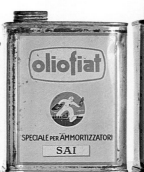

113

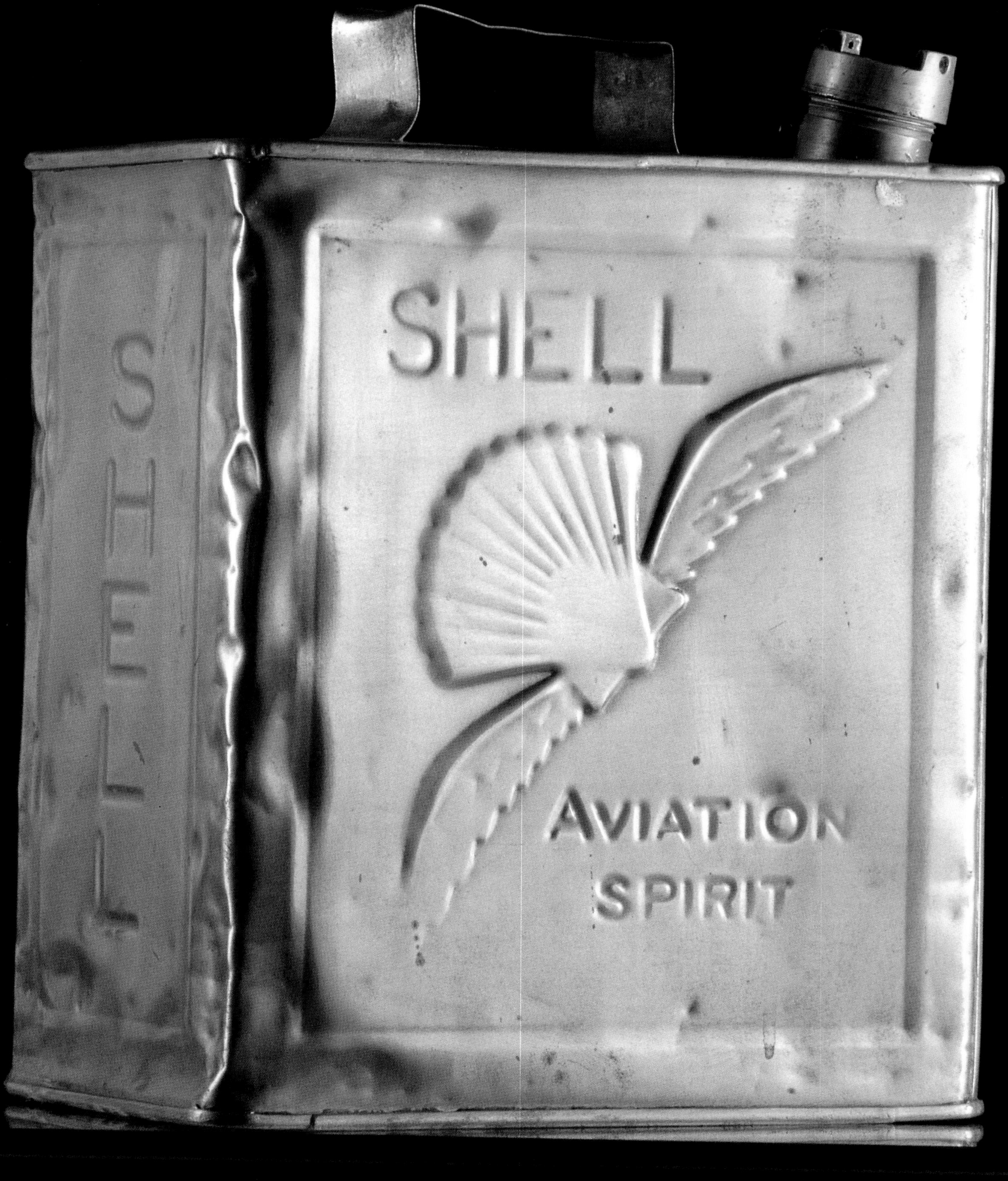
SHELL
SHELL
AVIATION
SPIRIT

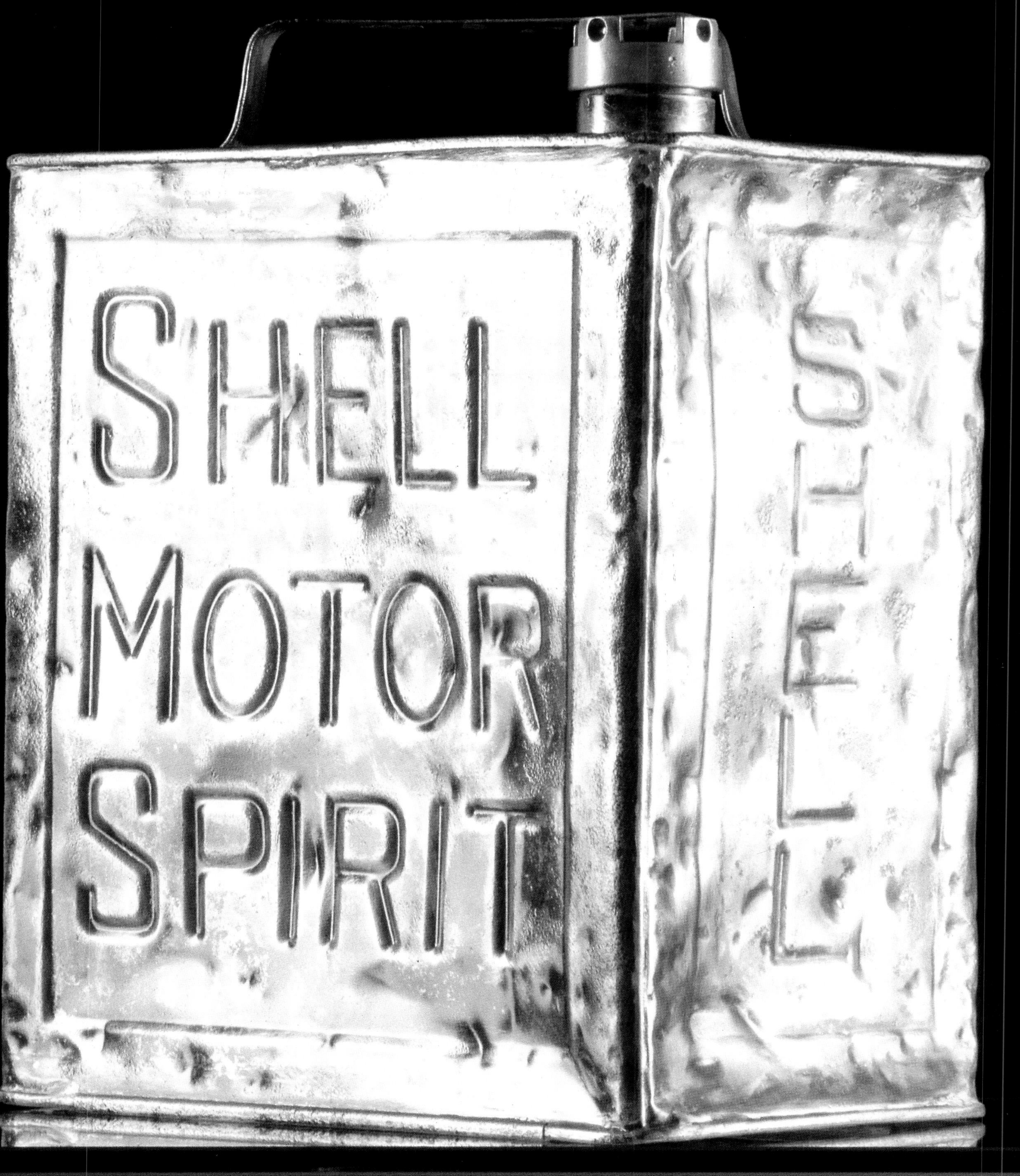
SHELL
MOTOR
SPIRIT
SHELL

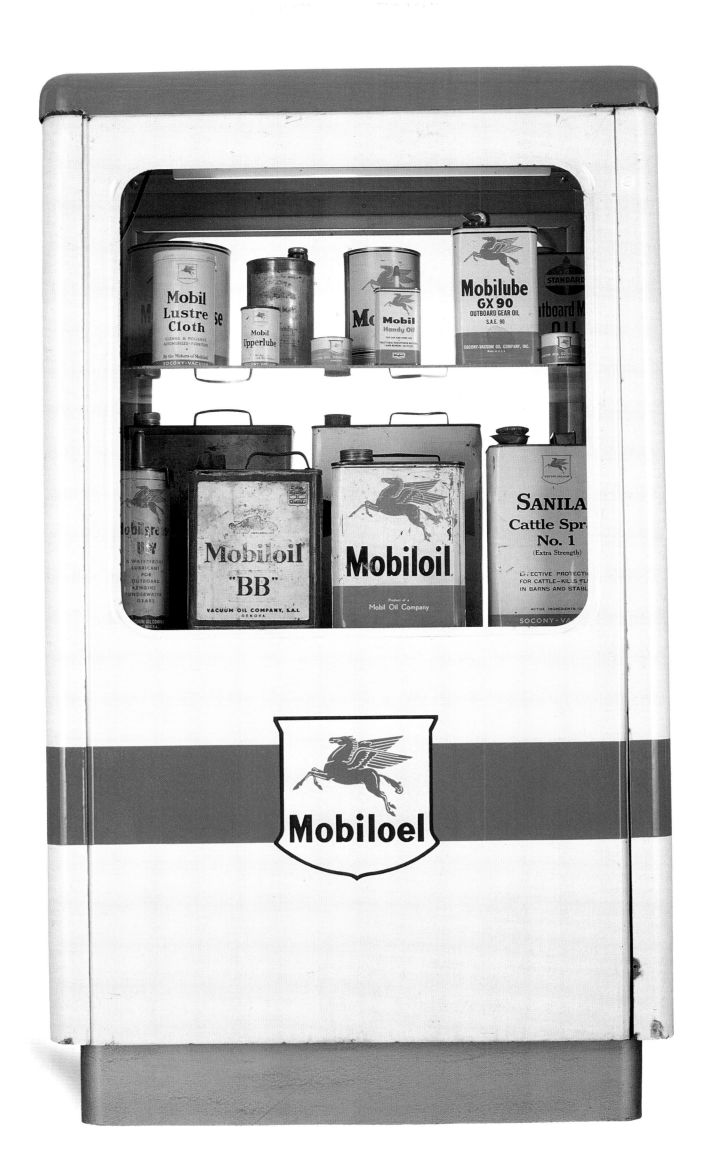

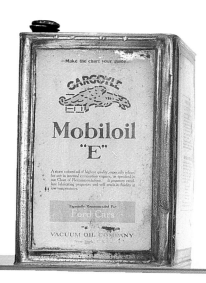

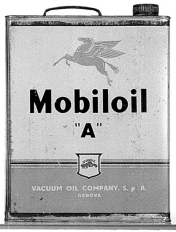
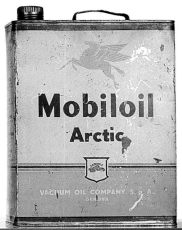

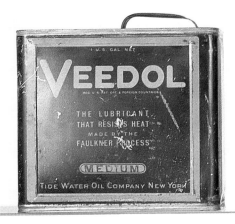

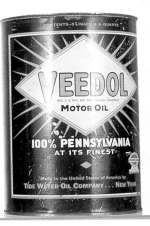
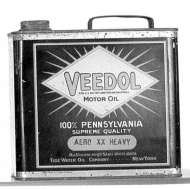

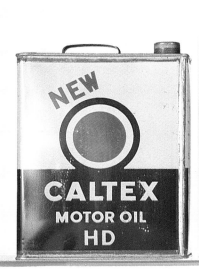

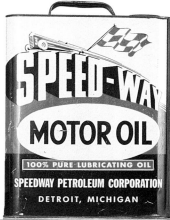

GULFLUBE
MOTOR OIL
PARAFFINE BASE
GALLONS
GULF
PROCESSED
GULFLUBE
MOTOR OIL

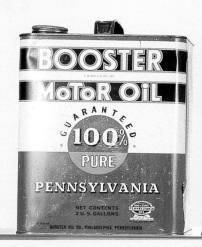

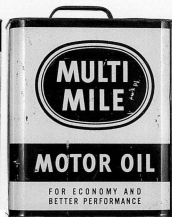

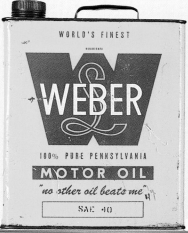

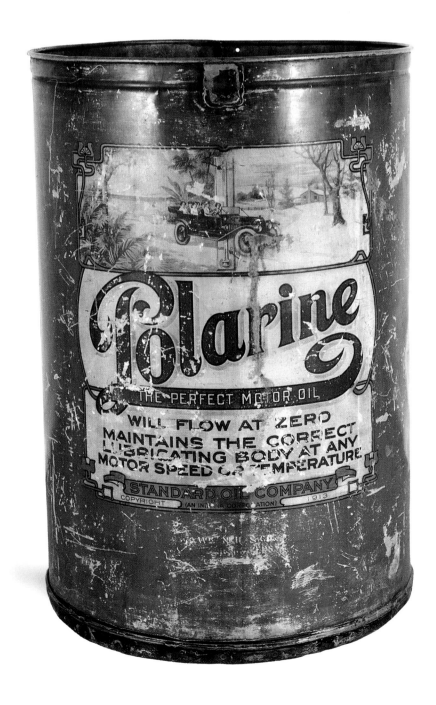

SIGNS

138

TOURING CLUB ITALIANO — CONFED. GEN. ENTI AUTARCHICI
RIOLO-BAGNI
m. 98 S/m.
LAMPO BENZINA SUPERIORE

42141 · TOURING CLUB ITALIANO
RECOARO Km. 20
ROVERETO Km. 46
LAMPO BENZINA SUPERIORE

LINEA AUTOMOBILISTICA
MILANO-OLEGGIO
PARTENZA DA OLEGGIO ORE
ARRIVO DA MILANO " "
BENZINA SHELL MOTOR OILS

SERVIZIO PUBBLICO AUTOMOBILISTICO
MILANO-OLEGGIO-BELLINZAGO
FERMATA DI CASTANO PRIMO
BENZINA SHELL MOTOR OILS

91788 TOURING CLUB ITALIANO
PASSAGGIO A LIVELLO
LAMPO BENZINA SUPERIORE

TOURING CLUB ITALIANO — CONFED. GEN. ENTI AUTARCHICI
BRA-SANFRÈ
LAMPO BENZINA SUPERIORE

LAMPO
BENZINA SUPERIORE

LAMPO
RIFORNIMENTO
SIAP
BENZINA SUPERIORE

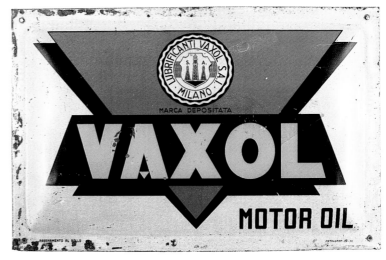

AGIP

SERVIZIO
LUBRIFICAZIONE

ROL

Extrasport

olio auto superiore

OIL

AUT. QUEST.MILANO - 30/11/53 N.517151   SMALTERIA PEREGO-TREZZO (Milano)

TOURING

S.A. LUBRIFICANTI
E. FOLTZER
GENOVA

OIL

OLEOBLITZ

LUBRIFICANTI REINACH - MILANO

OLEOBLITZ

RIFORNIMENTO

WAKEFIELD
Castrol
REGD. MOTOR OIL
(PATENTED)

THE MASTERPIECE IN OILS

PHILLIPS 66

The Gasoline that won the West!

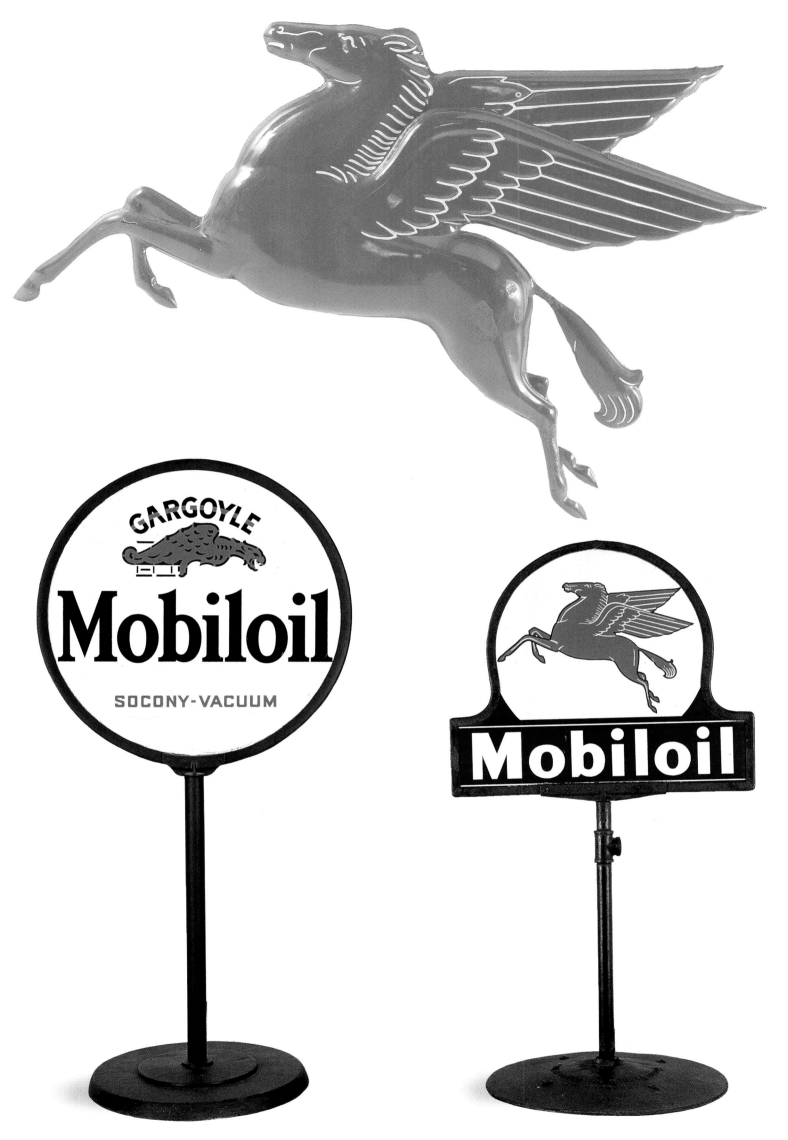

153

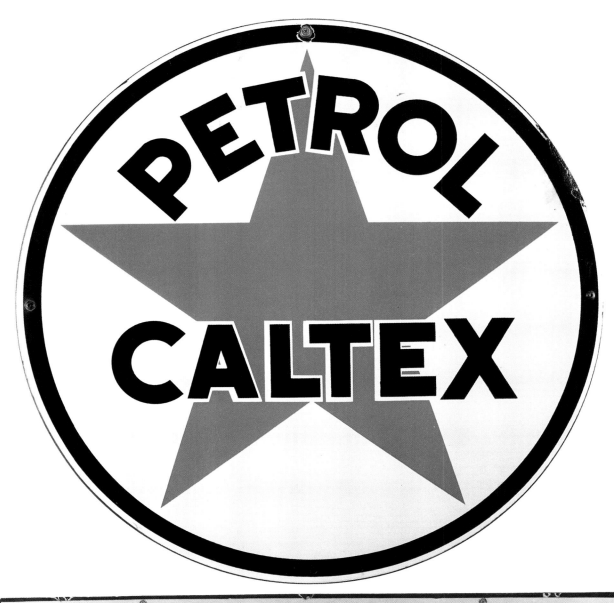

AMERICAN

RICHFIELD
REG. U. S. PAT. OFF.

THE PURE OIL
PURE
COMPANY, U.S.A.

1866
VALVOLINE
MOTOR
OIL

CHAMPLIN
MOTOR OILS

BLUE
SUNOCO

158

162

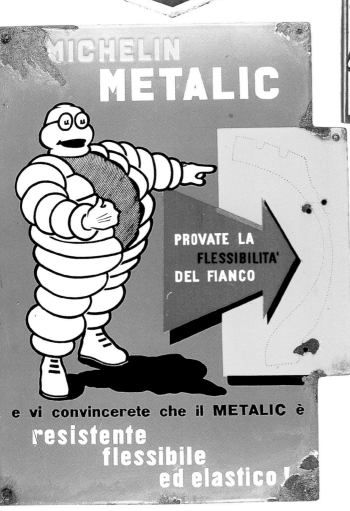

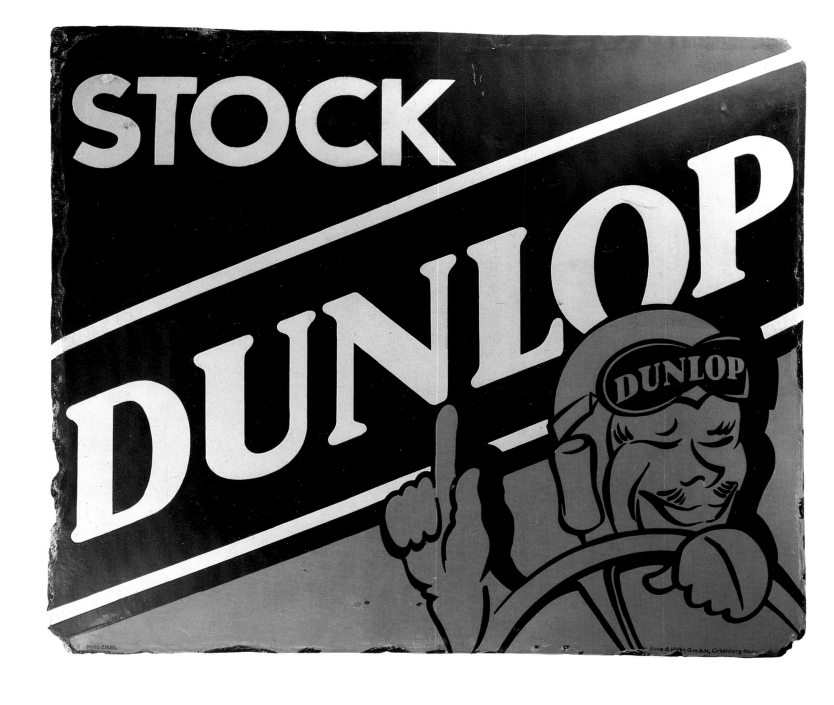

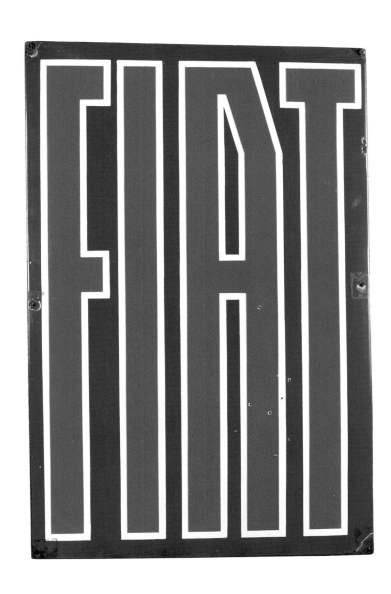

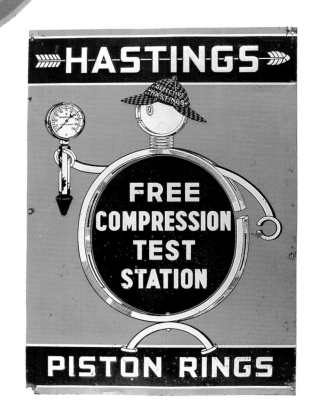

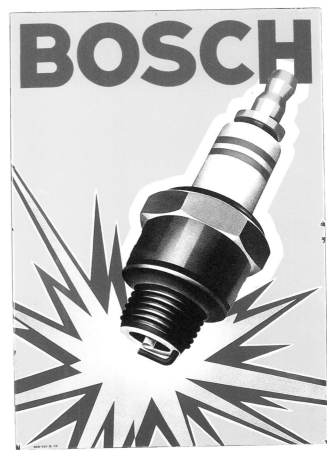

PRESSURE GAUGES AND AIR PUMPS

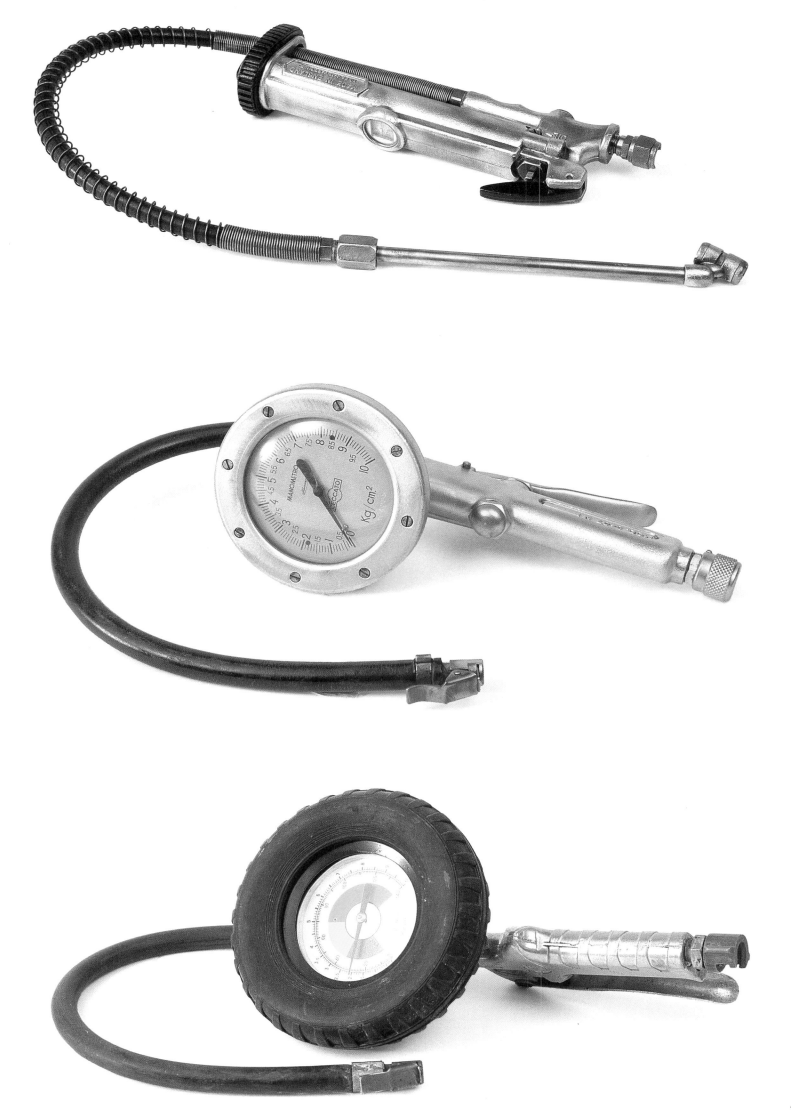

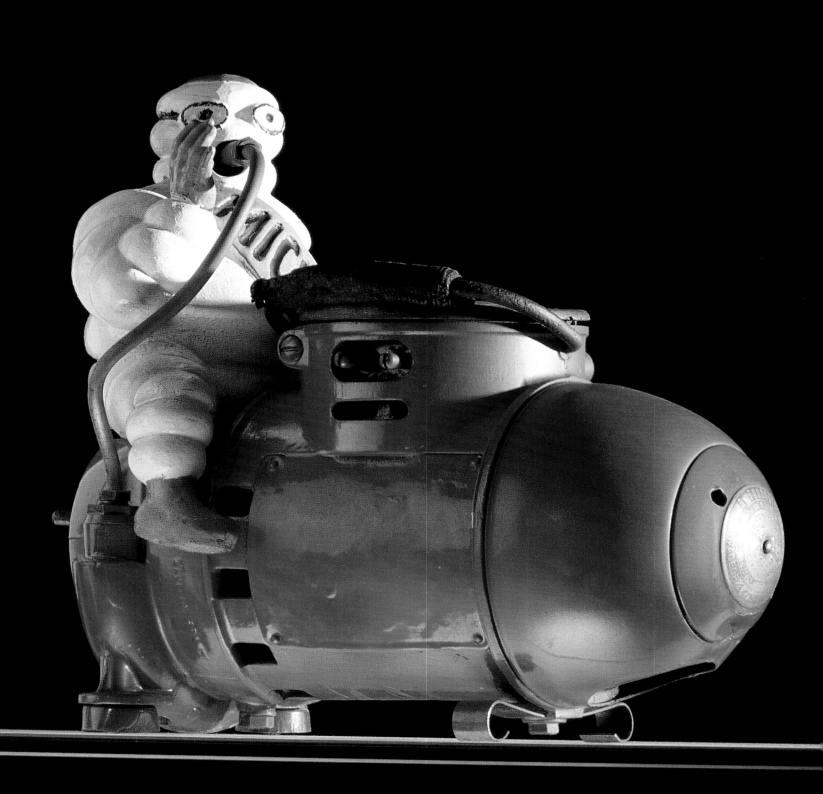

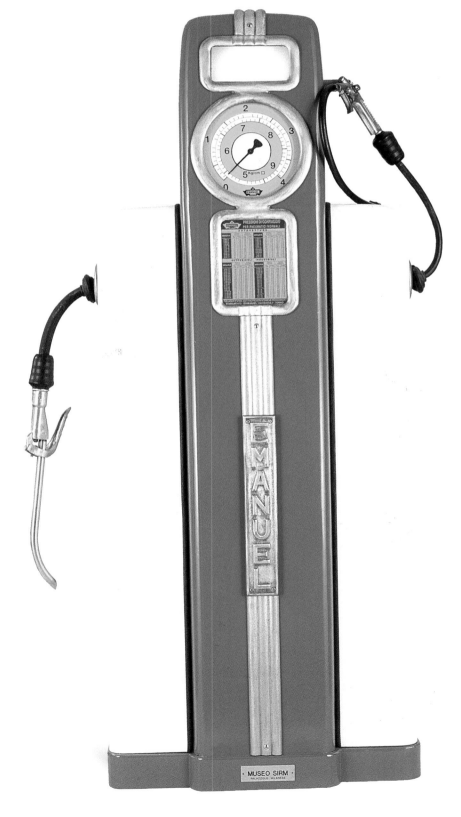

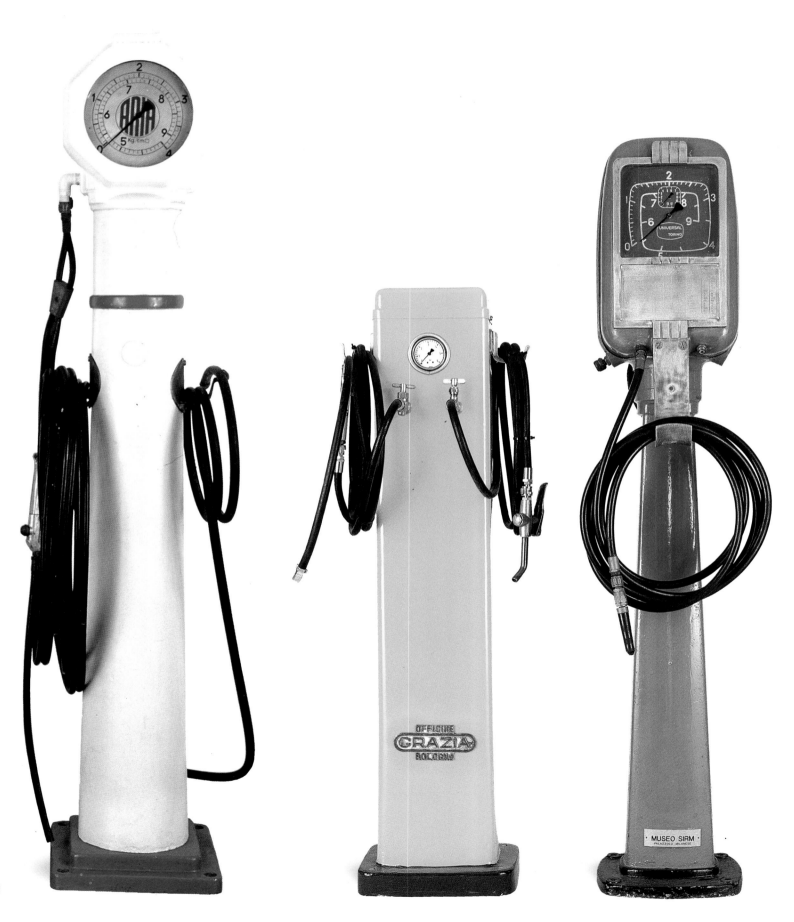

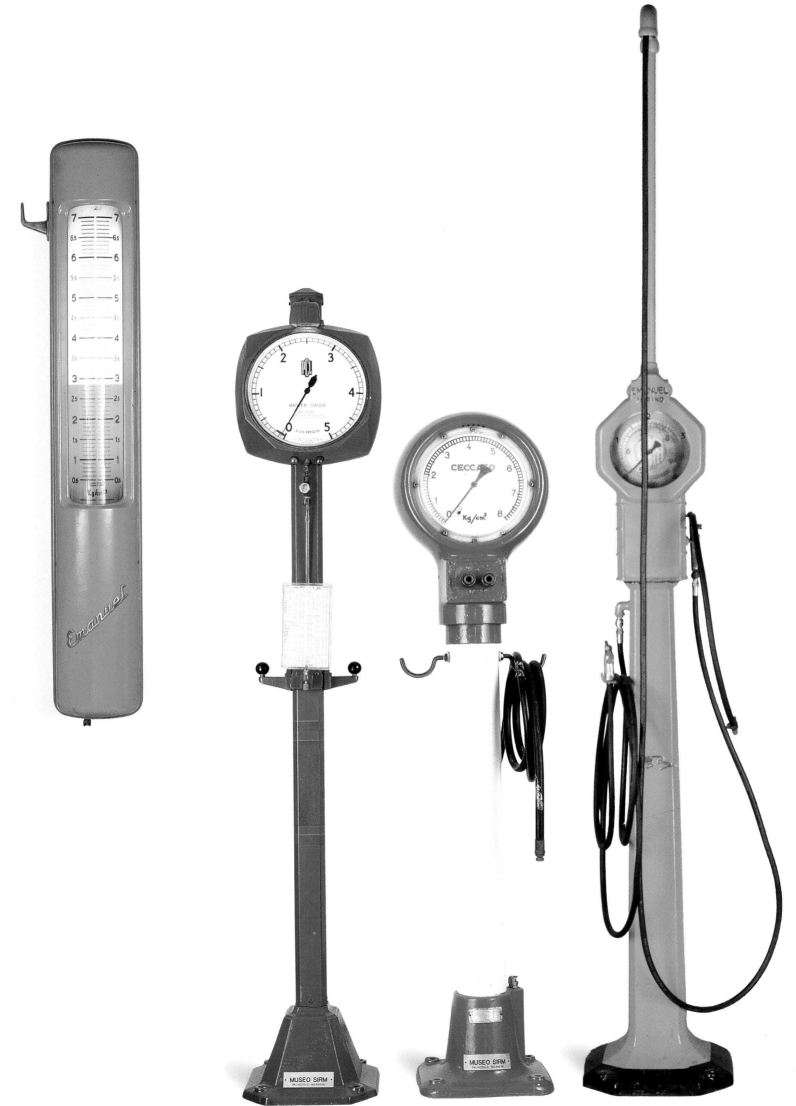

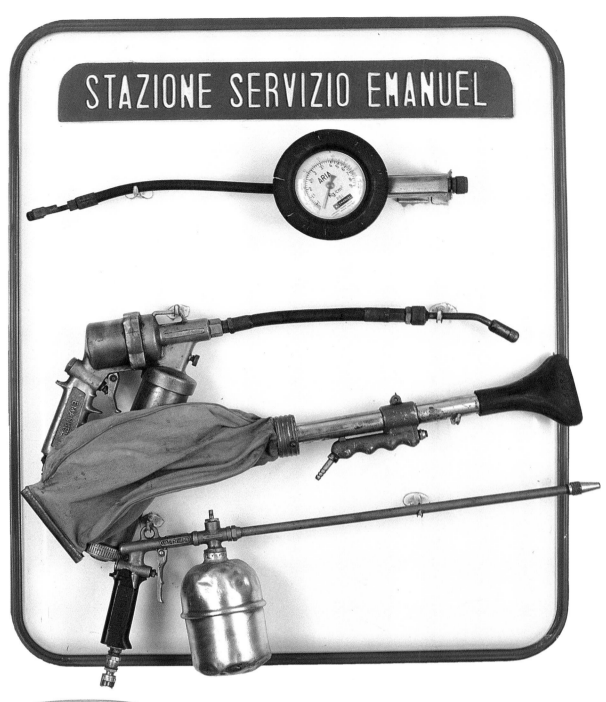

TOOLS AND GADGETS

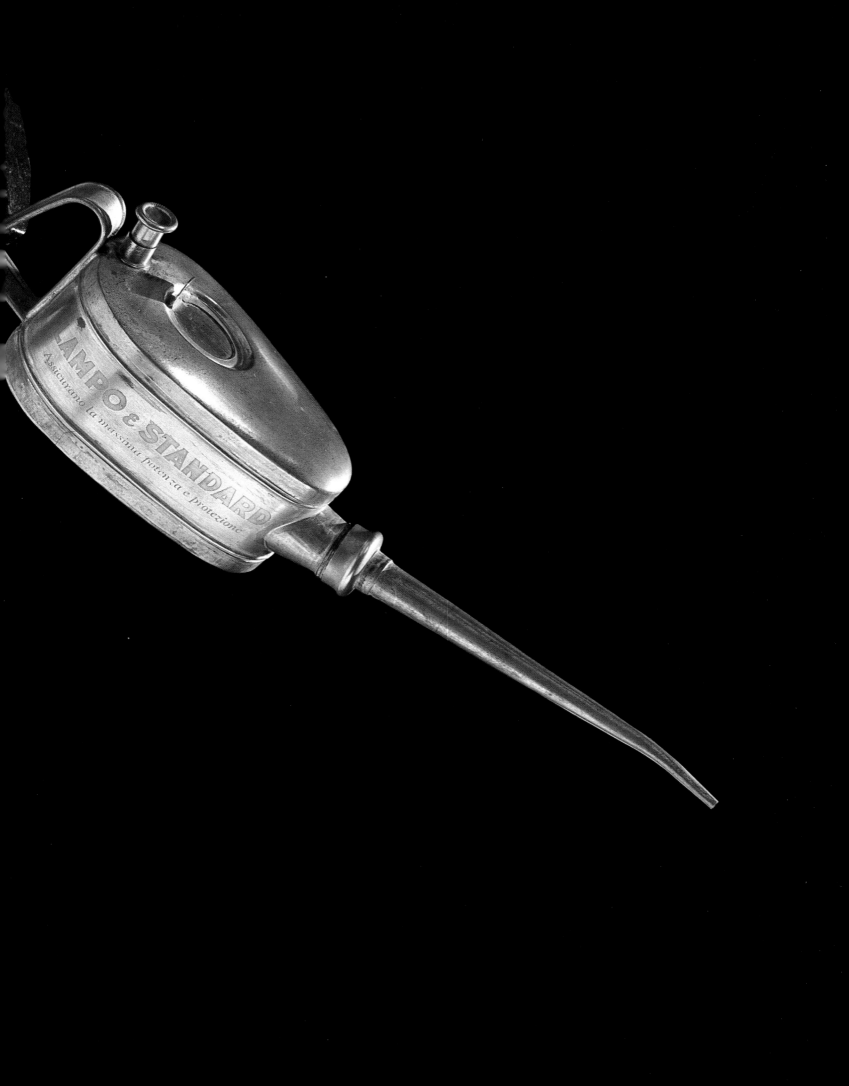

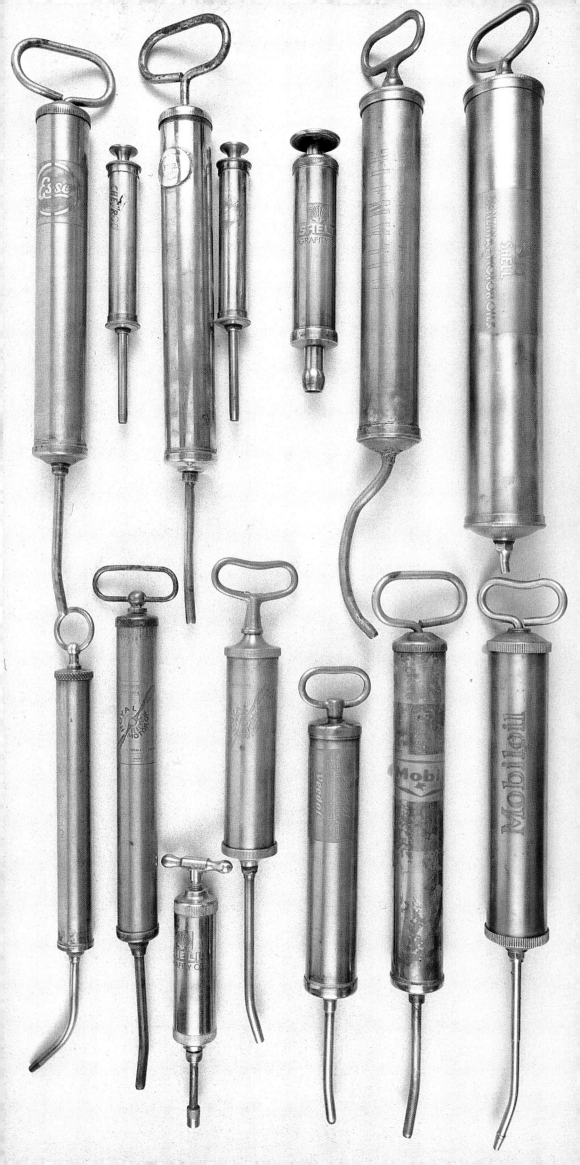

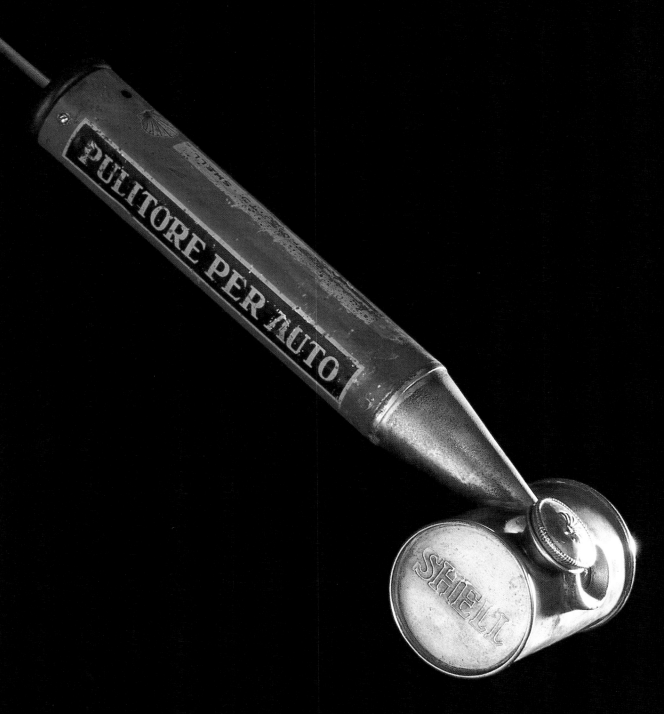

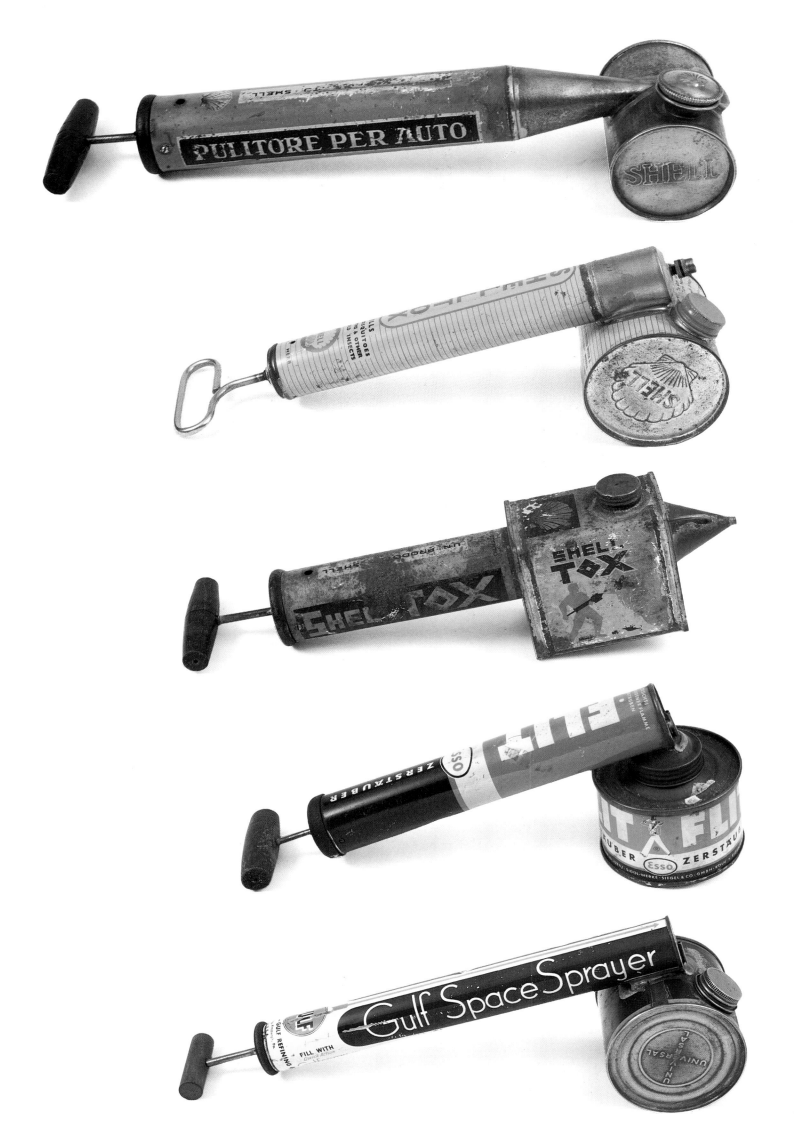

PULITORE PER AUTO

SHELL

SHELL TOX

Gulf Space Sprayer

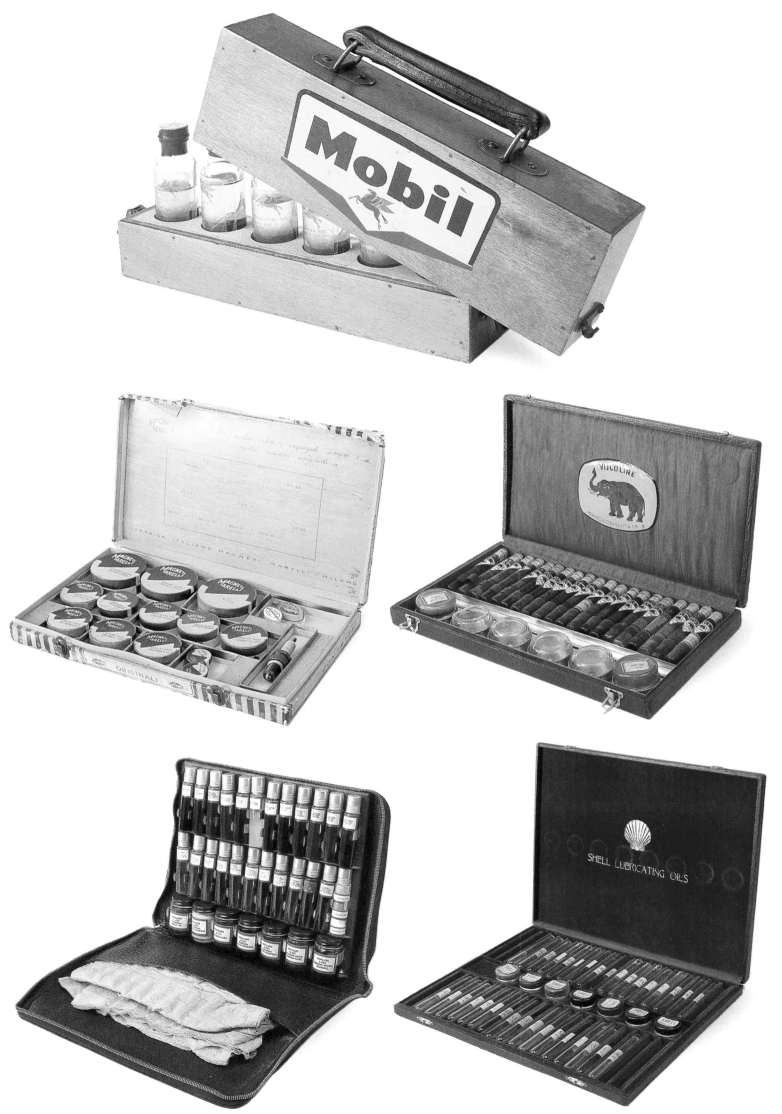

REPLACE THIS
VALVE CAP
AFTER USING
SCHRADER
GAUGE

SCREW ON TIGHTLY
BY HAND

KEEPS DIRT OUT
AND AIR IN

PRINTED MATTER

TRUCK GAUGE—VALVE REPAIR TOOL
PUMP CONNECTION   STAR WRENCH   VALVE CAPS

REGULAR GAUGES   VALVE INSIDES

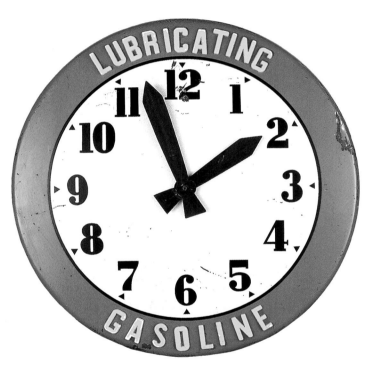

205

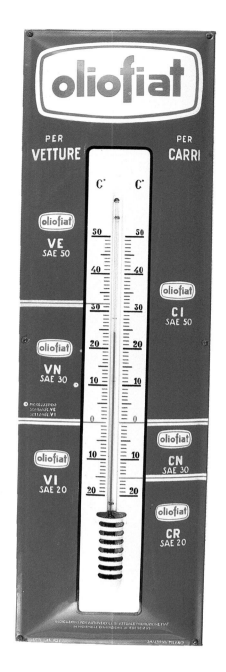

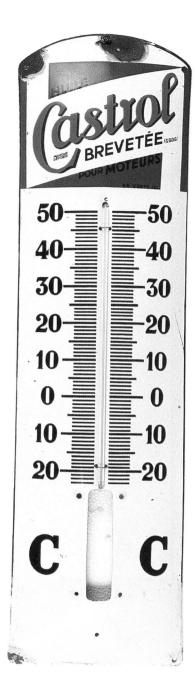

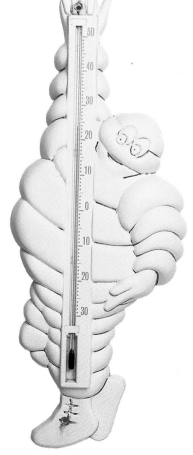

209

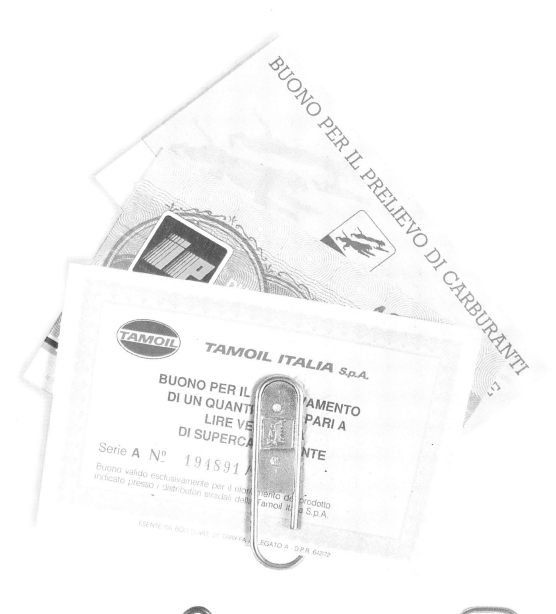

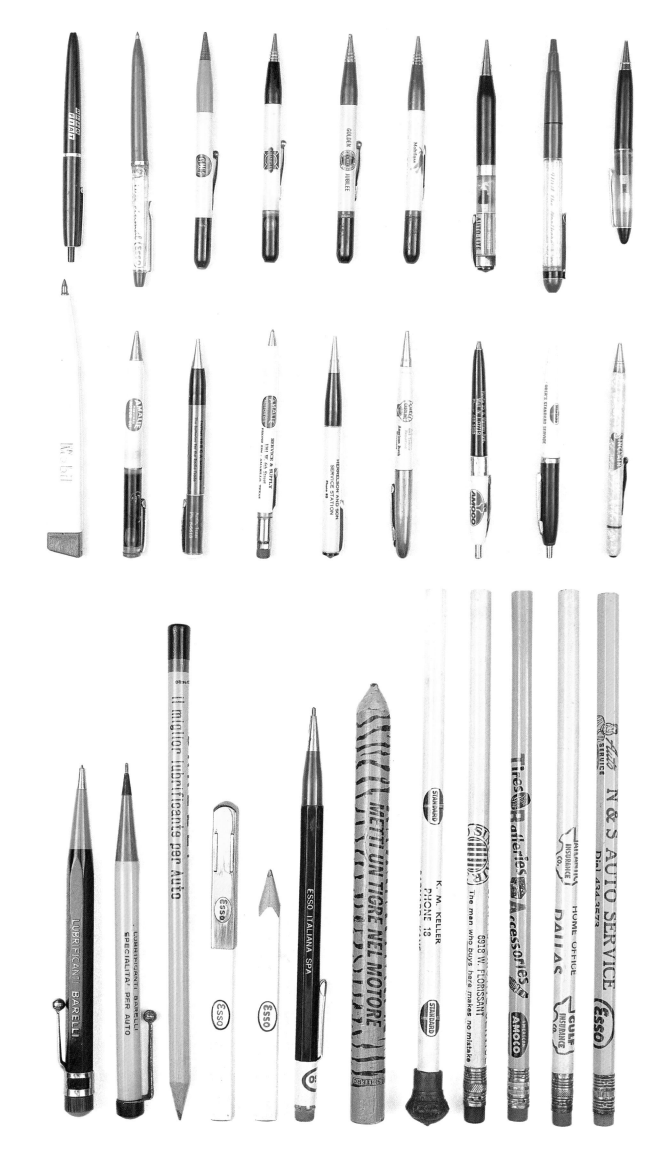

214

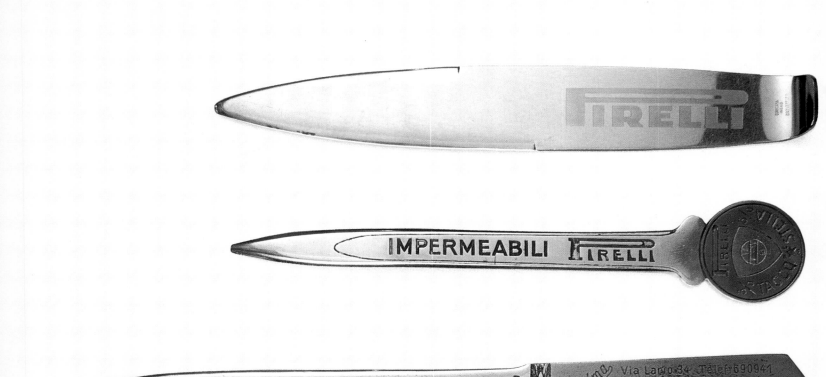

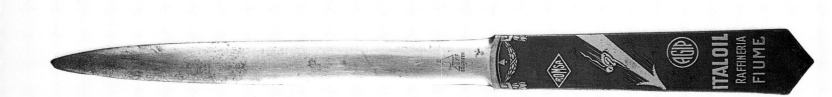

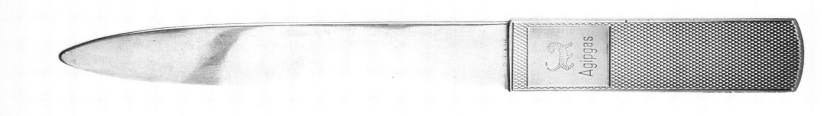

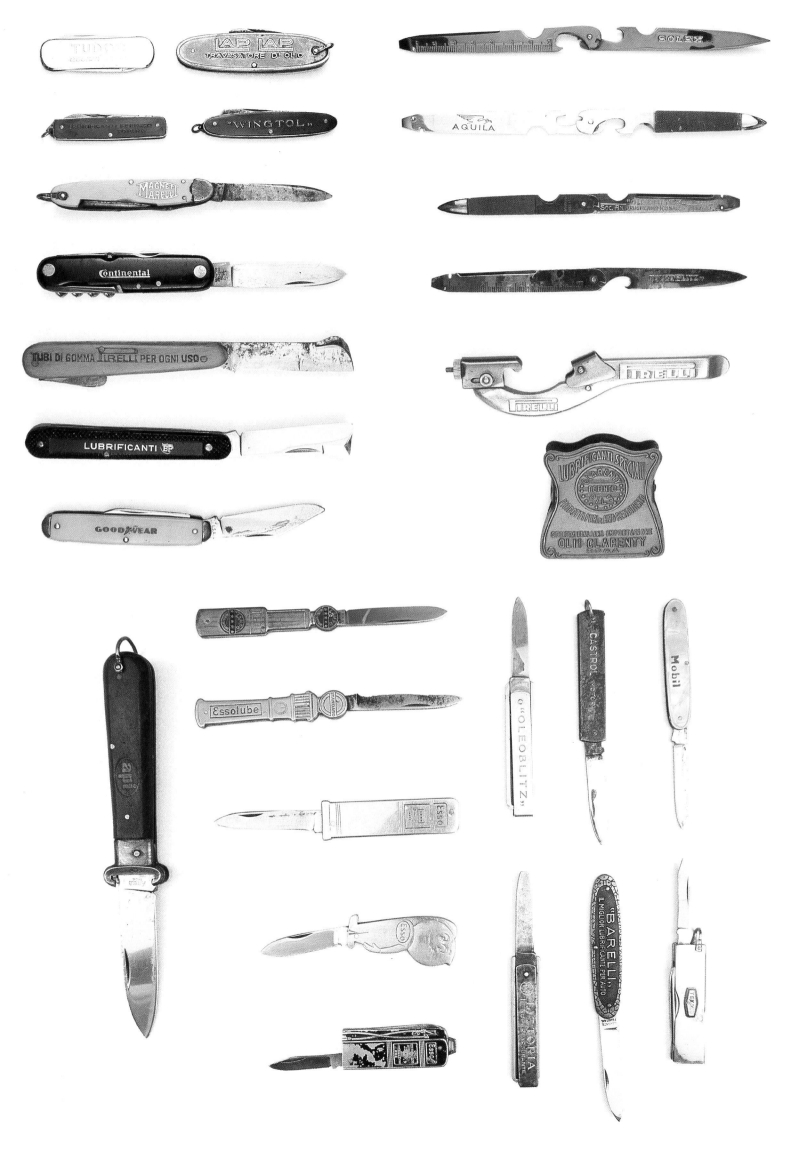

221

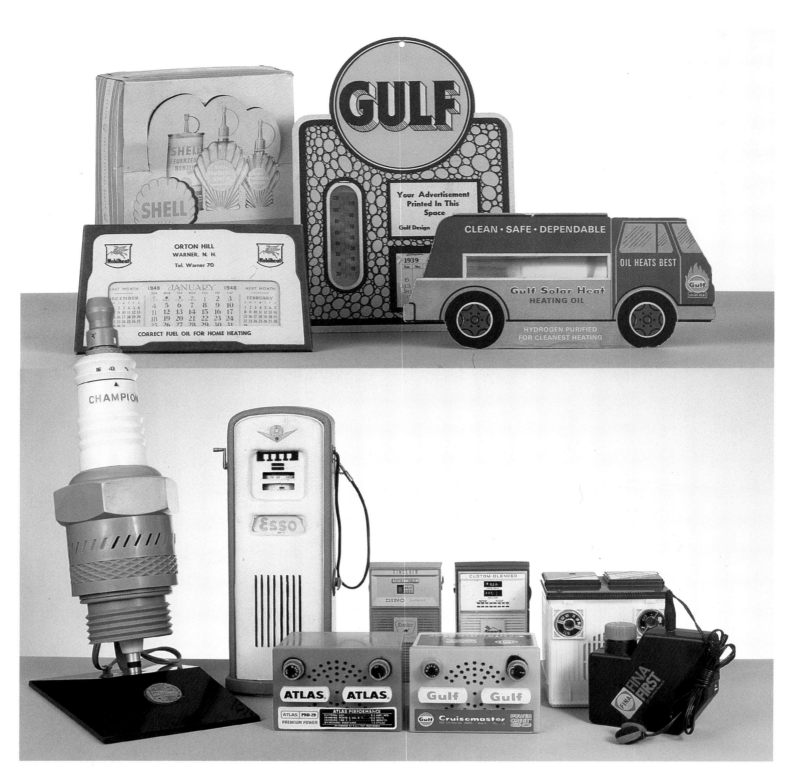

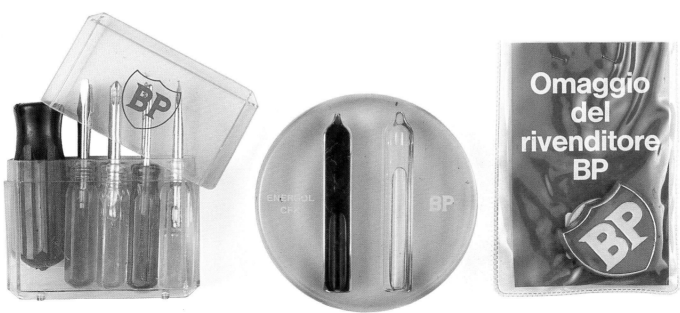

OSCAR **Esso** 1957
JUBILÉ du M.Y.C.C.A
1932-1957
- CANNES -

ADVERTISING PARAPHERNALIA

232

ANNO XXVIII - N. 11   NOVEMBRE 1922

RIVISTA MENSILE DEL TOVRING CLVB ITALIANO
MILANO - CORSO ITALIA, 10

LE VIE D'ITALIA

ORGANO UFFICIALE      PER LE INDUSTRIE
DELL'ENTE NAZIONALE   TURISTICHE

LEGGE 7 APRILE 1921 N. 610   ROMA, VIA MARGHERA, 6 – ANGOLO VIA DEI MILLE

MISCELA con Essolube Esso per MOTOSCOOTERS

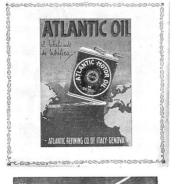

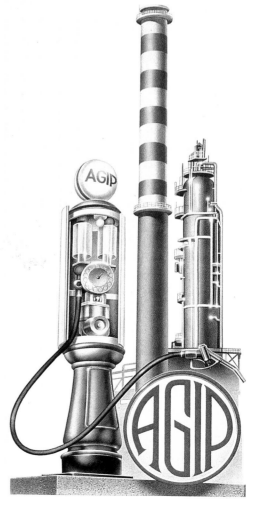

STANDARD

SOCIETÀ ITALO-AMERICANA PEL PETROLIO - GENOVA

ESSO

RIFORNIMENTI OVUNQUE

Società Italo-Americana pel Petrolio Genova

Esso

L'ANONIMA INFORTUNI è particolarmente raccomandata dal T.C.I. col quale ha accordi speciali a favore dei Soci

PER L'ASSICURAZIONE DEI DANNI ALLE VOSTRE AUTOMOBILI RIVOLGETEVI ALL'ANONIMA INFORTUNI MILANO - PIAZZA CORDUSIO 2

DANNI PAGATI DALLA FONDAZIONE DELLA SOCIETÀ: L. 123.709.313,13

RIVISTA MENSILE DEL T. C. I. — LE VIE D'ITALIA

ATLANTIC OIL

"IL LUBRIFICANTE CHE LUBRIFICA,,

ATLANTIC REFINING CO. OF ITALY - GENOVA

5-12 SETT.BRE MONZA 5-12 SETT.BRE

GRAN PREMIO DELLE 24 ORE

CAMPIONATO DEL MONDO

GRAN PREMIO MILANO

19 SETT. GRAN PREMIO MOTOCICLISTICO

LUBRIFICATE CON *Italoil*

TUTTO IL MONDO È

LUBRIFICATO
DA SHELL MOTOR OIL

Lubrificate con
Italoil
ROMSA

Victoria
LA BENZINA DEGLI ITALIANI
LITTORIA
IL SUPERCARBURANTE
Petrolina
OLIO COMBUSTIBILE FLUIDISSIMO

AGIP

IL NUOVO DISTRIBUTORE
ADOTTATO DALL'A.G.I.P.
CONTROLLA AUTOMATI-
CAMENTE LA QUANTITÀ
DEL CARBURANTE ACQUI-
STATO INDICANDONE
ESATTAMENTE IL PREZZO

M 25 AR38

AZIENDA GENERALE ITALIANA PETROLI · ROMA

Preferite il bidone
a rendere
- il più autarchico
dei recipienti!

Acquistando Mobiloil
in bidoni da 2 litri a
rendere non pagate
il costo del recipien-
te, avete la garanzia
della genuinità del
prodotto e contribuite
al successo della lotta
per l'autarchia.

l'olio che resiste e dura di più:
Mobiloil
Mobiloil
PRODOTTO NELLA RAFFINERIA DI NAPOLI

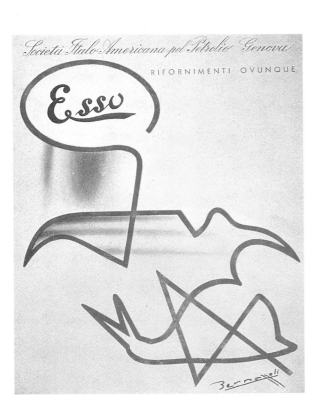

241

TECHNICAL DRAWINGS

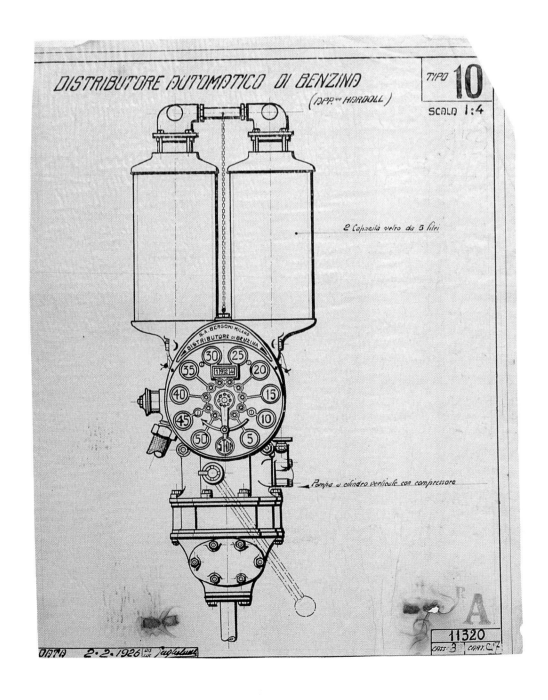

243

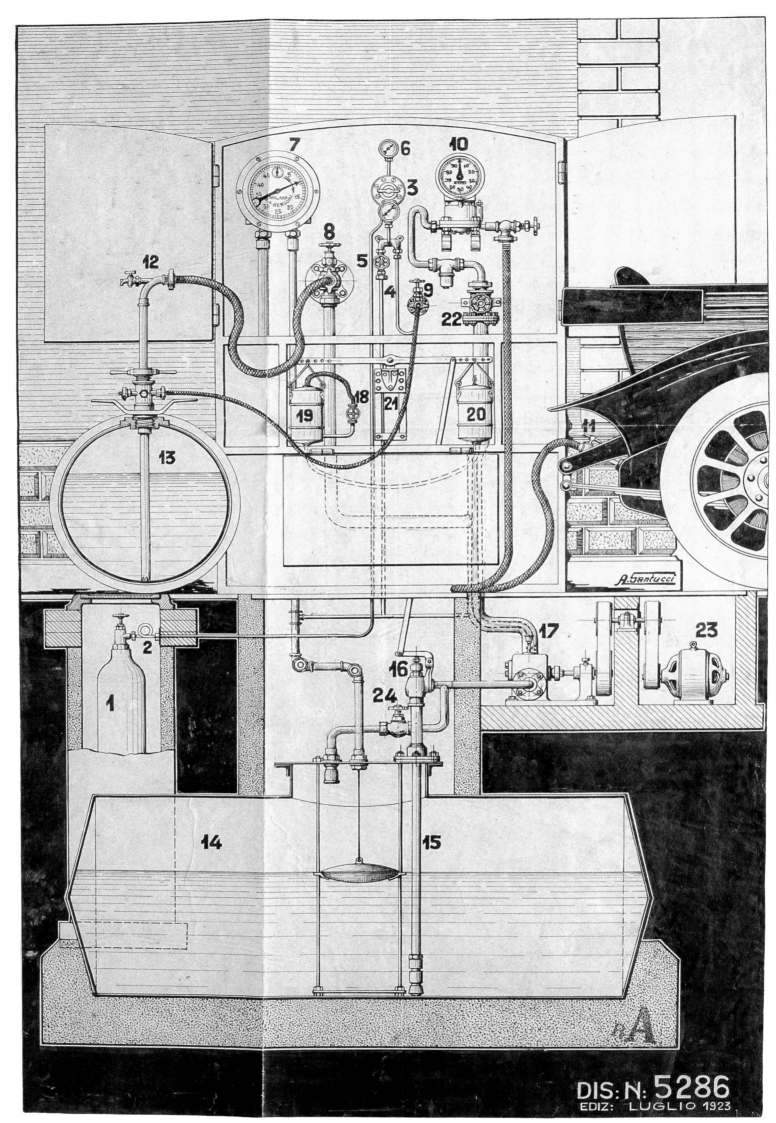

DIS: N: 5286
EDIZ: LUGLIO 1923

POMPA MISURATRICE per olio, petrolio ecc.

portata per colpo di stantuffo l!

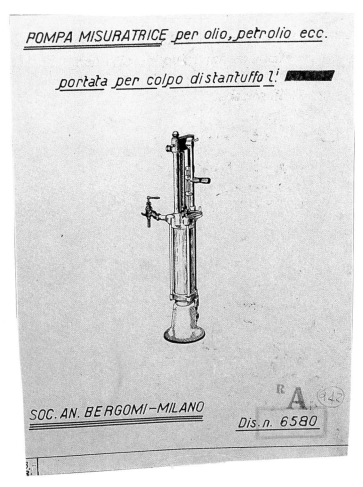

SOC. AN. BERGOMI—MILANO

Dis. n. 6580

DISTRIBUTORE di BENZINA

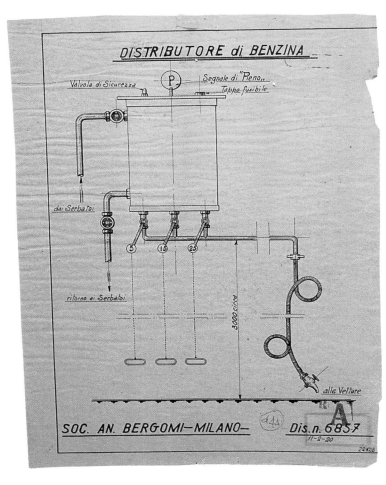

SOC. AN. BERGOMI—MILANO—

Dis. n. 6857

Distribuzione e Misurazione visibile di BENZINA

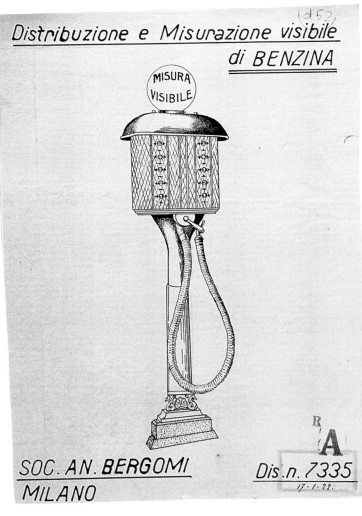

SOC. AN. BERGOMI
MILANO

Dis. n. 7335

POMPA MISURATRICE per Benzina ed Olio applicata su fusto.

SOC. AN. BERGOMI
MILANO

Dis. n. 7527

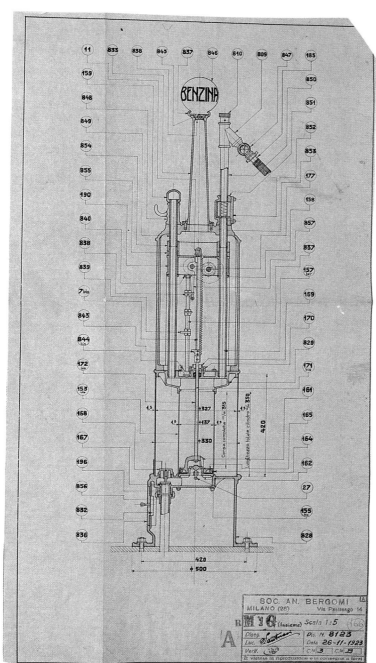

BENZINA

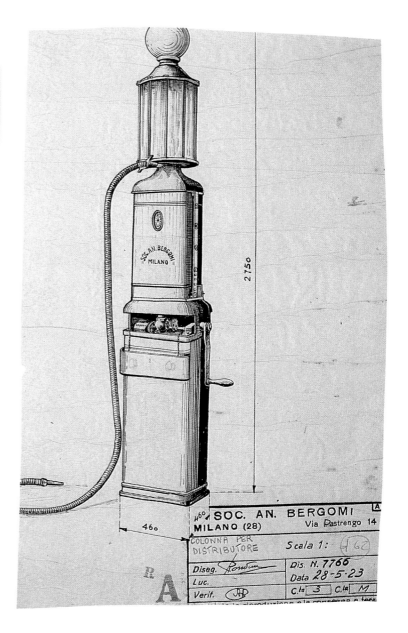

2750

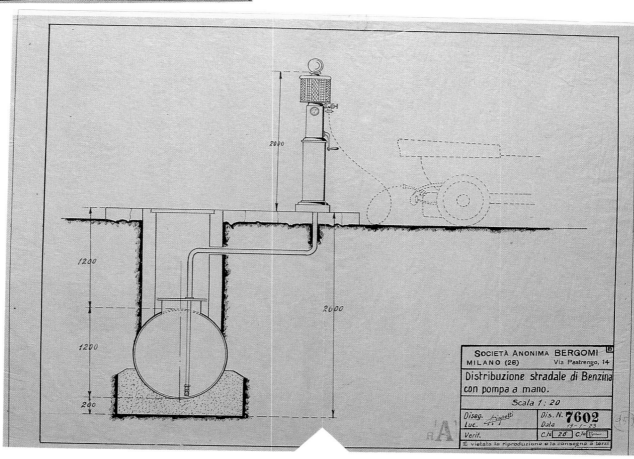

2000

1200

1200

2600

200

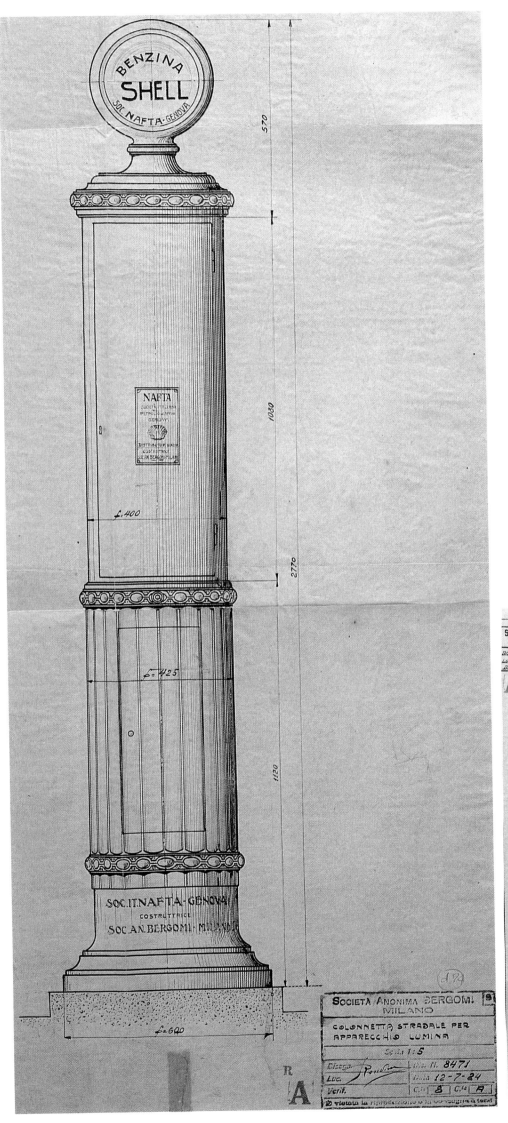

BENZINA
SHELL
SOC. NAFTA - GENOVA

570

1080

2770

1120

NAFTA
SOCIETA ITALIANA
PETROLIO e AFFINI
GENOVA

DISTRIBUTORE BENZINA
COSTRUTTRICE
SOC. AN. BERGOMI - MILANO

ℓ. 400

ℓ. 425

ℓ. 600

SOC. IT. NAFTA - GENOVA
COSTRUTTRICE
SOC. AN. BERGOMI - MILANO

SOCIETA ANONIMA BERGOMI
MILANO

COLONNETTA STRADALE PER
APPARECCHIO LUMINA

Scala 1:5

Diseg. | Dis. N. 8471
Luc. | Data 12-7-24
Verif. | C.- 8 C.14 A

È vietata la riproduzione e la consegna a terzi

R
A

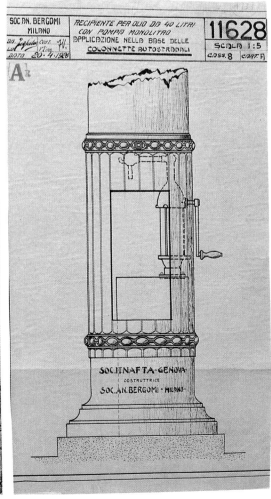

SOC. AN. BERGOMI
MILANO

RECIPIENTE PER OLIO DA 40 LITRI
CON POMPA MONOLITRO
APPLICAZIONE NELLA BASE DELLE
COLONNETTE AUTOSTRADALI

11628

SCALA 1:5

CLASS. 8 CART. A

A

SOC. IT. NAFTA - GENOVA
COSTRUTTRICE
SOC. AN. BERGOMI - MILANO

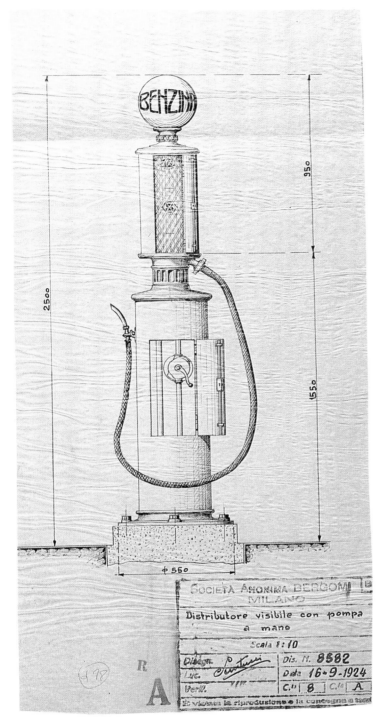

SOCIETÀ ANONIMA BERGOMI
MILANO

Distributore visibile con pompa
a mano

Scala 1:10

Disegn. _____ Dis. N. 8582
Luc. _____ Data 16-9-1924
Verif. _____ C.¹ 8 | C.¹ A

È vietata la riproduzione e la consegna a terzi

R
A

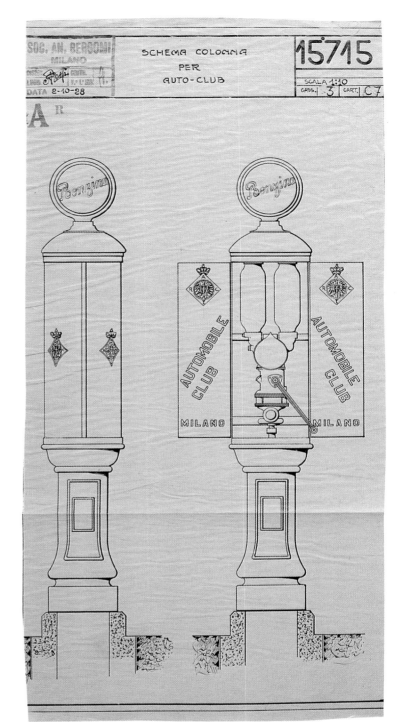

SOC. AN. BERGOMI
MILANO

SCHEMA COLONNA
PER
AUTO-CLUB

15715

SCALA 1:10
CASS. 3 | CART. C7

DATA 2-10-28

Benzina — Benzina

AUTOMOBILE CLUB MILANO — AUTOMOBILE CLUB MILANO

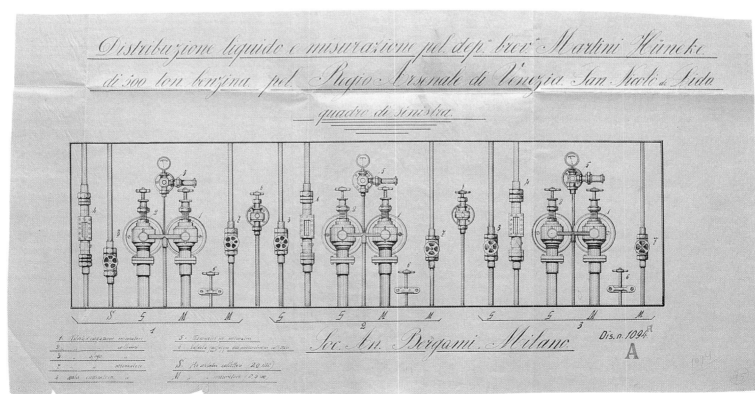

Distribuzione liquido e misurazione pel dep. brev. Martini Hüneke
di 500 ton benzina pel Regio Arsenale di Venezia San Nicolò di Lido

quadro di sinistra

Soc. An. Bergomi Milano

Dis. n. 1094

750

450

600

400

1000

2600

270

730

900

200

3200

600

Portelle ribaltabili

A

SOCIETA' ANONIMA BERGOMI – MILANO (28)
VIA PASTRENGO N:14

COLONNA STRADALE PER DISTR
BUZIONE BENZINA A DUE CON=
TATORI

(184)   SCALA 1:10=

DISEG: Pasturai Q.
LUCID: Pasturai Q.
CONTR: Rondin
V. L'ING:

DATA
DEL
DISEGNO

5-12-1924

A R

8752

CASS.to 8 | CART.lla A

BENZINA

249

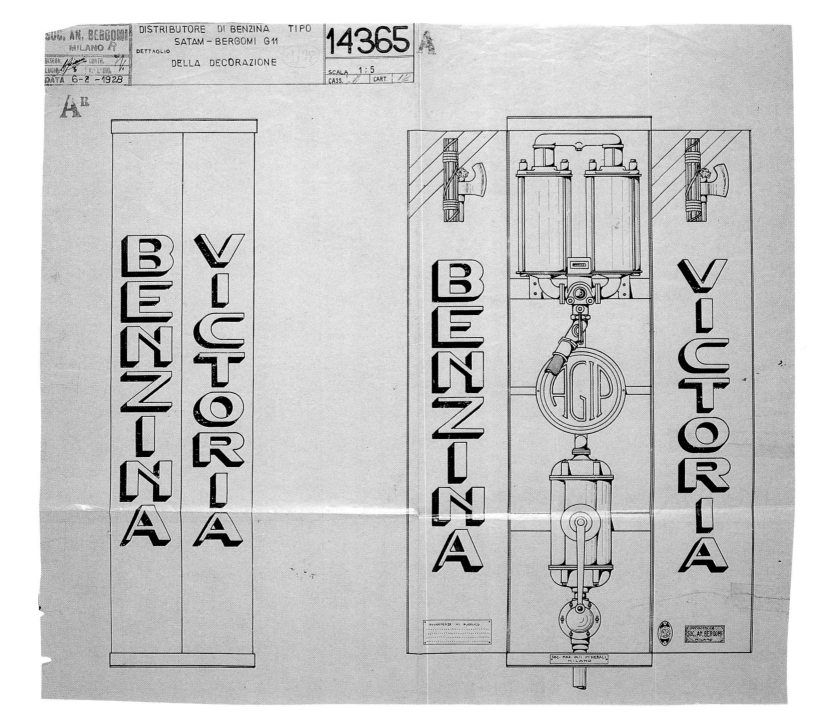

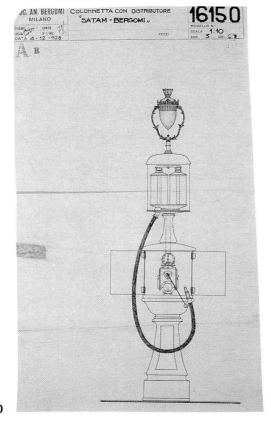

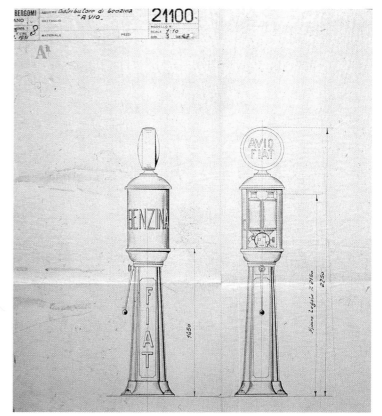

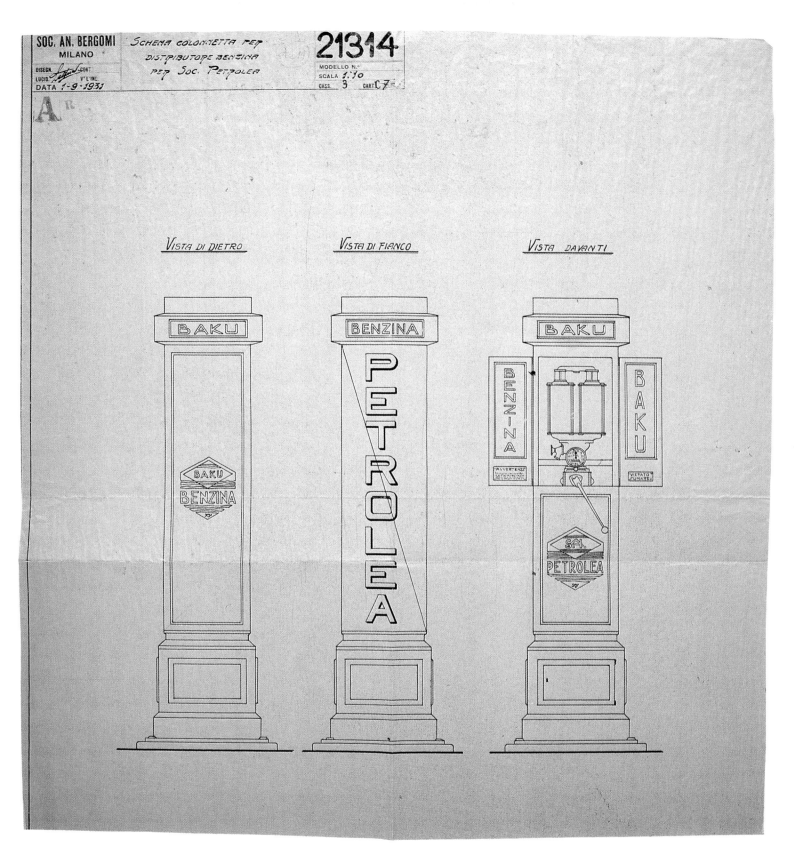

Schema colonnetta per
distributore benzina
per Soc. Petrolea

21314

MODELLO N.°
SCALA 1:10
CASS. 3   CART C 7

A

VISTA DI DIETRO   VISTA DI FIANCO   VISTA DAVANTI

BAKU   BENZINA   BAKU

BAKU   PETROLEA   BENZINA   BAKU
BENZINA
                                     AVVERTENZE   VIETATO FUMARE

                                     S.A.
                                     PETROLEA

TOYS

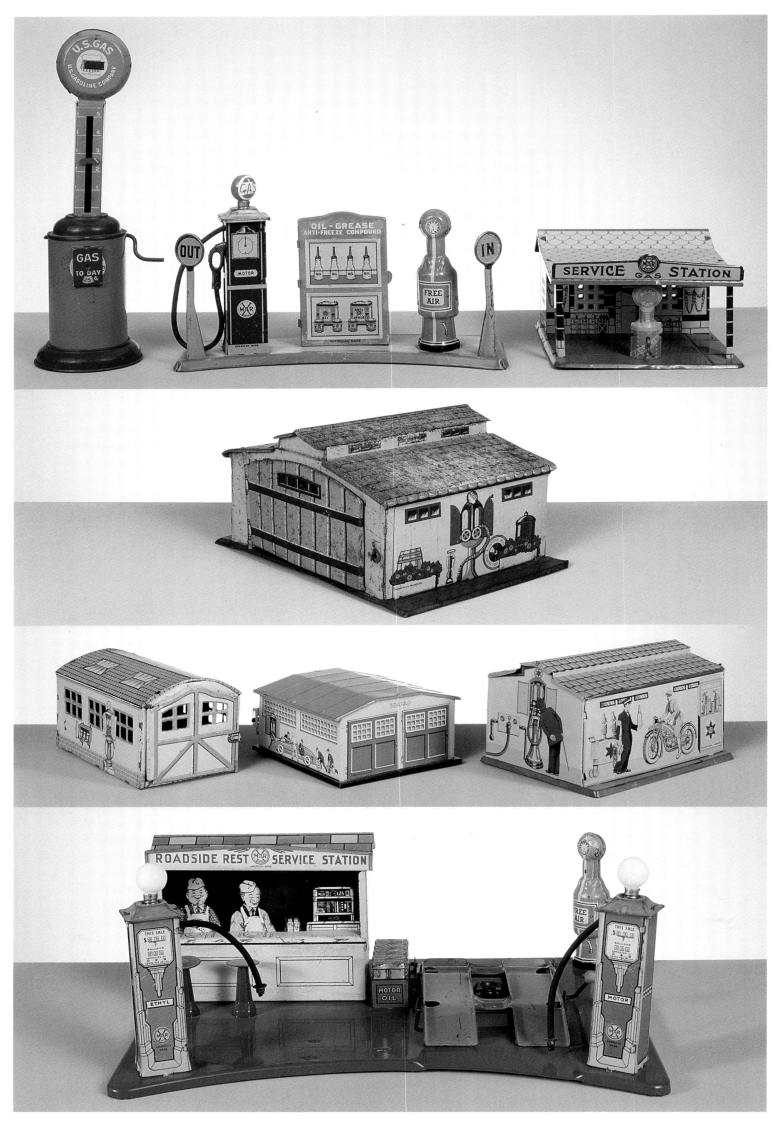

This book was printed by
Fantonigrafica - Elemond Editori Associati